MORAL EDUCATION
THEORY AND PRACTICE

MERIEL DOWNEY & A.V. KELLY

Harper & Row, Publishers

London   New York   Hagerstown   San Francisco   Sydney

Harper & Row Ltd
28 Tavistock Street, London WC2E 7PN

British Library Cataloguing in Publication Data
  Downey, Meriel Elaine
    Moral education.
    1. Moral education
    I. Title   II. Kelly, Albert Victor
    370.11'4   LC268

ISBN 0-06318079 0
      0-06-318080-4 Pbk

Designed by Richard Dewing, 'Millions'

Printed by A. Wheaton & Co. Ltd., Exeter

Contents

Introduction

"Teachers can only escape from their influence over the moral and spiritual development of their pupils by closing their schools." These words from that section of the Newsom Report that deals with moral and spiritual development draw our attention to what is perhaps the most significant feature of moral education in schools, and that is that, more than any other area of the curriculum, more even than language development, moral education is the responsibility of every teacher, and indeed of every adult, and truly runs right through, as well as across, the curriculum.

This is one of several features of moral education that makes it different from all other curriculum subjects, in fact a unique area of the curriculum generating its own peculiar questions. There are several other features too that make it a quite distinctive area of the curriculum. It is not an area for which it is possible in any way to delineate a corpus of knowledge that can be regarded as constituting its essential elements, since it is affected in a more fundamental way than any other subject by claims that are made for the subjectivity of knowledge. Nor is it a form of knowledge or a body of learning in any of the usual senses.

It is an area to which no pupil comes "cold" since moral learning, the development of values and attitudes, begins at birth and is fed from many sources. For this reason also it is not something that can be delayed, like, say, the learning of Latin, until we feel that pupils have reached an appropriate stage of mental development to cope with the demands which it will make upon their intellectual abilities. For the same reason too we must be constantly aware that moral learning is a function of everything that we do in schools and not just of the content of certain kinds of lesson. It permeates all aspects of school life, both formal and informal; it is as much a result of how we organize and plan the activities of the school as of any decisions we make about the content of individual syllabuses; and it is probably influenced far more by the examples teachers offer pupils through their own attitudes and behaviour than by any amount of moral exhortation or open and free discussion of moral issues.

Furthermore, it is an aspect of development in which the emotions play at least as crucial a role as the intellect. It is an area in which the feelings of pupils and sometimes of their parents often run high, in which, certainly with older pupils, there can be a good deal of heated involvement and which affects the life-style of the pupil in a more fundamental way than any other aspect of his or her education. Finally, that autonomy that so many education theorists speak of as a basic aim of education, an underlying principle of all educative activities, is in essence moral autonomy; it is the ability to make decisions on controversial issues of value, to make choices as a result of one's own thinking. Thus it can be seen that moral education continues to be the central core of education itself or, to put it differently, all education continues to be at root moral education. If we add the claim that to be morally autonomous is part of what it means to be a human being rather than an object acted upon by external forces or an animal driven by instinct or desire, we can see how central education is to human development and how basic is the role of moral education in that process.

For all of these reasons, moral education is both a central concern of education and a unique and peculiar curriculum subject.

It is our contention, therefore, that moral education is and must always be a vital issue in any discussion of education or of the school curriculum. It is also a complex area to understand so that the making of adequate practical provision for it is very difficult. On the other hand, not to make adequate provision for it is not merely to ignore it; it is to ensure that, since moral learning will take place anyway, moral miseducation is more likely to result. For this reason, it has to be seen, as our opening quotation from the Newsom Report states, as the concern of every teacher and, indeed, of every adult.

It is our intention in this book to attempt to spell out some of the peculiar characteristics of this area of the curriculum in detail and to examine the implications of these for the practice of teachers and others concerned with the upbringing of children. We will attempt first of all to analyse the notion of moral education itself to discover what is involved in the process and what it means to be morally educated. We shall then consider the place of reason in morality, the problems created by the sequential nature of moral development in children, the influence of the emotions on moral behaviour, the many sources of moral influence and learning. In each case we shall be concerned to draw out the implications of these facets of morality for the teacher and the task of promoting moral education. Finally, we shall look at the curriculum and endeavour to pick out the contribution that other subject areas might make to moral education and to consider some of the attempts that have been made to set up particular curriculum projects in this area, to establish moral education as a curriculum subject in its own right.

Throughout we shall of course try to ensure a proper linking of theory to practice in order to provide all teachers with the kind of basic understanding that will enable them to achieve a properly conscious and clearly thought-out influence over the moral development of their pupils.

CHAPTER 1

WHAT IS MORAL EDUCATION ?

"They should be brought to know and love God and to practise in the school community the virtues appropriate to their age and environment." These words from the Plowden Report on primary education (1966, §572) not only highlight the importance of moral education, they also illustrate very effectively the confusion that surrounds a good deal of thinking about both moral and religious education and especially about the relationship between them.

Any discussion of the theory and practice of moral education must begin, then, by attempting to define in some detail what is meant by moral education and what are its fundamental principles. It will be equally clear, however, that in order to do this we must first endeavour to discover what kind of relationship exists between moral education and religious education and, indeed, whether there is or should be any such relationship. A clarification of that issue might of itself take us some way towards a definition of moral education.

At all events it is a question we should deal with first before turning our attention to the question of what moral education itself is. When we come to that question, it will be helpful to consider it from at least three points of view. To begin with, we must look for some of the reasons for the recent upsurge of interest in moral education. For if we can discover why it is coming to be regarded as so important, we may be able to find out what it is hoped it will provide. Secondly, it will be useful to ask what is implied by calling it moral education rather than moral instruction or moral knowledge, since, as we shall see in the next section, a failure to distinguish these three terms in the teaching of religion is symptomatic of, and perhaps a major cause of, the confusion that has existed or has come to exist there. Thirdly, it may well prove profitable to approach the problem from the other end, as it were, and ask what we would regard as the essential characteristics of a successful product of a process of moral education. Whom would we regard as a morally educated person? If we can produce some answers to that question, we may have found a further source of clues towards our definition of what moral education is. All of these approaches we will explore in turn in an attempt to get some answers to the question, "What is moral education?".

Moral education and religious education

The links between moral behaviour and religious beliefs that have been established over the ages in the traditions of most religions but perhaps especially in the Judaeo-Christian tradition have been so strong that many people still regard the two as inseparable. There is little doubt that the requirement of the 1944 Education Act in the United Kingdom that religion be the only compulsory curriculum subject was prompted as much by a desire to promote the moral education of pupils as by any intention to propagate the Christian religion itself. We have already seen the same attitude and approach reflected in the recommendations of the Plowden Report published over twenty years later and it can be seen as a major factor in the continuing demands from parents and others that religion should be taught to all pupils compulsorily.

The church and its officials, too, still consider this area of education their own preserve and appear to be of the opinion that there can be no proper discussion of morals nor of moral education unless the church is fully represented. This view is usually also supported by those responsible for the media, so that, on the one hand, many "religious" programmes on both radio and television turn out to be discussions of, or pronouncements on, moral questions and, on the other, it is unusual to see a moral issue tackled without reference being made to the "expert" opinion of a clergyman of one denomination or another.

The same confusion is compounded by the practice of many schools, since often the compulsory "daily act of worship" nowadays is replaced by some kind of humanist, secular and non-religious event—the playing of a piece of classical music, the reading of a poem or the telling of some "morally uplifting" anecdote—, the approach to the compulsory period of religious education is often very much, if not entirely, concerned with moral issues and there is still a tendency for many teachers and headteachers to regard moral education as the private domain of the RE teacher.

It is not surprising, therefore, when this kind of link is assumed by those whose thinking on these issues ought to be lucid, that parents, politicians and even the intelligent and educated man in the street continue to regard the two as inextricably linked. Thus there emerges a danger, some of the results of which we are witnessing today, that when religious beliefs are rejected there appears to be no longer any basis for moral principles and the baby goes down the drain with the bathwater. It is important to consider, therefore, whether such links are necessary or merely contingent.

However, it might be worthwhile in doing so to ponder first of all some of the confusions that have surrounded our understanding and practice of the teaching of religion itself. This confusion is reflected in the fact that schools have used a variety of terms to denote the religious component of their curricula. Religious Instruction, Religious Knowledge and Religious Education are all terms quite commonly found on school timetables and they seem to be used almost indiscriminately according to the whims of individual head-teachers or heads of the relevant departments rather than as a result of any awareness of the semantic differences between them. Yet those semantic differences are crucial. To describe this area of study as Religious Knowledge begs all kinds of epistemological questions concerning the status of knowledge in this field; it also makes certain claims about the truth content of what is offered. To call it Religious Instruction, on the other hand, neither begs these questions nor makes these claims; what it does do is to suggest that, regardless of the epistemological status of religious knowledge and of questions concerning its truth, children will be instructed in it and will, one presumes, therefore, be taught to accept it. In contrast to this again, the term Religious Education suggests a more open approach to the teaching of religion. What precisely it implies is, of course, the subject of much heated debate, but in general it does invite such debate and requires that we approach it with an open mind.

It is this latter term that is now most common in schools and this suggests that our approach to the teaching of religion in schools has become over recent years more liberal and open-ended.

One development that illustrates this is the increased incidence of the study of Comparative Religion in schools and colleges. We no longer regard religious education as concerned to teach only the Christian religion. It is clear that this was the intention of the 1944 Act, since there could be no other reason for allowing parents to withdraw their children from RE lessons. It is also clear from the quotation with which we began this chapter that this was the intention of the Plowden Committee in its approach to RE in the primary school, a point which is emphasized by the refusal of some members of the committee to go along with its recommendations on this issue and the submission of a note of reservation by A.J. Ayer and several others. However, in spite of Plowden and even the 1944 Act, which is still in force, this is not usually any longer the practice of the schools, not least because many of them are catering for the kind of multi-ethnic community for which this sort of approach would be totally unsuitable. The approach to religious education in schools, then, like the approach to religious assemblies, is today far more open.

Two further points must be made about this trend in the teaching of religion in schools which are of crucial importance for moral education. Firstly, it is a trend which reflects a distinction that has come to be made by some theorists, theologians and educationists alike, within religious knowledge. Our attention has been drawn to the fact that all religious utterances are not of the same kind and are not, as a result, subject to the same kinds of verification procedures. In other words, what we call religious knowledge is a body of assertions of several different logical types. We need, for example, quite different methods for testing the truth of such diverse kinds of assertions as "Moses led the Israelites out of bondage in Egypt", "Jesus Christ is the son of God", "God is love" and "Goodness is treating one's neighbour as oneself". A broad distinction can be drawn, therefore, between what might be called "historical" or "factual" assertions, a category which would include statements concerning the history, the social significance and the ritual of a religion, and those that have been called the "parahistorical", a category which includes the doctrinal, the mythological and the ethical (Smart 1968).

Furthermore, not only has it been argued on the basis of this view of religious knowledge that we should adopt the more liberal and open approach to it that we have already discussed (Smart 1968); it is further argued by some that no justification can be found for teaching the second kind of religious knowledge at all (Hirst 1965a). Some would even argue that it is not really knowledge. There are good reasons, it is claimed, for teaching *about* the Christian religion (or any other religion if it comes to that), since it is part of our heritage, has played a major role in the development of our civilization and has the same claims to be included in the curriculum as English literature, history or any of the humanities. There is no justification, however, for teaching its doctrines or for attempting to establish faith or belief in them, since to do so is to discourage that open and critical approach to knowledge which is the essence of education and to offer as "fact" "knowledge" whose bases are highly problematic.

The importance of this for moral education will be clear. For, where links between morals and religion have been claimed, these links are forged with the doctrinal aspects of the religion not the historical. It is because "God is love" that we are urged to love our neighbour, not because Moses led the Israelites out of bondage in Egypt. It is because "Jesus Christ is the son of God" that we are encouraged to follow his moral teachings, not because he lived at the beginning of the first century AD.

This general development draws our attention, then, to the problems surrounding moral assertions as well as those of religious knowledge. It also puts moral education at risk. For it raises the baby and bathwater problem to which we referred earlier. If we cannot justify teaching the doctrinal aspects of religion, then we cannot justify teaching the moral precepts that are based on them. If our approach to the teaching of religion is liberal and open-ended, the implication of this is that pupils are to be encouraged to make up their own minds on religious issues, to accept or reject, "to stand on their own feet in such matters" (Smart 1968, p.99). If, however, their considered choice is to reject religion, the result of a linking of religion and morality will be the rejection of morality too. Not only is this undesirable, it is also a logical and psychological impossibility. For, while it is possible, as many people demonstrate daily, to live without religion, it is clearly not possible to live, except at the level of animal existence, without any set of moral values or principles to guide one's behaviour, one's human choices. This in itself must cast the greatest possible doubt on the validity of any linking of morality with religion.

It is for this reason that recent years have seen the development of what has been called "secular morality", an approach to morals that is independent of all religions. This term is used as though it denoted something new and unusual; it also suggests that it represents merely an alternative kind of morality. It is our contention that this is the only approach one can adopt to the problem of morals.

There is no logical connection between morality and religion. Any connection that exists is merely contingent. We have just discussed some of the dangers of this contingent connection, particularly those consequent on any rejection of religious beliefs. There is another danger too, however, which may be of even greater significance. A religious morality must essentially be an authoritarian morality. Our reason for accepting those moral principles that have their basis in religion and for adopting as a consequence certain kinds of behaviour must be that they are recommended, if not demanded, by the godhead. This is true of any religious code of ethics no matter what religion it emanates from. For if our reasons are other than these, then by definition our morality is not a religious one. If, for example, I believe on other grounds that I should treat my neighbour as myself, then my code of morality is not a religious one. If I believe this because God or Jesus Christ demands it of me, then I am tacitly accepting that the only reason for acting in that way is that it is required of me by an authority whose right to make such demands I recognize. Any morality that is based on religion, therefore, is authoritarian in essence.

Further problems will arise if one tries to avoid this difficulty by suggesting that there are reasons for these principles other than the arbitrary commands of God, that God's role is to reveal to us certain eternal moral truths. For if these moral truths exist in some way independently of God's will, then there are important implications for his omnipotence. If loving one's neighbour as oneself is right independently of God's will, then God is not omnipotent, since there exists something that is beyond his control and to which he may even be subject himself (O'Connor 1957). In any case, to argue thus is to acknowledge that the basis of any set of moral principles is independent of religious beliefs.

Thus the linking of morality to religion either creates enormous theological problems or must lead to the acceptance of an authoritarian basis for one's moral code. It is for this reason that over the centuries religion and theology have inhibited rather than enhanced moral debate, since they have focused attention on questions of the interpretation of the word of God rather than on how man could set about thinking for himself on moral issues.

Why is this not acceptable? Primarily it is unacceptable because it denies to the individual the right to choose his own beliefs, moral principles and behaviour on his own terms and in the light of his own thinking. The same arguments that have been put in favour of making up one's own mind on religious questions must apply with at least equal force in relation to moral principles and choices. In order to do this, one must reject any morality that is based on the blind acceptance of any kind of authority.

Secondly, it is unacceptable because it does not allow for the evolution of moral knowledge or understanding. It does not allow for the fact that moral "knowledge", like all other knowledge, will develop and change. Its model for all knowledge is that of a progressive revelation by God to man of eternal truths and such a view would seem to be no longer tenable in any area, least of all that of morality. To put it differently, our moral understanding must be such as to enable us to adjust to changing social circumstances, to meet new moral problems and modify our principles to deal with them. This is not possible with a morality that is based on authority.

For adjustment becomes a matter of interpretation and this is usually difficult and sometimes impossible, as the ambivalence of the church and its slowness to pronounce on such issues as contraception and abortion indicates. To leave such questions to the judgement of the individual is to admit that religion itself can provide no firm basis for moral decisions.

Thus a proper morality has to be seen as independent of religion. If there is a connection it is not that morality is dependent on religious beliefs, it is much more likely that man's religious beliefs are a result of his moral awareness. As Kant said, "Belief in God is grounded in the moral consciousness rather than the moral law on belief in God".

Because of the dangers inherent in the rejection of religious beliefs, therefore, and in the adoption of an authoritarian morality, we have begun in recent times to consider moral education independently of the teachings of religion. This is one of the reasons for the growing interest in moral education. It is our intention in this book to examine what is involved for teachers in facing up to the task of providing a moral education on this basis. In order to do that we shall begin by attempting to discern what moral education is, since we have now established that it is not religious education, and, firstly, what other reasons there might be for its growing importance.

The importance of moral education—in traditional theory and practice

From earliest times in educational theory and practice moral education has been seen as the very core of the educational process, and moral upbringing has been regarded, almost without question, as the central feature of education itself. The truth of this is immediately apparent from an examination of the work of any or all of the great theorists and practitioners of education.

All of the great theorists throughout the centuries have been quite explicit on this point. For Socrates virtue was knowledge of the good and, in Plato's elaborate development of this theme, the role of education, its whole point and purpose, was to help people, those at least who were blessed with the necessary intellectual capacity for it, to acquire the kind of knowledge that would of itself bring virtue in its train and lead to the attainment of that wisdom that comes from knowledge of the good. All other forms of intellectual activity were regarded as means to that end. The coping stone of all knowledge for Plato, that which bound all knowledge together into one unified whole, was knowledge of the supreme "Form" of "beauty, truth and goodness". Not only, therefore, was morality seen as the central feature of education, "goodness" also was regarded as the focal point of all human knowledge.

For the Roman Quintilian, too, the development of virtue was the core of educational practice. Quintilian's concern was with education in rhetoric, the education of the orator, a concern which reflects not only the more practical approach that he himself takes in discussions of education but also the major difference in "the national genius of the two peoples, Greek and Roman" (Rusk 1957, p.38). Nevertheless, the primary aim of this training in rhetoric is the production of the good man rather than merely the good politician or lawyer. "The perfect orator must be a man of integrity, the good man, otherwise he cannot pretend to that character; and we therefore not only require in him a consummate talent for speaking, but all the virtuous endowments of the mind....Let therefore the orator be as the real sage, not only perfect in morals, but also in science, and in all the requisites and powers of elocution." In this way Quintilian attempts to give an educational rather than a purely vocational dimension to the training in rhetoric by introducing into it as a central core the notion of moral upbringing.

The Judaeic tradition likewise stresses as the focal point of education an upbringing according to the law enshrined in the Torah and a commitment to living according to its demands. Christianity, as a fusion of these two traditions, similarly regarded character training as the central task of education and even condoned practices that we might be inclined to see as far from moral in themselves if they appeared to be conducive to the establishment of a proper sense of moral rectitude in children. As a result, most of the great educational theorists have seen moral education in one form or another as the hub of any activity that was to merit description as educational. Indeed, the term "Humanities" as used to designate a very large section of the curriculum (for a long time, in fact, the whole of the curriculum) indicates by its derivation that relations between man and man were seen as the central, or even the only, concern of education in the full sense. Moral upbringing, or character training, therefore, was for long the central feature of what education itself was understood to be by the great theorists and, indeed, by the great practitioners.

Thus Comenius tells us that the curriculum should include "all those subjects which are able to make a man wise, virtuous and pious". Locke claims, "'Tis a virtue, then, direct virtue, which is the hard and valuable part to be aimed at in education." This is echoed in Rousseau's assertion "Life is the trade I would teach him", and taken up by Pestalozzi with his claim that the ultimate goal of education is preparation for life, by Herbart who tells us that "the one and the whole work of education may be summed up in the concept—morality", and by Froebel's recommendation that the main purpose of education should be to bring out and develop to the full the innate goodness of the child (Rusk 1957).

It was probably with the development of education for all and the concomitant introduction of a vocational component into the curriculum that moral education lost in part this central role. There was, of course, an element of "gentling" of the masses in the early thinking about education for all, some kind of training for everyone in obedience and good behaviour, but much stronger was the need to provide every member of society with the basic skills that a developing industrial community needed and to tap as efficiently as possible the human wealth of the nation. Most practical decisions in education as elsewhere are made on economic grounds. Thus schooling came to be seen rather less as the education of the cultured gentleman and rather more as a national investment. New subjects came to be added to the curriculum whose prime justification was social or vocational, rather than based on their contribution to moral development, so that moral education or character training lost its central place and was no longer seen as the focus of the school's activities, although continuing to be the concern of some aspects of school life, particularly those extra-curricular activities that most schools have promoted. Within the curriculum, as we suggested earlier, it came to be regarded as the concern almost solely of lessons in religion.

The importance of moral education—in current theory and practice

Recent years, however, have witnessed a revival of interest in moral education as such, as evidenced by the establishment of several curriculum projects in this area and by the appearance of Moral Education as a subject on the timetable of many secondary schools. There would seem to be several reasons for this. One must be the decline in religious belief or at least in allegiance to institutional religion that has characterized the development of many societies in recent times. If morality is too closely linked to religion, then, as we have seen, a growing tendency to reject religion will raise difficult moral questions and may even suggest *prima facie* a rejection of morality. Hence, faced by an increasing reluctance on the part of many pupils to accept what Religious Education has offered them, especially in the way of moral teaching, schools have been forced to consider other ways in which their responsibility for the moral education of their pupils might be fulfilled. A good example of this process has been the increased secularization of the compulsory daily "act of worship" in many schools at all levels in the United Kingdom.

An equally cogent factor, however, has been the change that has taken place in our view of morality itself. The ideas of the theorists we mentioned earlier are based on a theory of morality that few today would regard as tenable. That theory is one that sees moral precepts as objectively valid and, as a result, regards it as sensible to speak of moral knowledge or knowledge of "the good" and to talk about "right behaviour". It results, therefore, in a view of moral education as a kind of character training and such a view is only tenable if one accepts the theory of morality at its base as fixed and objective. This, as we have seen, is inevitably the kind of view of moral education that emerges when it is too closely associated with religious education, since most religions include a relatively fixed code of morals within their tenets. It is a view, therefore, which leads to the notion that the morally educated person is one who has come to recognize the truth of certain particular moral values and to act on them and that the purpose of moral education (or rather moral instruction) is to instil these values in pupils, to bring them to a "knowledge" of them. Few would now subscribe to such a view of morality, since not only is it based on an outmoded theory of knowledge, it also leads, as we saw in our earlier discussion of religion, to an authoritarian morality.

The conflict between the traditional view of education as essentially concerned with moral upbringing and the change that has taken place in our attitude to morality itself is clearly reflected in the work of John Dewey which must be seen both as a culmination of the ideas that were first proferred by Rousseau and then developed by other theorists in the nineteenth century and at the same time within a new intellectual setting, characterized by such major intellectual advances as theories of evolution and the "revolution" in philosophy. For Dewey the central concern of education is still life or living itself, so that its main purpose is still to provide man with control over all aspects of his environment. But now the environment is seen as a changing one and the prime need is to produce people who can adapt to and control those changes; this they will do by learning to make decisions not in the light of some notion of fixed values and unchanging moral standpoints but from the point of view of moral positions that must be seen as themselves subject to the same process of continuous change and evolution. For Dewey, then, the central purpose of education is to enable human beings to make the necessary adjustments to meet a constantly changing environment and the most important (and most difficult) adjustments to be made are adaptations to changing moral values.

Herein lies the major clue as to the changes that have taken place in our view of education and especially of the role of moral education within it. The traditional theory of morality as fixed and unchanging which formed the basis of so many educational theories, as we have seen, is no longer adequate. One reason for this we have also just seen to be an acceptance of the notion of the evolution of all things. However, there have been several other contributory factors and, since they all combine to offer further perspectives on our main question of what is moral education, we must look at each of them briefly in turn.

The first of these is the fact of social change. Not only have we come to recognize evolution as a theory; we have come to see it also as an ever-present reality. Society in every respect has changed dramatically in recent years. Major advances have been made in technology and these have transformed life in all parts of the world to the point where most adults today take for granted features of their daily existence which in their own childhood they would have regarded as science-fiction. Worldwide television networks, landings on the moon, supersonic travel are no longer the prerogatives of Flash

Gordon or Dan Dare; they are a part of the lives of all of us.

However, technological change brings social and moral change in its wake; at the very least it raises moral questions for which tradition can provide no ready-made answers and for which new answers must be found. The development of the ability to transplant organs from one body to another, to abort a birth or to prevent conception has presented us with many new moral problems and these are among the more obvious examples of the way in which improved technological skill creates moral and social change by forcing us to adjust our systems of values to meet these changes. This is the reality of the point that we described as central to John Dewey's philosophy. Technological change is a fact and so, therefore, is the social and moral change that it engenders.

Furthermore, it is quite clear that on all of these issues many different stances are possible. There is no single hard and fast answer to them. Even established religions fail to offer solutions to them that all can accept and this must be seen as one factor in the decline of the influence of organized religion. Indeed, many societies now are multi-ethnic and thus contain a variety of religions which often offer a corresponding variety of moral codes. Most advanced societies, therefore, can now be described as pluralist; that is, they can be seen to contain groups and individuals who differ very markedly from each other on certain questions of value. As a result there has grown an awareness that moral issues cannot be dealt with in a once-and-for-all manner by the offering of universal moral answers, but that each individual will reach his own conclusions on most moral questions. This is true at least of most Western societies. If this is so, then it becomes the task of the schools to help children to acquire the ability to engage in the kind of thinking necessary to reach conclusions that are sound.

It should be quite clear by now that we cannot prepare pupils for this kind of world by offering them set answers to those problems we are aware of at that point in time when we happen to be attending to their moral education. A good deal of the moral turmoil and confusion that we have witnessed in recent times is a result of attempts made in the past to offer a moral upbringing in these terms. Even if we think we have the "right" answers to current problems and can persuade young people to accept them, this will not help them when new problems come along. It is for this reason, among others, that people who have had that kind of moral training find it difficult to respond to moral problems for which they have not been prepared. The Crowther Report (1959) suggested that the rapidity of technological change required not a vocational training for young people in specific skills but the development of a "general mechanical ability" that would enable them to cope not only with the technology of the present but also with that of the future. The rapidity of the social and moral change that is a concomitant of technological change requires us to approach moral education from a similar perspective. People need to learn how to adapt, to think for themselves, to be fully autonomous beings. If this is so, if this is the force of current social change, then we cannot, even if we might want to, set about the moral education of our young by trying to teach them what to think in a manner that does not invite their critical appraisal.

However, there are perhaps good reasons why we should not even want to approach moral upbringing in this way. For a second, and closely related, reason why our thinking about moral education is changing is that we have come to take a different view of the nature of man, a different model of man as a basis for our thinking. The pressures for this can be traced to a number of sources. One of these is, of course, the experience of social change which we have just been discussing. Another is the thinking of those philosophers, often dubbed "existentialist", whose view of individual autonomy goes back at least as far as Immanuel Kant and who have stressed the uniqueness of each human being and his consequential right to make his own decisions and thus determine his own "essence". As a result, there has emerged a growing hostility towards any theory, especially within education, which, like the views of the behaviourist psychologists, for example, is based on a passive view of man, as a being who is acted upon, shaped and guided, like an inanimate object, by forces external to himself rather than on a view of him as an active, dynamic being in charge at least to some extent of his own destiny and therefore responsible for his actions and behaviour.

Certainly in the Western world this has come to be a dominant feature of our way of looking at existence. For it is, of course, closely bound up with the ideal of social freedom that is fundamental to the explicit philosophy of what has sometimes been called the "free world". Such an ideal entails the notion of man as an active agent responsible for his own destiny and entitled to make his own moral choices according to his own moral values. Clearly, if acting on such choices, putting his beliefs into practice, is likely to lead unjustifiably to harm or threat of harm or loss of freedom to others, then his freedom of action must be curtailed. But a man's freedom of thought, his right to his own beliefs no matter how unacceptable or even distasteful they may be to others in theory, is not to be denied since it is fundamental to what is seen as the democratic way of life, one of the great freedoms of the Atlantic Charter.

If this view of man is taken, then an authoritarian approach to morality cannot be adopted. A man's values must be his own since he is not free if his behaviour is controlled by a code of values imposed by others. This, as we have already seen, is the source of the great tension that has always existed in Christian theology between the notion of free will, of the freedom of the individual to choose or to reject God, and the idea of an authoritarian code of morality set for man by God. This in turn is the source of some of the moral dilemmas the Christian church has faced — not always successfully — in recent times. If an authoritarian view of morality cannot be accepted, then an approach to moral education that derives from it cannot be accepted either. And so we have here a second major reason why moral education can no longer be viewed as a process of telling children what to believe and how to believe.

We have tried to show, then, that among the reasons for the recent revival of interest in the moral aspects of education are, firstly, the changing nature of society and, secondly, consequential changes in our view of what it means to be a human being. In doing so we have begun to discover part of the answer to our question of what moral education is, since we have seen that if it is to be a response to the demands of a changing society and suited to our concept of man as a free and active being, then this will to some extent determine the form it must take. Not only, then, must we recognize this as a demand for the freedom and autonomy of the individual; we must also acknowledge that nothing less than respect for that freedom and autonomy can enable us to help people to live in society as we know it. Hence not only are we made aware of an increased need for moral education; we are also made aware of the need for a different concept of what it is, the first aspect of which we have now discovered to be that it must enable people to do their own moral thinking rather than encourage them to conform to an externally imposed moral code.

The concept of education

The same conclusion is forced upon us if we approach this question in a different way and ask what is involved in using the term "education" to denote this process rather than speaking of moral instruction or moral knowledge. We saw earlier how crucial were the semantic differences between these terms for the teaching of religion in schools. There must, then, be similar significance in using the term "education" to denote the school's contribution to moral upbringing. Again the implication is that this is not a matter of instruction in certain moral tenets nor is it a matter of being introduced to certain moral values which are fixed and unquestionable and, as a result, the objects of moral knowledge, but that it is a process of learning to think for oneself on moral issues, of becoming morally autonomous.

However, an examination of the implications of the use of the term "education" in this context will take us further than that or, to put it differently, it will begin to reveal in further detail and at further levels of complexity some of the features of this moral autonomy.

Philosophers such as G.E. Moore and Ludwig Wittgenstein have suggested that the meaning of a term is to be discovered by exploring how it is used, and have further proposed that, if we wish to discover the similarities, the differences and the connections existing between related terms, we must do so by looking for significant differences or similarities in the contexts in which they are used. Acts of teaching are described as instruction, training, conditioning or indoctrination as well as education, according to the context in which they are used. Clearly everyone chooses his terms in this area according to some definite criteria. To discover the differences between them, therefore, we need to discover what those criteria are. Our particular concern here is to establish some of the conditions that must apply before we feel it appropriate to use the term "education".

The concept of "education" as it is used in wider contexts has been very well unpacked by Richard Peters (1965, 1966) and it will be helpful if we consider some of the general points he makes in the specific context of moral education.

What are the main features of education that make it different from other processes that teachers put pupils through, processes such as training, instruction, conditioning and even indoctrination? Fundamentally, of course, as we have already asserted, education is concerned with the developing autonomy of the individual as these other processes are not. To set about training or instructing someone in something is to ignore any consideration of that person's autonomy; such considerations just do not arise; in some cases they may even be irrelevant and inappropriate, as in training someone to drive a car. Processes such as conditioning or indoctrinating go even beyond this. For, whatever else is implied by the use of these terms, they would appear from their normal usage to be deliberate attempts to stifle the individual's autonomy. A man who has been conditioned or indoctrinated in some respect does not by definition think for himself in that area. Attempts to indoctrinate people into the blind acceptance of particular social and political systems are deliberate attempts to discourage and prevent them from questioning the validity of these systems. If successful, this kind of process will result in what Bertrand Russell, in commenting on Plato's theory of education, once described as "good behaviour with the wrong emotions" (Russell 1908). This provides further confirmation, therefore, of what we have already asserted, namely that to educate someone morally rather than instructing or indoctrinating him is to endeavour to promote in him the ability to think for himself on moral issues.

However, this can be developed further, as Richard Peters shows. For several things are involved here. To begin with, there is implied the development not only of knowledge but, further, of understanding, the acquisition of what Richard Peters calls "cognitive perspective" and the development of critical awareness. For in order to engage in one's own thinking on any issue it is necessary to possess as wide an understanding of that issue, and, indeed, of all relevant and related issues, as it is possible to gain as a basis for a critical analysis and review of the opinions held by others in this sphere. To be educated, then, is not merely to be given autonomy—one has that anyway—it is to be assisted to use that autonomy effectively. What distinguishes an educated man from an uneducated man in any area is that, while both have their opinions and enjoy their freedom of thought, the former's opinions are informed, based on a breadth of knowledge and understanding and thus qualitatively quite different. One of the "aims" of education, therefore, one of the principles that should inform all activities that are to be called educational rather than instructional, indoctrinatory or whatever, is that it represents an attempt not only to develop in pupils the ability to form opinions but also to improve the quality of the opinions they form.

What this implies for moral education, therefore, is that we are committed to promoting in people a desire to achieve the greatest possible knowledge and understanding of whatever kind will help them to reach autonomous choices which are based on careful and informed thinking about the issues involved. Autonomy of itself is of little value if it results in thinking that is done out of the top of the head or through the elbow. This crucial distinction is well illustrated by the basic pedagogy of the Schools Council's Humanities Curriculum Project, which we shall look at in greater detail in a later chapter. The authors of that project, which is concerned to encourage discussion amongst older secondary school pupils of moral and social issues of current relevance, have stressed that, while on the one hand the teacher must be neutral with regard to the conclusions that pupils reach on these issues, his job is certainly not to remain neutral with regard to the standards of the discussion, "that the teacher accepts the need to submit his teaching in controversial areas to the criterion of neutrality at this stage of education, i.e., that he regards it as part of his responsibility not to promote his own view", but "that the teacher as chairman of the discussion should have responsibility for quality and standards in learning" (Schools Council 1970, p.1).

Thus there is an important distinction to be made between the manner and the matter of education (Peters 1965, 1966). An examination of the concept of education tells us a good deal about the manner in which it is to be conducted. Indeed, this may be the only thing it tells us much about. When we apply this to the concerns of moral education, a crucial distinction emerges between the form and the content of moral education, which makes it clear that the moral educator's job is to teach pupils how to think rather than what to think on moral issues.

There is another aspect of this distinction that also needs to be mentioned here. Not only is it important that we should take care over the manner in which we set about the moral education of our pupils, the form of what we offer them; we must also pay close attention to the manner in which they come to hold their moral beliefs. We shall discuss at some length in Chapter 3 the theories of those developmental psychologists who have studied the stages through which children must pass if they are to reach the goal of moral autonomy. In broad terms, they have suggested that from a state of anomy which is without rules, children pass to the stage of heteronomy at which rules are seen as emanating from others, from people in authority, especially parents and teachers. The next stage is that of socionomy or conventional morality, at which rules are seen as based not on arbitrary authority but on social utility. Only after that can they come to the stage or autonomy of what Kohlberg calls "self-accepted moral principles" (1966).

The important thing to notice at this point in our discussion is that not only do these represent stages of moral development. They also represent qualitatively different levels of response to moral choices or dilemmas, different kinds or definitions of moral behaviour, all of which can be observed at all ages and in all people. In other words, it is an oversimplification to see this scheme as chronological, as tied to age. We must recognize that the point that is being made is epistemological as well as psychological. Few people, no matter how well educated they are morally nor how skilled at moral debate, will not hold some of their moral principles in an uncritical manner, having accepted them unthinkingly from those who have exercised authority over them or from the society in which they live. If moral education is concerned with the manner in which we hold our moral beliefs, then, it must endeavour to ensure that we reflect critically on all of them. This was one of the reasons we gave for arguing the unsuitability of a religious base for moral education. It is a point we will need to take up in greater detail in Chapter 5.

Furthermore, it will soon be clear that among the factors involved in teaching pupils how to think about moral questions, among the criteria we should appeal to in making judgements about the quality of people's thinking in this area will be such things as logical coherence, respect for truth and breadth of relevant knowledge and understanding. A moment's thought will reveal that we do not respect a man's opinion on any issue unless we are convinced that he has given proper thought to the matter and "knows what he is talking about". If he doesn't, we regard him as "not worth listening to" and certainly "not worth arguing with". Moral education, therefore, should be concerned not only to encourage pupils to think for themselves on moral issues but to help them to do this in an informed and intelligent manner.

Another feature of education to which Richard Peters draws our attention is that it involves bringing the pupil to the point where he comes to care about the activities we have engaged him in and values them; further, that he values them for their own sake, comes to regard them as having "intrinsic value". Again we must note that with other activities that involve teaching this feature need not be present. We can train someone to drive a car or instruct him in motor mechanics without any concern for the question of whether he likes such activities, cares for them or values them at all. From the psychological point of view, of course, our task will be easier if he does enjoy what he is doing and is thus motivated to work hard at it, but, conceptually speaking, such considerations are not crucial. On the other hand, it would be strange and perhaps illogical to speak of a man as educated while at the same time asserting that he places no value at all on any of the knowledge and understanding that he had acquired as part of that process of being or becoming educated.

Again, we must note that this has several implications for moral education. For it will be clear that the moral educator must be concerned to develop in his pupils a conviction of the worthwhileness of moral behaviour, a sense of moral responsibility. It will not be enough to teach pupils how to carry out their moral thinking at a high level if we do not at the same time bring them to the conviction that it matters.

Furthermore moral behaviour above all has a "caring" dimension to it. The man who "goes through the motions" of behaving morally is usually regarded as a pretty cold fish and is unlikely to be considered morally educated at all, not least because behaviour of this kind is prompted by considerations of a purely intellectual kind and can sometimes lead to the sort of "moral rectitude" that does more harm than good. This feature of human behaviour is well illustrated in a number of works of the Greek tragedians, this ability to cause mayhem by inflexibility of values untempered by any kind of human feelings being for them a significant source of truly tragic consequences. Thus Sophocles, for example, in his *Antigone* depicts the conflict between the desire of Antigone herself to act from the heart out of love for her dead brother, Polyneices, and the rigid intention of her uncle, Kreon, to maintain his ruling that Polyneices, who has died in battle fighting against the state, should not be accorded the rights of a proper burial, a conflict which results in the death not only of Antigone herself but also of Haemon, Kreon's own son, to whom she is betrothed. In this way too rigid an adherence to the dictates of the head, to what appear to be the demands of reason, is shown to be productive of harm rather than good. Moral behaviour has to be seen as involving the heart as much as the head.

Indeed, it may be the case that autonomous moral thinking as such cannot be carried out at a purely intellectual level since, if there is no real valuing of other people and of one's relations with them, one of the principal ingredients of a moral decision would appear to be missing. Every viewer of *Dr. Who*, young or old, knows that Daleks cannot make truly moral decisions and that this is precisely because they are "all head and no heart". Their leaders make decisions based on purely scientific or utilitarian considerations (usually involving the extermination of various beings who stand in the way of the attainment of their goals) and the others, with loud and repeated emotionless assertions of "I obey!", trundle off to carry these orders out.

This draws our attention, then, to an important feature of moral education which is often overlooked but which reflects what is probably the most complex and least understood aspect of morality, namely the extent to which it involves not just the intellect but also the emotions. As far as education is concerned, this means that it is not just a matter of cognition; there is an important affective dimension too. It thus opens up a new and important area of concern for the moral educator.

A related point emerges from an examination of what we mean by "morality", what counts as a moral action. For a moment's reflection will reveal that one crucial element in this is the intentionality of the agent. There are two aspects of this. In the first place, we do not regard a man's actions as moral—nor as immoral, if it comes to that—, as subject either to praise or blame, unless we have first established that he acted of his own free will. It must be an act that he is in the full sense responsible for, if we are to make any kind of moral judgement on it. This is the practice of every court of justice, which must establish not only whether a defendant did in fact commit the crime with which he is charged, but also whether he did it knowingly and can thus be held responsible for it and criminally culpable. Aristotle made a distinction between actions performed "willingly" and those done "not unwillingly" and claimed that only the former were moral actions in the full sense. Aquinas too makes a similar distinction between "human acts" and "acts of man".

Secondly, however, when we come to the question of apportioning praise or blame, the kind of motive also becomes important and we do distinguish between actions performed because the agent thinks they are right and those performed because he thinks they will bring certain advantages. It is not only the action that we weigh when making a moral judgement, it is much more the motivation. This is what Kant meant when he said "Nothing can possibly be conceived in the world, or even out of it, which can be called good, without qualification, except a Good Will." Actions can be and usually will be performed out of mixed motives; certainly they are susceptible to a variety of interpretations. Only the good will can be free of any such real or imagined flaws. This is why Kant also distinguished between actions performed *for the sake of* duty and those performed *in accordance with* duty. A grocer in reducing the price of his goods may make them more accessible to the hungry poor but he may do so not for this reason but to boost his sales and thus his profits. If the latter is his intention, then although his action is in accordance with his duty it has not been done for the sake of duty, so that it is not a truly moral act. Crucial to moral behaviour, therefore, is that it should be motivated by the desire to do what is right and not by considerations of expediency.

It has, of course, been argued throughout the ages that morality is only a matter of expediency, that we treat other people properly only because we are frightened of the consequences to ourselves if they were to cease to treat us in the same way, that we do unto others that which we hope they will do unto us and that, as a corollary, we also do unto them that which we think we can get away with. This theory has a long and distinguished history in the annals of Western philosophy. The whole of Plato's *Republic* is an attempt to demolish the view put in the early stages of the dialogue by the sophist, Thrasymachus, that justice or morality is "the interest of the stronger" and the "social contract" view of morality that is also put there. Men create and obey rules only to promote their own interests, usually of self-protection, and, if they do not need that, then they are above morality. This is illustrated in the *Republic* by the story of Gyges, a Lydian shepherd, who, on acquiring the power to render himself invisible, kills the king of Lydia, seduces the queen, becomes king himself and lives happily ever after. The question posed is "Who would be stupid enough to behave otherwise in such circumstances?". The behaviour of the Gods in Greek literature, especially in the early works, such as those of Homer, also supports such a view and one of the major features of the works of the Greek tragedians is an attempt to take up this issue and resolve it in a more satisfactory manner. It is a theme that has reappeared frequently down the ages, in the social contract theories of men such as Thomas Hobbes, for example, and it is a view that is not very far from acceptance by many people today.

What refutes this view (if "refute" is the word) is that it does not fit with the way in which people do behave and the way in which they view moral behaviour. The distinction we are referring to here between actions performed from a sense and conviction of their rightness and those done out of considerations of pure expediency, those done for their own sake and those performed as means to some other end, is one that we do make. Some of the behaviour of all of us is prompted by prudential motives, by considerations of expediency, but not all of our behaviour is of this kind. Some actions are performed because of a conviction that they are right and sometimes these are actions that cannot in any sense be regarded as in the interests of the agent. Furthermore, it is only actions of this latter kind, those done for the sake of duty, that are regarded as moral actions.

The relevance of this to moral education will be clear. If we believe that what is called moral behaviour is entirely explicable in terms of self-interest, self-protection or expediency, then we can have no interest in moral education at all; we can have no concept of moral education even. For our task can only be that of any animal mother of providing her offspring with the skills necessary for survival in a world characterized by being, as Hobbes suggested, "a war of all against all", in which there is "continual fear and danger of violent death" and in which the life of man is "solitary, poor, nasty, brutish and short". If we do have a concept of morality and thus of moral education, this must include centrally the notion of actions to be performed because they are felt to be right and not merely expedient. The importance of this to the practice of moral education we must examine later.

Our brief examination of some of the features of what we mean by "education" and "morality", then, has taken us some way further towards answering our question, "What is moral education?" It has provided further evidence of the importance of moral autonomy and it has taken us beyond this by drawing our attention to the need to develop in our pupils the knowledge, the understanding and the respect for morality that will help them to use their autonomy to best effect, to achieve informed moral opinions and values based on a full appreciation of their implications and a critical appraisal of the possible alternatives. It has also drawn our attention to the important role played by the emotions in moral behaviour and has suggested that this cannot be ignored by the moral educator.

Some of the facets of this will become plainer as we now turn to our last angle of approach to the question of "What is moral education?" by considering what might be regarded as the essential features of the morally educated person.

Who is the morally educated person?

So far we have tried to gain some idea of what is involved in moral education, first of all by considering why it has come to be regarded as so important and then by examining what is entailed by the use of the term "education" to denote it. Both of these approaches have brought some results. We must now finally try to discover what can be learnt by approaching the question from the other end, by asking what characteristics we would expect to find in a man or woman we would be willing to describe as morally educated. For if we can discover what qualities would be regarded as essential in a morally educated person, we will have gained a clearer view of the qualities we should be concerned as moral educators to promote and the principles which should, as a result, inform all of our activity in this field. This is an approach that proved very useful to John Wilson and his colleagues of the Farmington Trust Research Unit into Moral Education as a preliminary to the framing of their own proposals for moral education which we will discuss in detail in Chapter 7 (Wilson, Williams and Sugarman 1967).

To begin with, we must note that this approach will emphasize and offer further evidence for the importance of several of those features of moral education that our earlier discussions have revealed. We would be unlikely nowadays to describe as morally educated the person who has had the kind of moral upbringing we referred to earlier as the result of traditional views of the purposes of moral education, the man who has been taught what to believe and how to behave, who has been exposed to character training rather than moral education. For a moment's thought is sufficient to reveal that we would be unlikely to describe someone as morally educated who either was incapable of reaching his own autonomous moral decisions or who reached them without any kind of thought or consideration of relevant factors. The former person we would regard as totally indecisive, the latter as merely prejudiced. Nor would we regard it as satisfactory if a person made such decisions without a high degree of understanding, of awareness of possible alternatives and the ability to review these critically at some depth and in the light of the fullest possible knowledge as a preliminary to reaching his own conclusions. Thus this approach brings further confirmation of what our earlier discussions revealed.

However, it is possible that by asking what other features we would expect the morally educated person to display we may be able to go beyond this. For example, asking this question may be the best method of getting beyond the mere declaration of the need for knowledge and understanding to some idea of the particular kinds of knowledge and understanding that are needed.

In the first place, we would expect the morally educated person to possess a good deal of factual knowledge or at least to be aware of the kinds of factual knowledge relevant to each issue on which a decision needs to be taken, what A.J. Ayer once called the "non-moral" facts of a case (Ayer 1936, 1946). For, although ultimate choices themselves cannot be deduced by any process of logic from factual premises, this should not be taken to imply that factual knowledge has no kind of relevance to these choices. In particular, for example, we need in full the kind of scientific knowledge that will indicate the likely consequences of certain alternative courses of action. The morally educated person, therefore, must be aware of the need to take account of such factual evidence in reaching his conclusions; he must be aware of the need to be as fully informed on these matters as possible; and, in particular, he must recognize the importance of not basing his choices on actual misinformation. John Wilson offers us the example here of the man who might "through sheer ignorance... believe that (say) because negroes have less nerve-endings or thicker skulls they do not get hurt so easily" (Wilson, Williams and Sugarman 1967, p.193). It will be clear how that kind of misinformation can, and often does, affect the decisions people make. Thus the morally educated person will recognize that he must be as fully and as accurately informed as possible on the non-moral facts of each situation.

He will also need certain skills if he is to be able to act in a moral way as well as to think things through morally; he will need to know *how* as well as knowing *that*. It will not be enough for him to be able to work out intellectually and theoretically that a certain course of action is right if he lacks the necessary skills to put his decisions into practice. Some of these skills will clearly be social skills, the ability to relate to people, get on with them, even communicate with them. Others will be skills of a rather more basic and practical kind. It is not enough, for example, to decide that you should help the old-age pensioner next door to redecorate his living room if you either make a total and hideous botch-up of it or, worse, lack the social graces to avoid making him feel awkward, ill at ease or patronized all the time you are with him. These are further kinds of knowledge, then, that the morally educated person will need to possess. At the very least he must be sensitive to their necessity and importance.

This leads us, thirdly, to suggest that the morally educated man will also need knowledge and understanding of the feelings of other people. However, this is a kind of knowledge that is of little value if it never gets beyond the intellectual or cognitive level. If we recognize other people's feelings as facts and calculate accordingly what our behaviour towards them should be, there will be a coldness about our relationships that few would wish to characterize as moral. Consideration of the need for this kind of knowledge and understanding, then, takes us, as we suggested earlier, into a consideration of the affective dimension of moral behaviour and the part played by the emotions.

There are several features of this which we must take account of since they would seem to be essential elements in the equipment of the morally educated person and therefore of prime concern to the moral educator. The first of these we referred to earlier when, in looking at the significance of the use of the term "education" in this context, we suggested that it was important not to lose sight of the need to bring pupils to regard moral behaviour as important, to feel that relationships with others matter. Clearly, this is a feature that will be equally apparent when we are considering the qualities that should be evinced by the morally educated adult. It would be an odd kind of morality that resulted in decisions being made with no corresponding emotional commitment to them. It would result not so much in good behaviour with the wrong emotions as good behaviour with no emotions at all. This, as we shall see in a later chapter, is one of the criticisms levelled at Kant's view of morality and particularly at the kind of rationalist theory that it led such of his successors as Hegel to produce. In fact, it was this feature of rationalism more than any other that sparked off the existentialist reaction to it.

One aspect of this ability to recognize that moral behaviour is important, of course, is that it involves accepting the significance of other people's feelings. To recognize that other people have feelings like oneself is a matter of knowledge; to regard these feelings as important and as of equal value to one's own in any moral decision one takes is to have an attitude; it is to be emotionally rather than merely cognitively directed towards an acceptance of other people's rights, interests and feelings. The ability to do this, therefore, is not merely an intellectual attainment; it is another aspect of the emotional attitude towards moral behaviour we have just been discussing.

We might, however, take this even further. For it will not be sufficient for us to accept the importance of other people's feelings if we lack the ability at the same time to understand them. It happens quite frequently that people who do recognize the importance of the feelings of others cannot in particular situations appreciate the strength of someone's feelings and, as a result, do not let those feelings weigh with them as heavily as they should. We often "cannot believe he feels that strongly about it". Thus it is necessary in making moral decisions also to be able to see things from the other person's point of view, to get into his or her perspective on the matter at issue.

Thus far, therefore, we have established that the morally educated person will need to have a positive commitment towards the value of morality, towards the importance of other people's feelings, and the ability to understand as well as to recognize those feelings and their significance. There is, however, another way in which the emotions enter moral decision making. For our moral behaviour will be influenced by our own feelings and emotions even more than by a consideration of those of others. This feature of human behaviour has been regarded as of crucial importance at least since the time of Aristotle and it is vital that we do not ignore it in attending to the needs of moral education.

For Socrates and for Plato virtue was knowledge of the good. In other words, they were convinced, because of their total faith in and regard for man's rationality, that God-like quality that raised man above the animals, that once a person knew what the right course of action was in any given context he would follow it through without hesitation. Thus, as we saw earlier, for them moral education was a matter merely of bringing people to an intellectual recognition of the good. Once that was done, they believed, all else would follow, as the night follows the day. Aristotle, however, took a much more realistic view of man. He realized that it was not sufficient to have taken a moral decision at the rational and intellectual level. To do that is in many ways to have done the easy part. Once one comes to carry the decision out, other factors enter into the equation to make this far more complex and difficult than either Socrates or Plato had been willing to concede. These factors he called simply "pleasure", but by this he meant all of those emotional "pulls", those feelings that get between us and the implementation of our moral decisions. He was in fact asserting what St. Paul was later to confess, "The evil that I would not that I do and the good I would I do not". For Aristotle, then, moral education involved not only bringing up children to recognize the "right rule"; it also involved the kind of character training necessary to enable them to act on it once recognized.

This aspect of moral behaviour is clearly very important and it is again something we must discuss more fully in a later chapter. What we must stress here, however, is not merely that this is a feature of moral education that it is neither possible nor desirable to ignore, but further that it is one that we must develop a proper perspective on, a more sophisticated view than that of Aristotle. For it is not satisfactory to regard this emotional dimension, as Aristotle and many rationalist philosophers do, as an unpleasant reminder of human infirmity, as something, therefore, to be stifled and over-come, original sin to be stamped out. It must be seen as an indication of the necessary role the emotions play in morality. The emotional aspect of moral behaviour must be acknowledged and accepted as an essential part of it and not as an undesirable and unfortunate excrescence. As we said earlier, Daleks cannot behave morally since they lack the ability to respond emotionally to anything. Such response is the peculiar privilege of the human being; it is this that constitutes his humanity and enables him to live as a moral being. It is an aspect of moral behaviour that we must come to understand and value, therefore, rather than endeavour to stifle. This must also be the approach of the moral educator, since it is not his task to turn children into Daleks.

We cannot afford, then, to ignore this affective dimension of moral education and its many facets. For the morally educated person must be emotionally as well as intellectually attuned to his relation-ships with others. We must be concerned with the education of the emotions, helping people to acquire control of their emotions, but by developing an understanding of this aspect of human experience rather than by learning to stifle and suppress it. The message of Freud in this respect is clear and we must examine its precise significance for moral education in a later chapter.

This is another important feature of moral education, therefore, that emerges from an examination of what it means to be morally educated. Not only must we be able to understand the feelings of others; we must also be helped towards the greatest possible understanding of our own, which may, oddly enough, be much more difficult to achieve.

Summary and conclusions

We have attempted in this chapter to obtain a clearer picture of what moral education is so that we can begin to see what teachers have to do in order to plan and attend to the moral education of their pupils. We approached this question from three angles. Firstly, we tried to discover some reasons for the recent revival of interest in moral education and suggested that therein lay certain clues as to what its essential features are. In particular, we suggested that rapid social change has not only caused a revival of interest in moral education; it has also required us to approach it from a different point of view, to see its main concern as being with the development in pupils of the ability to think for themselves morally. Our second approach led us to a similar conclusion. For this involved us in an attempt to discern what was entailed by the use of the term "education" in this context. We suggested that in addition to reinforcing the need for moral thinking of an autonomous kind, this sort of analysis also alerted us to the need to promote understanding and critical awareness, a concern for the manner rather than solely the matter of education, a respect for truth and knowledge and a commitment to the importance of moral behaviour. Lastly, we tried to discover the main characteristics of the morally educated person, to see if this would add to our understanding of moral education. This approach in turn brought confirmation of what our earlier searches had revealed but it also opened up further considerations. It began to reveal in greater detail the kinds of knowledge people need to make moral decisions — knowledge of the non-moral facts, awareness of the likely consequences of their actions, skills of various kinds and understanding of the feelings of other people. This last point took us in turn onto a consideration of that very important but frequently ignored aspect of moral behaviour, the affective dimension, the role of the emotions, and we concluded by asserting the importance of helping pupils to develop not only an understanding and a sympathy for the feelings of others but also, of equal importance but perhaps of greater difficulty, an understanding and an acceptance of their own emotions.

All of these are aspects of moral education that later chapters will consider in greater detail. It is hoped that this chapter has succeeded in creating a clearer picture of what moral education is, upon which subsequent discussions can be based.

CHAPTER 2

REASON AND MORALITY

We concluded Chapter 1 by asserting that there is far more to moral behaviour than the mere application of reason to moral questions. However, we had pointed out earlier that reason does play a major role in morality. In fact, we suggested that it is man's ability to reason, to think rationally, that distinguishes him from the other members of the animal kingdom and it is the resultant ability to act purposefully, while at the same time considering consequences and alternatives, that constitutes in part what it means to be moral. In brief, it is because man can reason that he is capable of moral action, just as it is because animals cannot reason that they are not. It is man's rationality, therefore, that makes morality possible, so that reason must have a central role in the making of moral decisions.

It is the intention of this chapter to endeavour to throw some light on the difficult and contentious question of what that role is. What is the contribution of rationality to moral debate and, in particular, to moral behaviour?

What is rationality?

In order to achieve anything like a proper view of the place of rationality in morals we need first to clarify somewhat what we mean by rationality itself. Obviously, it is not possible to devote the rest of this book to the kind of detailed examination that this most interesting question warrants and requires, but it is necessary to attempt some kind of analysis—no matter how superficial it may have to be—if we are to get a sufficiently clear idea of the essential features of rationality to provide us with a basis for considering its place in moral decision making.

As we have just said, man, unlike other creatures, is capable of purposeful action, of acting deliberately on the basis of his own judgements, decisions, choices. He is not a passive creature whose behaviour is totally explicable in terms of instincts and the action of the environment on him (although we must not forget that some human behaviour—and in the case of some people almost all—is of this kind). He has the capability to behave positively, as an active agent rather than a passive recipient, in some respects at least controlling the effects of the environment upon him and even sometimes changing it to suit his own purposes. He has this capacity because of his ability to develop by the use of intelligence an ever-growing understanding of his world and a knowledge of the likely consequences of the different courses of action open to him. It is to the development of this kind of knowledge and understanding that the use of reason is directed and it is this basic notion of the function of rationality that is likely to offer us the most productive source of clues as to its nature.

For its prime features are essentially those encapsulated in the Hegelian notion of rationality as a dialectical process of argument and counter-argument, thesis and antithesis, leading to the emergence of the kind of synthesis that will add to our continuously developing understanding of the world. There are two features of this dialectical process and of the bodies of knowledge that result from it that are central to an understanding of what rationality is. For, in the first place, it will be obvious that the knowledge and understanding so developed should satisfy as nearly as possible such standards of truth as seem appropriate to it, so that suitable means need to be devised to test the truth of individual elements in the process. Secondly, we will need to be equally concerned with the validity of the process itself and of the bodies of knowledge it gives rise to. In other words, the process must be coherent and the links between one assertion and another must satisfy certain criteria of logical coherence. Clearly, questions of truth and validity are closely interwoven, but both are central features of what we mean by rationality.

We must not assume, however, that the definition of what will constitute truth or validity in any sphere will be easy or straight-forward. In fact, the case is quite the opposite, since there are many problems and difficulties over both, especially over the questions of what is meant by truth and what can be accepted as satisfactory criteria for testing the truth of any assertion. These, after all, are the central questions faced by philosophers, and in particular that branch of it known as epistemology or theory of knowledge. For, in the first place, there have been and still are many different theories as to what constitute acceptable bases for any truth-claims that are made and, secondly, there are also those who would wish to argue that truth and validity, in fact rationality itself, has several forms and that the tests for both truth and validity will vary according to the particular form of knowledge or understanding or "realm of meaning" we happen to have under consideration in any given context (Phenix 1964; Hirst 1965b). Mathematics, the physical sciences and the human sciences, for example, represent different kinds of knowledge, it is argued, distinguished from each other not only by the concepts they use but also by their logical structure and the truth criteria appropriate to them. Different verification proce-dures must be used in proof of Pythagoras' theorem from those appropriate to Boyle's Law or Gresham's Law. It has been claimed that as many as seven such distinct forms of knowledge may exist (Hirst 1965b).

However, while acknowledging the problems that exist, the disputes that rage and the traps and pitfalls that await anyone who ventures into such contentious territory, it is possible for us to pick out certain elements of rationality, certain essential characteristics which will be acknowledged by all, to identify certain features other than those that are the objects of disagreement and debate. Furthermore, it is important at least to attempt to do this, since, as we shall see later, it will only be an awareness of these features that will provide us with a secure basis for any conclusions we may come to about the role of reason in morals. Four such features spring immediately to mind.

In the first place, it will be apparent that, whatever views are held as to the precise nature of truth and validity, the exact tests for them or the form of these appropriate to the particular context of any discussion, there can be no doubting the need for any kind of rational process worthy of the name to be able to stand up to some appropriate tests of truth and validity. In other words, whatever precise criteria we have adopted, any body of knowledge or understanding to merit the description "rational" must hang together in some way; it must display coherence when measured against whatever tests are regarded as appropriate to those criteria and when viewed in relation to other assertions in the same field. We must all accept that rationality requires that any body of knowledge or set of beliefs we subscribe to must be internally coherent and consistent. For example, one test of any new "discovery" in science must be whether it fits in with other currently accepted theories. If it does not, then either it must be rejected or the theories adjusted to accommodate it in a rational, noncontradictory manner. A claim to rationality, therefore, requires at the very least a respect for the need for internal coherence and logic.

Secondly, the central concern of this process of developing bodies of knowledge and understanding that hold together in a rational way is the production of generalizations or universals, those general assertions without which no kind of prediction, no matter how tentative, would be possible and which must, therefore, be seen as essential prerequisites of purposeful action. For in order to act purposefully, as we said earlier, we must make choices and to do that we need to be able to make some calculation of the likely consequences of the different courses open to us. These calculations in turn cannot be made by reference to particular experiences we have had; they can only be based on the general conclusions those particular experiences have led us to make. Thus when the world's first streaker, Archimedes, ran though the streets of Syracuse shouting "I've found it!", this was not a comment on the discovery of an exciting and hitherto unnoticed part of his own anatomy nor even of something new about his own bath; it was the discovery of a general scientific law that excited him. Again, the rules by which such universal assertions are reached and the grounds for claiming their truth or the validity of arguments that make use of them may be open to dispute. What is not open to dispute, however, is the need for such universals to be established if any process of rational thinking is to be possible. Thus not only does the notion of rationality demand coherence in our thinking; it also requires that that thinking be productive of generalizations based on our experiences. For what else could "understanding" mean?

Thirdly, if the generalizations we reach and the arguments we base on them are to have any claim to truth or validity, there must be some grounds for them and this implies not only that they must satisfy the criterion of internal coherence we have already referred to; it implies also that reasons of many kinds be produced in support of them. In other words, to make any universal assertion for which one wishes to claim a rational basis is to be able to produce reasons for that assertion and, in some cases, evidence of an appropriate kind in support of it. Again we must stress that there is likely to be in many contexts a good deal of disagreement over what will constitute appropriate evidence or good reasons for any particular claim, but again of the need for evidence or reasons of some kind there can be no question. The ability to produce appropriate evidence or reasons is as crucial a part of what it means in most spheres to claim the truth of any assertion or the validity of any body of knowledge as any criterion of coherence.

Lastly, we must note the need for these reasons or this evidence to be public in nature and for the standards of coherence to be generally acceptable. If we wish to claim that a particular process of argument is rational, we must be prepared to have it tested by public criteria of rationality. For if it only satisfies our own personal criteria it will be an example of rationalization rather than rationality, a distinction the importance of which for morality we will see later. This draws our attention to a further very important feature of rationality, its relation to language and communication. There are those who believe that it is language that makes thought possible, that without the ability to express our thinking in words very little thinking worthy of the name would be possible (Vigotsky 1962). The converse of this is certainly true. For language is essentially a social activity and no kind of communication would be possible without common and shared standards of logic and rules of reasoning. Thus any claims we make for the rationality of our arguments imply by their very nature an appeal to some shared standards of truth, validity and logic, so that reasons we offer and the evidence we produce in support of our claims must be such as to be intelligible to others and seen by them to be coherent within the overall framework of our argument. It is for this reason that those phenomenologists who regard all experience as personal and subjective, believe that everyone's view of the world is unique and, therefore, deny the possibility of shared experience must reject not only the kind of universal rationality we are describing here but also the possibility of any kind of communication between individuals.

Thus what has been revealed by this brief and inevitably oversimplified account of rationality is that, while there are many problems and disagreements over its particular manifestations, over what constitutes truth, validity, logic and rationality itself in particular contexts, certain central features can be picked out and identified of a kind that cannot be denied by anyone who admits the possibility of shared meanings. Among these, we have suggested, are respect for the need for validity of some kind, a recognition of the necessity of producing universal assertions as a basis for decision making of all kinds, an acceptance of the need to give reasons and evidence in support of any claims of truth and validity we wish to make, and an acknowledgement of the requirement that all of these processes should be capable of withstanding the test of public intelligibility.

Our final point which prompted a brief consideration of the importance of communication in rationality brings us conveniently back to our central concern with morality. For it highlights the natural progression from thought through language to social behaviour and reveals these as the central characteristics of man's rationality, the three major aspects of that which differentiates him from other creatures, a threefold notion well expressed in the words of Sophocles. "Many are the wonders of the world and none more wonderful than man; for man has learnt the art of language, the use of thought swift as the winds and the temperament for social living."

These lines illustrate very well the interconnection as well as the importance in human life of both rationality and morality and, now that we have gained some idea of the major characteristics of rationality, we can return to the central question of this chapter, what we can learn from these general considerations that will help us to establish the place of reason in morals.

Rationality and morality

Throughout the first section of this chapter we have tried to maintain a crucial distinction between what can be said in general about the characteristics and the requisites or requirements of rationality in any sphere of knowledge and the difficulties which arise when we consider in particular contexts what will constitute appropriate criteria of truth and validity. We have suggested that, although it might be possible to reach a fair measure of agreement on the former general issues, many disputes and disagreements arise in almost all particular areas when we come to spell out what kinds of evidence are to be considered appropriate, what theory or theories of truth are applicable, what will constitute an acceptable logic, what criteria will be regarded as offering suitable tests of validity. We also drew attention to the disagreement that exists over the question of whether there are in fact different kinds of logic or rationality, different forms of knowledge, or whether the same tests for both truth and validity should be applicable in all contexts.

Nowhere is the importance of this distinction more clearly apparent than in the sphere of moral "knowledge". For while it may be possible to achieve agreement over the truth and validity of assertions in the fields of, say, science and mathematics, so that the possibility of disagreement there is less readily apparent, no one can after a moment's reflection fail to recognize the impossibility of this in morals. The process of establishing whether, for example, someone has stolen a loaf of bread is clearly far easier and less problematic than that of deciding whether he was right or wrong to do so, whether there were reasons, excuses, circumstances that should be accepted as mitigating, and so on.

Moral "knowledge", then, provides us with specially difficult problems and this distinction between the general requirements of rationality and the particular problems of its manifestations in any given field are especially relevant to any discussion of the role of rationality in morals. It is also the clue to where so many moral philosophers and others have gone wrong.

Moral "knowledge" provides us with particular difficulties because of the problem of establishing an appropriate logical basis for it and/or discovering its precise logical status. In particular, it is immediately apparent that it is not possible to state with any confidence of achieving general acceptance what would constitute "proof" of any particular moral position or belief, or what criteria would be accepted by all as appropriate to appeal to in order to resolve any moral dispute. Thus, although there is no real difficulty in demonstrating the stupidity of filling the bath to the brim if one does not want to be continually mopping up the bathroom floor nor of resolving any dispute one might find oneself in with anyone who regarded this as not stupid at all, there are enormous difficulties in demonstrating the rightness or wrongness of, for example, using contraceptive devices and in resolving those disputes which manifestly do exist between those people who approve their use and those who do not, unless of course their approval or disapproval is based merely on views they have about their efficiency or possible side-effects. What this amounts to is that whatever moral "knowledge" or moral discourse are, they are not like scientific knowledge or discourse nor, indeed, like mathematical knowledge or discourse.

It is precisely here that traditional moral philosophy went wrong, since its approach failed to recognize the unique problems of moral discourse and treated it as mathematical or as scientific or as analogous to one of these, as a matter of proving certain kinds of moral belief to be right or wrong, correct or incorrect. Whether by mathematical methods or by scientific methods or by some new and different kind of approach, the aim was to demonstrate the truth of certain moral positions.

The early rationalists, for example, adopted what is essentially a mathematical approach to morality, regarding it as a matter of deducing particular moral positions from higher order principles. Thus for Plato, as we have seen, morality is a matter of "knowing" and recognizing the "form of beauty, truth and goodness" and "applying" it in particular contexts, just as one might know and recognize the "truth" of Pythagoras' theorem and apply that to particular problems of a spatial kind. Indeed, Spinoza's *Ethics* is set out in the form of a series of theorems "proving" each moral point step by step and thus building up a huge quasi-mathematical edifice of moral "knowledge". Religious approaches to ethics, whether Christian or Judaeic, are also of this kind, as are metaphysical theories generally, since they all attempt, albeit in different ways, to establish "first premises" or "higher order principles" from which particular deductions can then be made.

The other main strand of traditional moral philosophy rejected this kind of rationalist metaphysics in favour of empiricism and took a scientific rather than a mathematical approach. In other words, it attempted to reach its first premises or principles not by some kind of mystical or purely intellectual means but by empirical observation. Thus the first premise of utilitarian ethics is man's observable tendency to seek pleasure and to avoid pain, so that it is claimed that what is right in any given context is that which promotes pleasure and minimizes pain. Evolutionary theories of ethics too, seeing the "fact" of evolution as the key to an understanding of human existence, deduce from this that what is right is that which will enhance and assist the evolutionary process. Such "naturalistic" theories, then, seek a basis for the proof of certain moral tenets in some empirical observation or other about human character or the human condition, and thus regard moral "knowledge" as analogous to the natural sciences.

Others have tried not to use an overtly mathematical or scientific approach but nevertheless to suggest that the approach to moral enquiry has to be seen as analogous to these, that the task is still to establish some basis of proof for certain moral positions, even if such proof cannot be achieved by mathematical or scientific processes as such. This is the approach of those theories that constitute what one might describe as "developed rationalism", theories which, taking their cue from Immanual Kant, endeavour to establish the truth of certain higher order principles by appealing to the nature of rationality itself and developing some kind of metaphysic of morals or, as we might say, peculiar moral logic. We will need to consider this approach again later. It will be sufficient at this juncture if we merely note this as an attempt to do the same job by different methods.

That none of these approaches is satisfactory is clear from several considerations. The first of these is the manifest fact that no such attempt has been successful in producing moral "knowledge" of a kind that is or can be universally accepted. On the contrary, one of the salient characteristics of moral discourse is the degree of disagreement it permits and tolerates. Secondly, it will be clear that one reason for this is that all of these approaches have perpetrated a logical fallacy, endeavouring to deduce moral conclusions from factual premises, committing what G.E. Moore (1903) called the "naturalistic fallacy" by endeavouring to define "good" in non-moral terms. This is equally the case whether these terms be metaphysical, scientific or logical. Thirdly, these theories do not allow for the fact of social change, to which we have already referred on several occasions. We now realize, as a result of our experience of change of all kinds and the moral issues it presents us with, that no hard and fast rules of a once-and-for-all kind are possible. We saw in Chapter 1 that the work of men such as John Dewey has drawn our attention to the hypothetical nature of all human knowledge so that, when we have come to regard even scientific knowledge as subject to modification, change and even rejection in the light of newly acquired evidence, the possibility of achieving anything approaching certainty in moral knowledge becomes even more clearly remote.

Whatever the role of rationality in morality is, then, it would seem clear what it is not; it is not the production of reasoned "proofs" of particular moral positions; it is not the establishment of a base upon which can be built a corpus of moral "knowledge".

An appreciation of this has led some people to go to the other extreme and claim that, since no particular moral beliefs can be "proved" and no moral dispute resolved in any final way, then anything goes, any one man's beliefs, no matter what they are, are as good as any other's.

This kind of view takes a number of forms. There are those, for example, who adopt a sociological relativism and argue that all moral beliefs are conventional, relative to the society in which they are held, that eating people is not wrong in every society, that having ten wives (no matter how stupid some of us may regard the practice) in some societies is the accepted thing and consequently right; in short that, since it is not possible to establish universal overriding moral principles, we must accept that what is right is what is in accordance with the accepted tenets of any given society.

One obvious difficulty which many find with such a view is that it makes comparisons between societies impossible; one cannot condemn cannibals nor headhunters nor Nazis; one certainly cannot justify such actions as the trial and condemnation of war "criminals"; nor can one claim that to civilize a primitive society is to improve it. This, however, is a difficulty that has to be faced once one adopts any kind of relativist stance.

The particular difficulty with sociological relativism is that there seems to be no basis for taking this kind of middle position. Once one accepts that there are no universal moral truths that transcend human societies, one cannot claim that there are nevertheless such truths to be found within particular societies which transcend the choice of individual human beings, since it is clear that there is seldom any real consensus and that, in any case, neither consensus nor majority opinion are any guarantee of truth. Furthermore, there is that feature of advanced societies to which we are constantly referring, namely their pluralism, the fact that many shades of opinion are to be found on most issues. Laws, rules and customs may vary from society to society, but values vary not only between societies but also between individuals in every society.

For this reason many have stressed that morality is an individual matter, that we must make our own moral choices in the light of fundamental moral principles which themselves have also been chosen by us. This is a basic feature of existentialist philosophy and of those phenomenological theories, to which we have just referred, which claim that, since everyone's experience of the world is unique and personal, everyone's reaction to that world must be of a similarly unique and personal kind.

Furthermore, many would argue that, although this is true, there are in fact no rational grounds upon which one can make such a choice of moral principles, that there are no reasons for taking one moral stance rather than another. This was the position taken by David Hume in relation to all human "knowledge", that there is no basis for believing anything in preference to anything else. "If we believe that fire warms or water refreshes, 'tis only because it costs us too much pains to think otherwise." This led to an emotivist view of ethics which saw moral principles as no more than those social norms that hold a society together because and for as long as the members of that society feel them to be right, regard them as conducive to those things they approve of and thus agree and assent to them. This is also the central feature of modern emotivist theories of ethics, which believe that ultimately moral value is a matter of individual feeling. It is also the source of the existentialist's nausea, that feeling of hopelessness that comes from the awareness that one must make choices to assert both one's existence and essence as a moral agent combined with the simultaneous awareness that there are no rational grounds for believing one thing rather than another, for adopting one set of principles rather than another, for behaving in one way rather than another.

All of this would seem to suggest that there is no place for reason in morality, that one might as well plump for any set of principles, that, since anything goes, it is of as much value tossing a coin as going through elaborate cerebral convolutions to reach a moral conclusion. In the very ultimate, there may be a lot to such a view, as the existentialist believes.

However, it is only necessary to take this as evidence that reason has no place in moral discourse if we are determined to adhere to the idea that that place has to be in establishing the content of moral "knowledge" or producing moral "proofs". For although there can be no ultimate criteria to appeal to in resolving moral disputes, it is not necessary to assume as a result that rationality has no place in moral discourse. The role or roles of rationality in morals can best be discerned if we return to a distinction we have referred to before between the manner and the matter of moral discourse, between its form and its content, its language and its literature (Oakeshott 1962, Peters 1963). For although any attempt to establish the matter, the content or the literature of morality is fraught with the problems and beset by the dangers we have briefly listed, the same is not the case when we try to apply reason to the question of its manner, its form, its language. The content of morality is changing, as we keep saying, and people must be allowed to be autonomous moral beings, but in order to become such they must learn the language of morals and be shown what rationality can reveal about its form.

It is important, however, to be clear what we mean by form, manner and language, especially since we are claiming this distinction to be crucial for moral education. To achieve this clarity we must refer back to what we said in the first section of this chapter about rationality itself. For we were at pains to argue there that there is a distinction to be made between the need for truth and validity and the question of what constitutes truth and/or validity in particular contexts. This is the distinction that is crucial, although it is often blurred. Richard Peters, for example, although, as we have seen, drawing our attention to its importance (1963), elsewhere (1970) loses sight of it and, in attempting to establish certain particular higher order principles, wanders back into the area of content, matter and literature, telling us "there are a limited number of principles which are fundamental but nonarbitrary in the sense that they are presuppositions of the form of discourse in which the question 'What are there reasons for doing?' is asked seriously. The principles which have this sort of status are those of impartiality, the consideration of interests, freedom, respect for persons, and probably truth-telling. Such principles are of a procedural sort in that they do not tell us precisely what rules there should be in a society but lay down general guidance about the ways we should go about deciding such matters and indicate general criteria of relevance" (Peters 1970, p.36).

However, these principles are not merely procedural; they are those higher order principles, those first premises from which rules of action in specific contexts can be deduced, which we saw just now it is both impossible to establish and wrong to seek after. In failing to adhere to this important distinction between form and content, Peters is thus following exactly in the footsteps of Immanuel Kant who in seeking for the role or roles of rationality in morals also went too far in this way. For it is not irrational to be partial, to refuse to consider the interests of others, to deny freedom, to fail to show respect for persons and even, perhaps, not to tell the truth; and our concern is not with what is unpleasant or distasteful or even contrary to the views of the majority; it is solely with what is irrational. An appeal to rationality, therefore, cannot establish these as principles and that is why they are not procedural and why in arguing this sort of case Peters and others are not confining themselves to the form or the manner or the language of morality but essentially involving themselves in its content, its matter and its literature.

In order not to make this same mistake but to adhere very closely to the distinction we are claiming to be crucial, we must stick rigidly to a consideration of what an examination of rationality as such can tell us about moral discourse, what it means to claim that such discourse must be rational, and there is a good deal of value we can learn from that. What procedural principles must we adhere to if our moral beliefs are to be regarded as rational? Or, conversely, what would lay us open to a valid charge of irrationality?

To answer these questions we need do no more than refer back to the general points we made about the nature of rationality itself in the early part of this chapter. For we claimed there that for any body of knowledge or beliefs, any kind of discourse, to lay claim to being considered rational it must, in the first place, display coherence and it will be clear that this is as true of moral discourse as of any other. It is not enough, therefore, for us to plump for a set of beliefs; it is necessary also that that set of beliefs should display an inner coherence and consistency. For that, after all, is what rationality is. Thus, for example, it is not rational for me to believe that all other human beings must respect my interests if I do not at the same time accept that I must also respect theirs. On the other hand — and this is the important point to grasp — it would be equally coherent, and thus equally rational, for me to believe that no one need respect my interests just as I do not respect theirs. There are many people who live their lives out on this basis and, whatever else we may think of their values, we cannot dub them irrational. Again we see how an appeal to rationality can help us to discern the form of morality, but emphatically not its content. Whatever one's own moral code is, it must be coherent and consistent and one's behaviour must "chime" with that code in all respects — at least as far as one is able to ensure that it does; certainly one must accept that it should.

Secondly, we argued earlier that rationality is concerned with the generation of universals or general principles. This point is, as it were, a subvariant of our first, since it suggests another way in which the idea of coherence enters into morality — we must act according to settled principles, whatever those principles may be. In short, I must not act on one principle today and another contrary one tomorrow — not at least without being prepared to produce valid reasons for my change of heart. The idea of a rational morality, then, requires that our behaviour evince an acceptance of universal moral principles, again without dictating what those universal principles must be.

Thirdly, we noted earlier the need to produce evidence in support of any claim that we wish to have considered as a rational claim. The question of what constitutes evidence in the field of morals is a vexed one. Certainly one must accept that it is more likely to be analogous to legal than to scientific evidence. It will also be extremely difficult to establish what shall count as good or bad reasons for a particular course of action, not least because this will depend very much on one's own point of view. Furthermore, it will be equally difficult to distinguish behaviour which is irrational from that which is merely unreasonable (Woods and Barrow 1975). I kick my dog every time West Ham United lose a football match (i.e., once or twice a week). This behaviour you may regard as unreasonable; but is it irrational? To resolve this kind of question in most serious contexts is very difficult. However, what we can say is that behaviour for which no reasons at all are or can be produced is irrational in the full sense and thus cannot be counted as moral. It is indisputable, therefore, that evidence that one regards oneself as relevant and reasons one regards as good should be produced, again because this is part of what we mean by a rational claim to validity. We are concerned with respect for the idea of evidence as much here as in any field of scientific exploration.

Fourthly, we argued that whatever was felt to be appropriate evidence should be so regarded in the light of publicly accepted criteria, that to some extent what constitutes appropriate evidence or good reasons must be decided by the test of whether others see it as such or at least can understand our reasons for claiming it to be so. This is Dewey's answer to the problem of ever-evolving values. For he does not feel it necessary to accept that anything goes in morals any more than in the equally rapidly evolving field of scientific knowledge. On his view, rationality requires that we look for some public agreement. If we are totally idiosyncratic the whole point of rationality is lost, since, as we also saw, it is essentially connected with communication. Reason requires, therefore, that we produce reasons for our moral beliefs and behaviour of a kind that others can understand. We need not go all the way with Dewey and require that they themselves accept these reasons or the beliefs and behaviour they are adduced to support (for that is to get into content again), but they must be able to recognize that there is a connection between them, that an overall coherence is being sought, even if it is not always attained.

One aspect of this is particularly important for moral education. We have already referred to the notion of rationalization and have contrasted this with rationality. Rationalization is at root the selective use of evidence to justify what we wish for other reasons to find justification for. In other fields this kind of selectivity is regarded as deplorable. It is a matter for front page headlines even in the popular Sunday newspapers when it comes to light that some eminent academic may have fudged the evidence to support his thesis that the palace of Knossos existed or that intelligence is innate. It is quite the worst crime that any academic can commit. Yet do we not all commit this crime in the moral sphere almost daily, when we "convince" ourselves that there are good reasons for doing what we want to do rather than what we ought to do? If the evidence we produce to support such decisions really will stand up to public tests of rationality then the danger is avoided. One of the major tasks facing the moral educator is to draw the attention of his pupils to this important distinction.

Lastly, we must note the role that reason must play in the calculation of the consequences of our actions and, indeed, in the mechanics and practicalities of carrying out our decisions. Whatever weight we give to these consequences, we cannot make any kind of decision that is at all positive or, indeed, rational, unless we have made some estimate of its effects. This, as we said earlier, is what rationality is all about; it is about behaving thoughtfully and purposefully and it is for this reason that it is crucial to moral behaviour. We must bring our reasoning powers to bear, therefore, on a good deal of knowledge and understanding that is not in itself "moral" but which is highly relevant to the moral decisions we make and the actions we perform.

We have argued, then, that although a consideration of rationality cannot provide us with any help on the issue of what moral principles we should adopt and act upon, it can tell us a good deal about the form, the manner, the language of our moral code, displaying the need for this to be coherent, consistent and subject to evidence and reasons of a public kind. This may seem somewhat disappointing to those who still want reason to tell them what to believe and how to behave. On the other hand, to ask this of rationality is in itself to be guilty of irrationality, since it is to ask that all real choice be removed and that moral answers be attained in much the way that answers to mathematical problems are reached, by the use of pure reason. To ask for that is to surrender one's autonomy and all claims to individuality. Not to be granted it is to retain autonomy and individuality and that must be a gain rather than a loss in real moral terms.

The distinction that we have been arguing for here is well brought out in what is perhaps the best summary of the place of reason in ethics, that given by Goldsworthy Lowes Dickinson in his dialogue, *The Meaning of Good* (1901, pp.86-87), and quoted by Stephen Toulmin at the conclusion of his examination of *The Place of Reason in Ethics* (1950, p.225).

> It is the part of Reason, on my hypothesis, to tabulate and compare results. She does not determine directly what is good, but works, as in all the sciences, upon given data...noticing what kinds of activity satisfy, and to what degree, the expanding nature of this soul that seeks Good, and deducing therefrom, so far as may be, temporary rules of conduct.... Temporary rules, I say, because, by the nature of the case, they can have in them nothing absolute and final, inasmuch as they are mere deductions from a process which is always developing and transforming itself. Systems of morals, maxims of conduct are so many landmarks left to show the route by which the soul is marching; casts, as it were, of her features at various stages of her growth, but never the final record of her perfect countenance. And that is why the current morality, the positive institutions and laws...both have and have not the value [sometimes claimed for them]. They are in truth invaluable records of experience, and he is rash who attacks them without understanding; and yet, in a sense, they are only to be understood in order to be superseded, because the experience they resume is not final, but partial and incomplete.

Stripped of its Victorian grandeur and related to the context of the developing morality of the individual, that quotation sums up very effectively the central point we have tried to make about the place of reason in morality.

If we now turn to a consideration of the implications of all of this for moral education, the first thing we must note is that it reinforces a good deal of what we said about moral education in Chapter 1. For it reasserts the need to develop in pupils certain cognitive skills and to promote in them a recognition of the necessity for their moral thinking to satisfy those requirements we have listed if it is to claim acceptance as rational. In short, we must recognize the need for moral educators to develop within the field of moral thinking and decision making those general features of rationality, such as respect for the need for coherence, consistence, public evidence and so on to which we keep referring.

This does, however, raise an important and difficult question for the moral educator, namely the degree to which these qualities can be developed by pupils of all abilities. If we may make reference once again to Plato's system of moral education (and we continue to do so because it illustrates better than any other single theory all of the issues that have subsequently come to be regarded as central to moral debate), there is no reluctance there to accept that a large proportion of the population of any state will lack the intellectual ability to attain a moral education in the full sense, to be able to do their own moral thinking. This is the real significance of his division of the populace into men of gold, silver and bronze, a myth which is deliberately created and fostered to ensure the acceptance by the men of silver and bronze of the right of those of gold to do their moral thinking for them. Only the latter, therefore, are regarded as being capable of being educated morally; the rest must be conditioned or indoctrinated into obedience and are thus offered an authoritarian form of moral training.

Nor must we see this as remote from our times and of merely antiquarian interest. We are only just ourselves emerging from a philosophy of differentiated curricula, of an "educational" provision for pupils of "average and below average abilities" that has been framed on different principles from those that apply to the more able pupil, principles that have been attacked by some as centrally concerned to achieve a similar kind of control through largely unquestioning obedience as that advocated by Plato (White 1968, 1973; Young 1971). From the advent of the idea of secondary education for all until very recent times, as a glance even at the title of the Newsom Report (1963), *Half Our Future*, will reveal, the idea of one kind of education for the bright and another for the rest has dominated our thinking, although—significantly enough—not always our practice, and there are still those who advocate this kind of approach and argue it strongly and quite vehemently (Bantock 1968, 1971).

This has been given a strange twist in relation to specific projects in moral education. For these, like most of the projects sponsored by the Schools Council and other bodies, have been directed mainly at the "less able" pupil. For the most part this has been the result of mundane considerations such as the unwillingness of schools to experiment with the curriculum of pupils on traditional examination courses and, conversely, their need to find something "relevant" and "meaningful" to keep the other pupils occupied, especially after the raising of the statutory school leaving age. However, its effect has been to suggest that brighter pupils do not need moral education — a somewhat bizarre notion — or that they are bright enough to sort moral issues out for themselves and do not need the help of the school in doing so, or else that the kind of moral "education" needed by the less able is precisely the kind that Plato advocated, a training in obedience.

In this context, it is worth noting that the Humanities Curriculum Project, as we shall see in Chapter 7, although its brief specifically directed its attentions towards pupils of average and below average ability, did start from the premise that such pupils are capable of the kind of abstract thinking we are suggesting a rational approach to morals requires, so that those responsible for the project did attempt, as we shall see, to develop materials that would demand this kind of fully autonomous moral thinking from all pupils.

Clearly, in the sphere of morality, as in all other spheres, intellectual ability will play its part. To reach moral conclusions of the kind we have tried to define one needs to be able to analyse situations, to recognize what knowledge is relevant, to apply that knowledge appropriately, to attempt some prediction of consequences and so on. All of these make demands on one's intellectual powers and here, as elsewhere, the ability of individuals to meet these demands will vary. This is confirmed, as we shall see in Chapter 3, by Lawrence Kohlberg's cross-cultural studies which indicated that moral development is slower in some societies, for example in rural societies, and that the final stages of moral development do not emerge clearly in preliterate communities.

However, with the right kind of environmental stimulus, progress towards moral autonomy will be maintained, and, if we are to say that some people will not be able to meet these demands at all and that as a result we must not try to educate them to the point where they can do so, we must recognize the seriousness of what we are claiming. For we are assuming not only that they cannot be morally educated but that *ipso facto* they cannot be educated at all. And we are further assuming that, if we were right to claim that it is the ability to think for oneself, to make choices and to act morally in the full sense of the term that constitutes what it means to be human, then those we regard as intellectually incapable of this are not fully human at all, an assumption which in turn could be held to justify differential and unequal treatment of them in many other contexts. Unless we are prepared to concede that point, therefore, we must make the attempt to bring all pupils to the level of autonomous moral functioning.

Finally, we must remind ourselves that intellectual qualities are not the only elements in moral choice and behaviour; other qualities, as we have seen and shall see, are equally important. Indeed, Plato recognized the need to look to more than intellectual ability in selecting the children of gold for moral education. Moral judgement and, in particular, moral behaviour are, as we shall see in Chapter 4, at least as much a matter of the emotional responses the individual is capable of making, so that this also would suggest that those who are highly endowed intellectually do not have the monopoly of moral judgement or moral behaviour. It is in any case unlikely that after observing the behaviour of some of the most intelligent members of our society we will still need convincing of this.

If we set out to offer any pupils a form of moral upbringing that is different in kind from the one we are outlining here, that difference must consist in attempting to tell them what to think, in short in a concern with the content rather than the form of their morality, and thus in treating them as though they were not capable of achieving a fully human level of existence. This would be disturbing even if there were empirical evidence to support it. Since there is not, it is particularly reprehensible.

This discussion of the place of rationality in morals, therefore, highlights not only what we must attend to as moral educators but also some of the pitfalls to be avoided. In particular, it draws our attention to the fact that many problems can arise when we approach moral education through a concern with its content, with what children should be encouraged to believe rather than the manner in which their beliefs should be reached and held. For we then enter the realm of what many would wish to describe as indoctrination rather than moral education and, since the distinction between these two notions is both highly important to the whole enterprise of moral education and the subject of much debate and disagreement, we must now give some attention to the question of what indoctrination is, particularly in the sphere of morality, and whether and how it can be avoided in attending to the moral upbringing of children.

Moral education and indoctrination

Problems of indoctrination are not restricted to moral aspects of education or schooling but they do loom very large in that area since, as the etymology of the word suggests, it is centrally concerned with the teaching of doctrines or values of some kind. In every area, however, difficulties arise mainly from the degree of disagreement that exists over the meaning of the term and the resultant impossibility of achieving anything like an acceptable definition. Yet without such a definition it is impossible to derive any kind of practical guidance from a discussion of the issue.

Disagreement appears to centre on three main questions, whether the term applies to the teaching of doctrines only or to a wider range of teaching, whether it is used always pejoratively and by what criteria we can recognize examples of it in practice. A view on each of these questions will emerge as we discuss the whole problem of indoctrination, but a few preliminary comments may help to dispel some of the confusion in advance.

The term "teaching" is a purely neutral term in that the use of it does not imply that one has any particular views on the process one is describing or referring to. Thus we can speak of someone as teaching his pupils Latin and another as teaching them the art of torture without the use of the term implying any attitude on our part to either of these pursuits. The term "education", however, since it encapsulates certain evaluative criteria, does imply much more than that. To speak of someone as educating his pupils is, first of all, to express one's approval of the process and, secondly, to suggest that it satisfies a number of criteria that we briefly discussed in Chapter 1, criteria such as respect for the autonomy of the pupil, the development of understanding, a recognition of the value of what is being learnt and so on.

The term "indoctrination" is evaluative in a similar way. In its normal current usage it is not neutral—not at least any longer, even if it once was (Gatchel 1972). For in the first place, it is normally used nowadays in a pejorative sense; we use it to condemn certain kinds of teaching which we disapprove of, and we never hear it used, except perhaps by certain educational theorists, in any other sense. If we wish merely to describe the teaching of anything in a manner which either ignores or even actively discourages the development of critical awareness and understanding in the pupil, we use the perfectly adequate word "instruction"; only if we want at the same time to condemn the practice do we use the word "indoctrination". There are some, indeed, who see the term "indoctrination" as synonymous with miseducation, a term we use of a situation in which education has gone wrong in some way (Crittenden 1972). Certainly, it would seem that its use does imply some kind of contrast with the notion of education. The question then arises of whether it is to be taken as denoting any kind of miseducation or whether it picks out certain particular features that may be present in a situation in which teaching is taking place.

If the latter is the case, the problem then centres on what these particular features might be, what evaluative criteria are encapsulated in the meaning of the word, what characteristics must be identified in an act of teaching if it is to be properly designated indoctrinatory. In offering answers to this question most theorists have concentrated their attention on three aspects of the teaching process—methods, content and intention—so that it will be helpful if we consider all of these briefly in turn.

The idea that indoctrination is to be defined in terms of the methods of teaching being used is a popular one and, superficially at least, attractive. For the man in the street when asked about indoctrination would almost certainly be reminded of the teaching methods described in Orwell's *1984* or Huxley's *Brave New World* or those said to be in current use in some countries, and would thus think first in terms of the methods used — subliminal suggestion, hypnotism, amplifiers hidden under bed pillows and so on (Wilson 1964). At a more sophisticated level it has been argued that the term has a purely descriptive meaning and does in fact describe those methods of teaching that are employed when an authoritarian form of teaching is adopted either from choice or necessity, such necessity arising either from the fact that the pupils lack in general the ability to think for themselves or — an important point we must take up later — are too young to have reached the age and stage of cognitive growth at which they can think for themselves (Moore 1972). Thus it is argued that when we speak of indoctrination we are referring to the use of certain kinds of teaching method. If this is the view one takes, then the term "indoctrination" is regarded as a neutral term used nonpejoratively to describe the teaching of doctrines by methods that do not invite any response of a critical kind from the learner.

However, it is clear that in most contexts the term is used not merely descriptively but also to convey disapproval. Most people, for example, in using the term of the teaching methods employed in *1984* or *Brave New World* are condemning those methods and many, too, in considering the kind of teaching Willis Moore describes would want to condemn it and would feel that by calling it indoctrination they would in fact be doing so.

If this is so, then on closer examination it quickly becomes apparent that the definition of indoctrination in terms of the teaching methods used is inadequate. For, as John Wilson goes on to point out, we would not regard it as reprehensible if these same science-fiction methods were used to teach pupils their multiplication tables or Latin grammar in a painless way nor would we use the term "indoctrination" of such processes. Nor is it the method we are concerned about in the kind of teaching that Willis Moore is describing. We must, therefore, look beyond method for the criterion we are seeking.

John Wilson himself suggests that the crucial difference lies in the content or subject matter of the teaching, that what we object to is not the use of these methods in themselves but the use of them to implant and ensure the uncritical acceptance of certain social roles or moral, religious or political beliefs. In short, he is arguing that, as etymology suggests, indoctrination is the teaching of doctrines and that we will recognize the truth of this if we consider the areas of subject matter of which it is normally used. For we usually use the term, he argues, of the teaching of politics, religion or morals, in other words, those areas which are concerned with doctrines, with sets of beliefs which are by definition uncertain rather than bodies of knowledge for which publicly accepted evidence can be produced (1964). Thus it is argued that the teaching of mathematics cannot be termed indoctrination, even if the methods used are of a subliminal kind, since indoctrination can only occur in those areas where doctrines, sets of values, are involved. Presumably, too, all teaching in these areas must by definition be indoctrination if this notion is to be defined entirely in terms of the subject matter of teaching.

There are two problems, however, with this approach. In the first place, it accepts that a clear-cut division can be drawn between those areas of the curriculum that involve doctrines or values and those that do not and that indoctrination is only possible in the former. But such a line would be very difficult to draw and, although in popular usage the term may be restricted to the religious, moral or political spheres, it would seem undesirable to deprive ourselves of the use of it to describe teaching that actively discourages criticism in any sphere, especially at a time when the status of all kinds of knowledge is seen as problematic.

Conversely, it suggests that all teaching in the areas of religion, morals or politics must by definition be called indoctrination and, since the term is accepted by John Wilson himself as pejorative, must therefore be condemned. However, it will be apparent that not all teaching in the realms of politics, religion or morals need or should be described as indoctrination. Indeed, we speak of political education, of religious education and of moral education, so that we must believe these expressions to be meaningful.

It would seem, therefore, that a definition of indoctrination in terms of content or subject matter still does not get us to the heart of the issue. It is for this reason that several people have introduced the notion of intention (Kilpatrick 1951, 1972; Hare 1964; White 1967, 1972), suggesting that indoctrination is not so much a question of what we teach pupils nor of how we do it but of what kind of change we intend to bring about in them and that, if our intention is to persuade them to accept what we are teaching them uncritically and blindly, then the process we are engaged in is one of indoctrination. It was this aspect of Willis Moore's account of indoctrination as a method of teaching that was disturbing. For what he was describing was more than just a method; it was an approach to teaching whose intention was authoritarian, to bring about learning and acceptance without encouraging or even allowing any kind of critical appraisal or any resultant possibility of rejection. Clearly, in this kind of account, although we will most often be concerned with those areas of teaching which involve doctrines or beliefs, the notion of indoctrination could be applicable in any field of knowledge, since even in relatively straightforward areas of the curriculum, such as mathematics or science, a distinction can still be made between uncritical acceptance and understanding. It is being suggested, therefore, that unless the aim is to bring about understanding and critical awareness or, at least, if the aim is to prevent the development of these, then the process is one of indoctrination.

One major drawback of this point of view, however, is that it does not allow for the possibility that some indoctrination might happen accidentally, and, since we will be arguing later that it is this feature of moral learning that is the most crucial for any discussion of moral education, we must look at some of its implications now. It will be clear that often, whether teachers or parents intend it or not, children do acquire quite uncritical attitudes, prejudices in fact, in the fields of morals, religion, politics and even aesthetics, not to mention those things they "learn" in other fields without achieving any level of understanding or real critical awareness. If this happens, they would seem to be as effectively indoctrinated as in any situation in which a deliberate attempt was made to achieve this kind of end — perhaps more so.

This consideration suggests, then, a further criterion we should take account of in attempting a definition of indoctrination and leads us again to consider the importance of a notion about which we have already said a good deal in this chapter. That notion is that of the manner of learning that takes place as a result of our teaching, the way in which children or others come to learn and in which they hold whatever beliefs they come to hold (Green 1972) or, in the sphere of morals, the style rather than the content of moral decisions (Atkinson 1965, 1972).

A consideration such as this illustrates very effectively the whole point of our argument in the last section. For there we were trying to establish that moral education is concerned not with what a pupil comes to believe but with how his beliefs are held. In particular we stressed that pupils should be helped to develop understanding, a respect for rationality, for truth and for relevant evidence. What we are now suggesting is that indoctrination involves the absence of these. It implies that knowledge or beliefs are held uncritically and without respect for rationality, truth or evidence. It suggests teaching that either by accident or by design precludes rationality, the central theme of this chapter. It implies the acceptance of a passive model of man. It encourages the development of minds that are closed to any consideration of evidence of a kind contrary to the beliefs that are held. It involves a violation of the criteria of inquiry appropriate to any given subject area (Crittenden 1972). That violation, that closing of minds, that precluding of rationality, that absence of respect for truth and evidence are vitally important whether they happen by deliberate intent or merely by accident or through inefficiency. It is likely, of course, that this will most often come about, especially in the field of morals, through that undue concern with the teaching of content that this chapter has endeavoured to show to be a misinterpretation of the notion of moral education. But, however it comes about, the uncritical acceptance of any kind of knowledge or any set of beliefs is to be deplored and it is this that most people have in mind when they speak of indoctrination, even though for the most part they use the term to denote deliberate attempts to bring about this undesirable state.

It may well be that in taking this view we are really supporting those people who have argued for some kind of amalgam of all the criteria we have discussed (Flew 1972; Wilson 1972), that in seeking out examples of indoctrination we must look to methods, content, intentions and manner or to any combination of these. Certainly it is from all of these sources that indoctrination or miseducation in some form is most likely to arise. The important thing, however, is to recognize that the main use of the term is to define miseducation, however it comes about. The growing usage is to describe as indoctrination those acts of teaching which violate what we have several times referred to as the essential characteristics or criteria of education. If education is concerned with the promotion of autonomy, understanding, critical awareness, respect for truth, a love of knowledge and so on, then indoctrination is teaching that results, for whatever reason and in whatever way, in the absence of these qualities.

Two final points must be made. The first of these is that we have accepted a definition that does not insist on intentionality but opens teachers to the charge of indoctrinating their pupils even if they do this accidentally or through inefficiency. A child is no less indoctrinated or miseducated if his teacher is inefficient than if he is a deliberate purveyor of his own beliefs, just as a patient is no less dead if his surgeon is inefficient than if he is a psychopathic killer. Teachers must, therefore, accept full responsibility for the education of their pupils and this implies accepting equal responsibility for any miseducation that occurs, although clearly we must acknowledge some difference between the deliberate and the accidental as much in this context as in any other.

The second point we must consider briefly in conclusion is the problem that this is said to create for the teacher of young children. We will be discussing in Chapter 3 what developmental psychology has told us so far about the stages of children's intellectual growth and in particular the import of this for moral development. Two things are clear. One is that we do not know as much as we would like to know and need to know about this whole question. The second is that, while it may have particular implications for the work of teachers of young children in all areas, it has especial relevance for their concern with moral development. For at any time before a child has the intellectual capacity, the cognitive skills, to cope with the tasks we are describing as endemic to education, to think for himself with all that this implies (and we must remember that some people never get to this stage), the question must arise as to whether everything a teacher does is indoctrination. For at this stage the child must have a "content" to his morality, a set of values by which he organizes his life and makes the choices open to him. What is more, he will already have such a set of beliefs when he comes to school, since he will acquire his attitudes and his values from many sources, his parents, his peers, the media and so on. How can the teacher avoid indoctrination at this stage?

It was of course in order to solve this problem that some people suggested that the key criterion of indoctrination is intention (Hare 1964), arguing that, although one does have to tell young children what moral positions to adopt before they are capable of thinking critically about them, this is not indoctrination if one intends that critical appraisal should follow at some later stage. Nor is it indoctrination, it is claimed, if children are taught to accept certain things before they can understand the reasons for them, provided that reasons are given so that they understand that reasons are relevant and appropriate and do not come to accept whatever they are told blindly. Thus they can be told not to steal, tell lies, hurt people and so on, so long as we give them reasons and intend that they should subsequently come to see the point of these precepts for themselves and, indeed, come to be able to relate them to particular contexts.

Clearly, this is a context in which intention is an important consideration, but it is naive to suggest it offers an adequate solution. For, as we saw just now, it is not enough to exonerate a teacher if his intentions were good if his practice resulted in the closing of his pupils' minds in any area of knowledge. The road to hell, as we know, is paved with good intentions of this kind and, while this may be acceptable if it is the road to one's own hell, it cannot be when one is paving such a road for others. To say that intention is all is to discourage thinking on the part of teachers as to a more positive role they might be expected to play in this respect.

If we accept the notion of stages in the intellectual growth of children, we must recognize the need to work at getting every pupil from one stage to the next and through to the final stage of autonomous thinking in all spheres, but perhaps especially in morals. This is the point of Richard Peters' comments on the work of Piaget on the moral development of children; to tell us about the stages does not help us a lot as teachers with the task of getting our pupils through them or, conversely, avoiding their becoming fixated at any one of them (Peters 1960). In such a context to say that we intend to do it is not enough; we must work in a much more detailed and practical way at the mechanics of the process itself.

In the moral sphere, this raises an issue that we have already referred to and one which we must examine in detail in Chapter 5, the issue of how we can offer some kind of moral content to our pupils before they are capable of looking at it critically and, in particular, how we can set about moral education, as we are defining it, when we know that our pupils have already acquired and are constantly acquiring moral beliefs, attitudes and even prejudices from many other sources.

It will perhaps be sufficient, therefore, at this point, to say that this is a far more complex issue than many seem to have been prepared to recognize and, secondly, that it is dangerous to assume that it is a problem that only confronts the teacher of young children, although it may well have a particular relevance for that stage of education. We all know many adults whose moral development has stopped short long before the autonomous stage. Indeed, if we will but confess it, it is true of all of us in some aspects of our moral lives. Conversely, many of us have observed quite young children displaying the beginnings of a critical approach to moral questions. As we suggested in Chapter 1, we may be wise not to tie what is being said about the stages of moral development too closely to chronological age. We will do better, therefore, if, instead of relegating this issue to discussions of primary education, we recognize it as being central to the whole process of moral education at every stage, since that process must be viewed as developing the rationality of the individual stage by stage towards moral autonomy. Only if we approach our task in that spirit will we avoid indoctrination and focus our attention on moral education in the full sense.

Summary and conclusions

We have tried in this chapter to gain some idea of the nature of rationality and of its place in morality. We have suggested than an examination of the relation of reason to morality supports an approach to moral education whose main concern is with how pupils hold their moral beliefs and how they reach them rather than with what particular moral beliefs they hold, that the attention of the moral educator should be directed towards the form rather than the content of morality, towards the manner rather than the matter of moral learning, and in particular that he should endeavour to promote understanding, critical awareness and an appreciation of the need for knowledge and skills of many kinds as a basis for the making of autonomous moral decisions that are sound and for thinking for oneself in the fullest possible way. Finally, we suggested that to fail to achieve this is to be engaged in a process of miseducation that is often called indoctrination, the result of which, whether intended or not, is the blind and uncritical acceptance of certain beliefs or values. In short, the essence of indoctrination is the absence of rationality, just as the essence of education is its presence.

We referred finally to the particular problems that face the educator when his pupils may not yet have reached the stage of cognitive development at which they can look in a properly informed, critical and autonomous manner at beliefs and values and to the task that faces him in leading his pupils from each of these stages to the next. We also noted the particular complications that arise here for moral education from the fact that pupils will have acquired moral values and attitudes from many other sources and will thus have a content to their morality (as, indeed, they must in order to live) before they can be brought to this position of critical and autonomous appraisal.

These are the issues that we must turn to in subsequent chapters. First of all, we must consider the stages of cognitive development and their implications for moral education and, then, using that as a basis, we must face the question of how we can convert moral learning into moral education of the fullest kind.

CHAPTER 3

MORAL DEVELOPMENT

If we wish to argue that one of the increasingly important tasks of education is to help children to develop the appropriate skills and judgement to cope with the variety of moral choices they have to face in today's complex world, then it follows that every teacher, regardless of his subject specialism, or the age range with which he is primarily concerned, must play a part in the moral education of his pupils. Morality is an area which permeates the whole life of the school. Moral issues may be dealt with formally as part of the curriculum, but they are just as pervasive in the informal or hidden aspects of the curriculum, in, for example, the organization of the school and in teacher-pupil relationships.

If we pursue the argument further, claiming that teachers should make a deliberate attempt to educate children morally, then questions are raised about children's levels of understanding, readiness for learning and modes of learning. Experience, as well as empirical research and developmental theory, have taught us that to base work for children on levels of thinking which are inappropriate to their developmental stage is educationally unsound, in almost every curriculum area. We should not hope to deal with the abstract concepts in mathematics or physics with five year olds any more than we should wish to limit our work with average sixteen year olds to purely fact finding or observational exercises or to the practice of simple skills. Such inappropriate choice of materials and methods leads on the one hand either to rote learning or complete incomprehension, resulting in a rejection of school work or feelings of failure, which have a detrimental effect on a child's self-image, motivation and involvement in school (Downey 1977). And on the other, where the level of material is too simple, boredom and frustration ensue, prompting the adolescent to regard school as a complete waste of time. To promote moral education, whether formally or informally, requires a similar understanding of the child's level of development and personality makeup.

With this in mind then, this chapter sets out to give some account of the main theories of moral development which will contribute to an understanding of the child's development, crucial to the planning of any kind of moral education programme.

Concepts of development

However, before we can consider some of the most useful theoretical approaches towards children's moral development, it will be illuminating to examine briefly what we mean by the term "development". The term itself suggests a progressive change towards some more complex level, a change usually of an irreversible nature. But whether it is possible to predict the end state of any developmental process depends on what it is that is developing. We can more or less predict with certainty that under appropriate conditions a caterpillar will develop through specific stages into a butterfly of a particular kind. The implication here is that there is some preexisting genetic structure which determines the end state, the culmination of the whole process, and also that there is a gradual unfolding which under normal circumstances is not arrested or reversed.

This model of development taken from plant or animal biology can be applied up to a point to aspects of man's biological development, but the same criteria cannot hold for man's social, intellectual or moral growth, precisely because of the very factors that distinguish him, as a human being, from other organisms.

Theories of the maturational or unfolding type, which presupposed a genetic structure that would gradually emerge as the child grew older, have been discredited, since evidence shows that man does not simply unfold without the help of outside influences. Children deprived of sensory stimulation, perceptual variation or adult contact (Bowlby 1975) are clearly hampered, since development depends upon accommodating to such influences, assimilating them and interpreting them. Social interaction and adult attention have been shown to be necessary factors in the developmental process.

Similarly, although it is possible to talk of an end state when referring to plant or animal life, few people now would want to claim any kind of end state in relation to human development. One reason for this is that human life offers a vast variety of possibilities and since its quality varies so much from one culture to another it is impossible to predict how any individual might turn out. But more important, man is an active agent, capable of making choices and interpreting his experiences in his own unique fashion. He is not merely at the mercy of genetic influences on the one hand or cultural pressures on the other.

Thus, as Hirst and Peters (1971) make clear in their analysis, development is a necessarily evaluative concept, rather than a purely descriptive one, when applied to man. If we talk of a morally developed person, we are presupposing some idea of what it means to be morally mature. This in turn depends upon a view of morality that one can justify, and ultimately upon the view of man that one adopts. It is not an empirical issue to be decided on the basis of what we can observe about a person's moral conduct. What we have to decide, as we saw in the first chapter, is what it implies to be morally educated.

An examination of three main psychological approaches to moral development—the psychoanalytical viewpoint, the learning theory approach and the cognitive developmental view—will show that, far from offering contradictory or incompatible explanations, as might be apparent at first sight, they are in fact complementary and offer insight into different aspects of a child's moral growth.

The psychoanalytical approach, as manifested in Freud's monumental work, sees morality as conforming to cultural standards through a process of internalization. Learning theories, as reflected for instance in the work of Sears, Bandura, Eysenck, assume that

moral behaviour is the result of reinforcement, rewards or punishments, and that much moral conduct is a result of a child's
modelling himself on an admired adult. Individual differences in
moral behaviour are explained in terms of differences in conditionability (Eysenck 1964). As with the psychoanalytical approach,
morality or moral conduct is seen as conformity to some sort of
cultural or social norm. Cognitive-developmental theorists, on the
other hand (Piaget 1932, Kohlberg 1964), view moral development
as an active, dynamic, constructive process leading to a state where
the individual is able to act according to moral principles which he
either accepts because he understands them and agrees with them or
which he has worked out for himself.

These theoretical stances have different implications for moral
learning and moral education and each will now be examined in
further detail.

The psychoanalytical approach

It is to Freud that we owe our awareness of the effects of the
unconscious on human behaviour. In the area of morality, Freud
assumed an end state of rationality and the main impetus of his
work in this area was to explain why some people deviate from
rational behaviour and show an exaggerated or distorted mode of
rule-following. The acquisition of morality was for Freud the
development within the child's personality of the super-ego, the
agency or mechanism which issues moral imperatives derived from
standards of adults close to him which the child has internalized.
These moral imperatives serve to control the impulses of the id (the
unconscious), especially those relating to aggression and to sex. The
super-ego he sees as having two prime functions: it acts as the
conscience and as what Freud calls the ego-ideal (Freud 1933).

The child's conscience is formed by means of identification with his
parents and internalization of their moral standards in such a way
that when the infant is frustrated or punished by his parents, his
aggression towards them is aroused. But rather than venting this
aggression onto those he loves and thus fears losing, he unconsciously turns his anger inwards onto himself. The conscience
henceforward operates when parents are not present to enforce
moral standards by punishing the child or by preventing him from

acting in a way that would infringe societal rules and norms. But what is difficult to explain is that the strength of a child's conscience does not appear to depend upon the severity or strictness of the actual standards or behaviour of his parents. Rather it seems to stem from the intensity of the child's aggression towards his parents and thus, when it has been internalized, towards himself. A strict or even over-severe conscience is thus found in children who have a close attachment to their parents, who thus do not vent aggression on them overtly because of fear of losing the loved ones and who, unconsciously, take steps to avoid showing aggression by being over-punitive to themselves. On the other hand, there are those of course in whom the close attachment is lacking who do give open vent to their feelings or displace hostility onto others. According to Freud's theory such children develop a less severe conscience themselves.

The super-ego also acts as the ego-ideal which provides a positive standard against which the conscience measures the standards required by society. Like the conscience, it represents the voice of the parents and thus of society, giving some guidance on moral conduct (Freud (1914). The failure of the ego-ideal to reach its own standards results in feelings of guilt which are frequently far more severe than the person's actual behaviour warrants. Thus many of Freud's patients who consulted him as adults because of some severe nervous disturbance were found to be those who, even as children, had suffered from severe guilt feelings for minor transgressions or even for thinking of indulging in socially unaccept-able behaviour, perhaps in the form of fantasy in the area of sexual activity. We are all familiar with those who suffer severe pangs of conscience for some trivial offence to others or even merely for thinking ill of others.

The value of Freud's theory of moral development lies in the fact that it draws attention to the importance of both aggression and attachments during the early years. As we have seen, his theory deals with the rather negative notion of taking the voice of prohibition into ourselves, but also the positive one of modelling our behaviour on that of an admired figure, albeit at an uncon-scious level. The theory thus deals with emotional aspects of moral development which later views, such as those of the learning theorists and of the cognitive developmentalists, tend to neglect.

Freud's concern was largely with those who exhibited such an exaggerated or distorted style of rule-following that the normal course of their lives was disrupted. To help such people, he sought to explain why they had not attained a rational level of rule following and suggested that their development was arrested through fixation at some critical stage of psycho-sexual development during the first five or six years of life. His explanation was in terms of unconscious emotions rather than in terms of variations in social or environmental conditions.

However, although he offers no positive theory of moral development by suggesting conditions under which such growth might be promoted, apart from the general notion of the importance of a proper love relationship with parents in the early years, his work nevertheless prompts us to ask certain questions which are of fundamental importance to the moral educator. For he does suggest that some early experiences can inhibit or even prevent moral development in the full sense. Thus Peters (1960), in comparing the contributions of Freud and Piaget to moral development, raises some important issues which recent research has attempted to shed light on. He asks whether certain child-rearing techniques lead to compulsive rule-following habits, blocks or breakdowns at some later stage, and whether a particular kind of training in early childhood tends to encourage blind conformity to rules, regardless of circumstances.

Learning theory approach

Since Freud did not concern himself with child-rearing techniques or social and cultural differences, but concentrated largely on the individual's inner states, we must now turn to the work of the learning theorists to see what light their work throws upon such issues.

Learning theorists with a behaviourist bent tend to argue that to postulate some kind of hypothetical construct like the conscience or super-ego to explain moral conduct is totally misguided since, after all, such a mechanism cannot be observed and must therefore remain hypothetical. Assuming that moral behaviour is learnt they set out to explain its acquisition in terms of the laws and processes of learning used to explain other kinds of behaviour such as retention, the aquisition of skills, the learning of habits. In their view then there is no need to call upon either hypothetical mental structures, such as the conscience, or cognitive structures and stages as suggested by developmental psychologists.

Moral behaviour can be explained in their view by three sorts of mechanism: reinforcement and rewards; punishment or the threat of it; and modelling or imitation. Following the Skinnerian pattern of operant conditioning, behaviour can be modified or shaped by the use of reinforcement techniques. The effect of rewards in this system is to increase the probability of a desired response or unit of behaviour. Such techniques are based upon animal learning under laboratory conditions and there is no dearth of evidence to demonstrate their success. Skinner successfully trained rats to operate levers and to learn mazes; he taught pigeons to turn in a circle and to play with a ping pong ball by administering food rewards at appropriate intervals, to reinforce the desired response. Children, he claims, can also be taught to adopt the kind of conduct their parents deem desirable or morally correct (such as telling the truth, helping others, being polite and considerate) as a result of parental praise and approval. Similar techniques are advocated by some psychologists for helping teachers to cope with deviant or disorderly behaviour in the classroom. Ward (1971) developed a training schedule for teachers, based on operant conditioning procedures and designed to help them eradicate disruptive behaviour of children in the infant and junior school. Teachers were taught to reward children's desired behaviour by praise, attention, smiles or approval and by ignoring unwanted behaviour.

Behaviour can similarly be shaped by punishment or negative reinforcement in the form of verbal rebuke, physical punishment, sarcasm, the withholding of privileges — in other words any treatment a child finds unpleasant or disagreeable. The desired effect of punishment is either to inhibit the undesired behaviour by operant conditioning techniques or, within the framework adopted by Eysenck, to arouse feelings associated with pain, fear or anxiety in the hope that, by association, the undesired behaviour will in future be refrained from.

Eysenck (1960, 1964) goes so far as to suggest that the learning of any moral values should be based on modern learning theory and attempts to explain the formation of a conscience in terms of conditioned responses. Conscience, in his view, is a set of conditioned responses built up during the formative years by the pairing of conditioned stimuli (arising from aggressive or prohibitive behaviour) with unconditioned stimuli (smacks, verbal admonitions) by a process of stimulus generalization; the two become associated so that in future when a child contemplates a forbidden act, conditioned feelings of anxiety prevent him from indulging in it. His "conscience", in other words, is acting as a moral rein on his behaviour. Individual differences in the force of this so-called conscience are explained in terms of inborn conditionability. Extroverts, Eysenck has demonstrated, are more difficult to condition than introverts. Experimental evidence to support such an explanation is drawn largely from animal studies. For example, the now classic work of Solomon and Wynne (1953) showed that puppies, punished for eating from a forbidden bowl of food, were in future inhibited from touching the forbidden bowl even though they were on the point of starvation and even in the absence of the experimenter who had administered the punishment. They had, it was suggested, developed something akin to what we call conscience in human beings.

Not only do children learn to adopt desired behaviour patterns as a result of rewards and punishments, but also by watching other people. Experiments have confirmed what we already know from everyday observation, namely that children readily copy or imitate what they see others doing, especially the actions of a parent or admired peer.

Bandura and Walters (1963) base their theories of social learning and personality development largely on the notion of imitation or modelling. Their claim that limitation plays an important role in the learning of deviant as well as conforming behaviour is well substantiated by cross cultural and laboratory studies. Young children learn to adopt sex-linked occupational and domestic roles typical of their culture, by observing their elders' behaviour rather than through deliberate instruction of any kind. Cross cultural evidence (Nash 1958, Bronfenbrenner 1970) demonstrates the fact that children not only learn from what they are told to do by adults, but also from what they see the adults doing. And not only do they learn by watching real adult models — symbolic models on film, television or in books can also have a similar effect. In fact, the use of film sequences in the laboratory is the main technique chosen by Bandura and his co-workers (1963) to demonstrate the effects of observational learning on children's behaviour.

Such studies suggest that observing the behaviour of models may have several effects. Firstly, the child may acquire new responses which he has hitherto not shown spontaneously. This seems another case of confirming what we already know from everyday observation. We are all familiar, for instance, with young children who play at hospitals or schools, adopting the role of doctor or teacher as they have seen it enacted. Bandura *et al.* (1961) carried out a study designed to test for delayed imitation of deviant models by young children. They exposed one group of nursery children to aggressive adult models and a second group to non-aggressive models and observed the children's spontaneous behaviour subsequently in a play situation. In a later experiment (1963) children's reactions to aggression displayed by real-life models, film models, cartoon-film models were compared. In all cases, children who had observed an aggressive model themselves displayed aggressive behaviour later on in a mildly frustrating situation, whereas such responses rarely occurred in control groups of children.

This kind of work does raise several important issues relating to moral learning. For instance, if part of what it means to act morally is to show consideration for others and not to vent aggression on them, what is the effect on children of being severely punished by an adult for their aggressive activity? An adult who loses his temper is perceived by the child as aggressive, so that, if the effects of modelling are as potent as Bandura would have us believe, this must serve to make a child even more aggressive and less considerate of others. Such work does imply too that much learning of social or moral conduct is likely to go on inevitably: children model themselves on adults they see around them, following the example they set. We shall consider some aspects of this in greater detail in Chapter 5.

However, not only do children learn new kinds of behaviour as a result of the observation of others. Bandura (1962) has demonstrated that children exposed to aggressive models subsequently display far more aggressive responses than they could possibly have seen during the course of the experiment. In other words, exposure to uninhibited aggressive behaviour may release responses which had hitherto been latent or forgotten. The model thus appears to have a disinhibitory or releasing effect. We are reminded here of the thorny question of the effects of violence seen on television on children's behaviour. Several studies have attempted to examine these effects (Himmelweit 1958, Belson 1977) but naturally methodology is difficult and so far results have been equivocal.

Studies of modelling or imitation go further in suggesting the vicarious effects of rewards and punishments on children's social or moral conduct. In yet another series of experiments (Bandura *et al.* 1963), four groups of nursery school children were observed under different conditions. One group watched a film model being punished for aggressive behaviour and a second group saw the model rewarded for the same kind of conduct. One control group was shown a highly active but non-aggressive model and a further control group saw no models at all. In subsequent observations of the children at play, those who had witnessed the aggressive model being rewarded indulged in significantly more hostile acts than children in any other group.

Learning theorists are divided in their views on the effects of punishment on moral conduct where this is seen partly as the conformity by children to norms and standards set by adults. Whereas Eysenck's conditioning theory assumes that children have to be punished before they learn to refrain from an "immoral act", Bandura's modelling studies suggest that children may equally well learn to inhibit undesired behaviour without committing a prohibited act and without themselves being punished. Watching a model being punished seems to suffice, at any rate in some cases.

In discussing the contribution of learning theories towards moral development, we have so far seen that the focus for them is on conduct or behaviour. Moral conduct is interpreted either as resistance to temptation involving the classical conditioning of emotional responses such as fear as in Eysenck's model, or learning to conform to certain standards as a result of rewards and punishments or through imitation learning. Since only conduct or behaviour is at stake, it could be argued that the explanation offered by learning theorists is applicable only to moral training rather than to any other aspects of morality. They omit to deal with moral feeling, reasoning or judgement. Their explanations fall into a mechanistic paradigm where children are regarded as passive learners, responding or reacting to the influence of others rather than acting and interpreting the world around them and progressively learning to form their own standards and apply their own moral principles according to the differing demands of prevailing circumstances. As we have already made clear, the growing dislike of a theory in which man is regarded only as passive makes the social learning approach untenable as a sufficient explanation of moral learning. It is therefore to the work of the developmental theorists that we must turn to seek an explanation for these more complex aspects of human moral development.

Cognitive-developmental approach

Among the early investigations into moral development, the work of Arnold Gesell (1940, 1946) deserves mention. Gesell sees development mainly as a maturational, unfolding process, which advances more or less regardless of environmental influences. His evidence comes from wide-scale longitudinal studies of children from birth to adolescence so that he feels confident in talking of the typical child at any age level as the titles of his books show, for example, *The Child from Five to Ten* (1946).

Nevertheless, although his way of thinking still deals largely with moral conduct rather than with reasoning or judgement, his scheme does hint at a stage sequence of morality. His work seems to suggest three distinct stages in moral conduct: the first is typified by obedience to adult instructions and commands; the second reveals rigid adherence to rules even in the absence of an authority figure; and the third shows a personal morality where the individual acts apparently autonomously. Gesell suggests that parents and teachers should expect different kinds of moral conduct with different age groups and that in school we must accommodate our attempts at moral education to the developmental level of the children we are concerned with.

This kind of thinking is, as we shall see, similar to that of Piaget and Kohlberg in a sense, but Gesell does not go as far as exploring the nature of children's thought processes to explain why their moral conduct is as he finds it at these three stages. He tells us more about what children think rather than how they think. Piaget, who views moral development as one aspect of a child's overall intellectual and cognitive development, sets out to explore the child's processes of thinking.

The work of Piaget

Piaget's own thinking was influenced by the ideas of both Durkheim, in a sociological context, and Kant, from a philosophical perspective. To Durkheim Piaget was indebted for the emphasis he placed on the social context of morality. For Durkheim (1960) claimed that we are moral beings only in so far as we are social beings and was concerned with the individual's relationship with society through his attachment to it, with society's discipline on him and with the individual's eventual autonomy within a social structure. Piaget also drew upon the distinction Kant made between the heteronomy and autonomy of the will; Piaget hoped to show that this distinction has practical application in the contrast he wished to make between conventional morality and a rational moral code.

In the former, children are at the stage of heteronomy where their conduct is dependent upon the wishes of others, while in the latter they have reached a stage of automony where they act according to their own moral choices for which they can give their own reasons.

Piaget's main aim was to explore the nature of children's moral judgements and, to do this, he worked in Geneva with individual children, talking to them and questioning them on three broad areas: their attitudes to rules; their judgements of right and wrong; and their assessment of justice and fairness. He established that growth in moral judgement is a gradual developmental process, involving not the learning of rules by rewards, punishment or imitation, but rather a progress of cognitive restructuring.

In order to make clear how his conclusions were reached, we shall look briefly at his empirical work in each of the three areas mentioned above.

In 1932 Piaget wrote that "all morality consists in a system of rules and the essence of all morality is to be sought for in the respect which the individual acquires for those rules." In view of this, then, one of the crucial questions for Piaget was how the young child's mind comes to understand and respect rules. He was concerned not only with the child's practice of rules (his moral conduct) but also with the way in which the child perceives rules as a restraint on his actions. For his investigations Piaget chose rules children follow in playing the game of marbles (universally popular among the child population of Geneva at that time), since this kind of rule is one seldom passed on by adults but learnt from other children during the game itself. He himself joined in their games adopting the position of one ignorant of the rules and conventions, and in conversation with children, discovered how their approach to rules changes as they mature.

The very youngest children play haphazardly with no regard for rules at all, but later, up to the age of about six, they become more and more aware of the rules of the game, now regarding them as immutable and following them rigidly. This reflects the child's heteronomy, obeying rules laid down for him externally which are not to be quesitoned. But later he gradually begins to realize that rules are not sacrosanct and have been formulated in order to regulate the game. Rather than being untouchable they can be modified by mutual agreement with the other players. It is during this stage that heteronomy begins to give way to autonomy and around the age of eleven or twelve children begin to show an interest in how and why rules are formulated. They are not now concerned with putting them rigidly into practice, but are ready to modify them by mutual agreement according to circumstance.

In Piaget's view, one of the main factors contributing towards this developing autonomy is the child's growing ability to cooperate with others. Where rules were seen, at an earlier stage, as emanating from some authority figure, respect for them was unilateral rather than mutual. It is only when children experience relationships with their peers, meeting together as equals, that the opportunity arises for mutual consent and cooperation and the scene is set for the growth of autonomy. But in order to move towards autonomy it seems essential for the child to be released from constraints imposed by authority figures where adults use their superior force. Cooperative activities and mutual understanding between peers are, in Piaget's view, necessary conditions for autonomy to develop.

If we now examine some of Piaget's work on children's judgements of right and wrong, we again find a gradual progression from a stage of heteronomy to one of autonomy. Actions are at first regarded by young children as right if an adult approves of them, wrong if he disapproves. Children at the heteronomous stage judge conduct according to its material consequences, rather than the intentions behind the act.

To explore children's judgements of right and wrong Piaget used a story technique, presenting the children with pairs of incidents and asking them to comment on the behaviour of the characters portrayed. For example, children were asked whether a girl who accidentally cut a large hole in her dress when she was trying to help her mother with some dressmaking was naughtier than a child who deliberately played with scissors when she had been told not to and made a small snip in her dress. Younger children almost without exception judged the first case as more severe and more deserving of punishment: the act was judged as naughtier because the girl made a bigger hole. Piaget terms this stage in the formation of moral judgements "moral realism"; the child is forming his judgement on the basis of what he can observe happening around him in his reality, that is, on material consequences. Similarly, on hearing stories about a boy who stole a roll to give to a hungry friend and a girl who stole a piece of ribbon, judgements were made on the basis of the cost of the stolen article — that which was immediate and real to the child.

This tendency of young children to focus on external, observed consequences of actions and to ignore intentions can be explained by reference to the child's egocentricity. In Piaget's stage theory of cognitive growth, a child at the egocentric level is still limited in his ability to distinguish himself and his own feelings from those of others. He is capable of seeing things only from his own point of view, does not always distinguish fact from fantasy (dreams, to him, are real) and thus cannot conceive that other viewpoints are possible. He cannot internalize rules and apply them to actions in a flexible enough manner to take into account factors which might be variable; for example, other people's intentions or the different demands made by varying circumstances. It is only as he emerges from this state of egocentricity and begins to be able to focus on more than one aspect of a situation at a time, and, in particular, on unobservable aspects, that his moral judgements become more flexible. Thus an older child, confronted with the anecdotes about stealing, might argue that whereas it is usually wrong to steal, it is not so bad if your friend is starving. Consideration for others is now assuming an important part in a child's life, as a result, Piaget argues, of peer group cooperation and interaction.

To come now to the third field of investigation, we shall look at some of Piaget's work on children's sense of justice, the development of which, he claims, is also dependent upon mutual respect between peers. As he writes: "the sense of justice, though naturally capable of being reinforced by the precepts and example of the adult, is largely independent of these influences and requires nothing more for its development than the mutual respect and solidarity which holds among chidren themselves." Again, very young children interpret justice to mean that which adults tell them to do. Losing or breaking something deserves punishment, even if done by accident. Fairness involves being given equal shares, even if needs differ. A closer examination of Piaget's findings reveals the same progression here as in other areas, namely from an egocentric stage, where children's judgements stem from moral realism and where rules, duties and obligations are dependent upon adult constraints. They pass from this stage of heteronomy, which, as we have seen, indicates dependence upon others, to that of autonomy as a result of cooperation on an equal basis with their peers.

It is this development of mutual respect that enables a child to begin to see the world through other people's eyes. It is only when he can consider all possible circumstances and points of view before making a moral judgement, one that fits a particular set of circumstances, that he can truly be said to have reached a stage of autonomy or to practise a rational moral code instead of being tied to a conventional morality.

In summary, then, Piaget distinguishes between two kinds of morality. Conventional morality is reflected in an obedience to adult command and an uncritical adherence to rules. This is described as a stage of moral realism or heteronomy, characterized by unilateral respect for and dependence upon others for guidance in moral issues. Rational morality is reached where children are able to formulate their own moral rules by mutual agreement and to apply them according to circumstance rather than rigidly and immutably. Kay (1973) sees this kind of morality as creative, that is, applied flexibly according to the unique set of circumstances in operation at the time.

Children do not practise either conventional or rational morality to the exclusion of the other, but move from one to another by a process of maturation, development and cognitive restructuring. Thus Piaget assumes that a child's development in moral judgements is paralleled by his cognitive development in other spheres. A stage theory of development is thus postulated with the observation that children pass through stages in an invariant order even though not all at the same rate. Some do not ever attain the final stage of absolute autonomy, as we shall see later.

A stage theory of development is characterized by several unique features. Firstly the concept "stage" supercedes that of chronological or mental age and although it is possible to say, for example, that children do not begin to emerge from the stage of heteronomy until about the age of eleven or twelve, it must be remembered that age is only a very rough guide. Children do not all develop at the same rate, so some will progress more rapidly through the stages than others. Secondly, the sequence of stages has been demonstrated as being invariant: it is not possible either to miss out a stage or to pass through them in a different order, though exceptional children, as Williams and Williams (1969) have shown, will show flashes of insight characteristic of an advanced stage long before they are firmly established in that stage. Thirdly, progression from one stage to another does not involve simply an addition to what went before, but implies a reorganization or restructuring, enabling the child to see problems and thus to make moral judgements from a different and more complex perspective. Fourthly, as we suggested in Chapter 1, the concept of stages should not be taken in a literal or chronological sense. All adults will respond to some situations in a heteronomous manner.

The great value of Piaget's work on moral judgements lies both in the methods he used to investigate children's thought processes and in the fact that he was the first to view moral thought as a developmental and restructuring process depending largely on a child's growth towards abstract thinking and interaction with his environment and with those with whom he comes into contact. Important questions, left unanswered by his own work, have stimulated further research. For example, although he demonstrates that children move from one stage to another in a fixed sequence, he does not examine the conditions which might facilitate or impede this progress, nor does he explain why some children are apparently arrested in growth before they reach the stage of autonomy. And although teachers and educators have drawn widely upon Piaget's work for guidance in planning work for children, Piaget himself never suggested ways in which parents or teachers might help children to develop further. Thus Piaget offers no deliberate guidance to teachers concerned with their responsibility for the moral education of their pupils. However, he did lay the foundations for later investigators to build upon.

Research stimulated by Piaget's theory

So vast is the wealth of research stimulated by Piaget's theory of moral development that only a few examples can be referred to here before we consider one of the major contributors, Lawrence Kohlberg. Many of the empirical studies set out to replicate Piaget's investigations and did in fact substantiate his findings (Morris 1958, Johnson 1962, Loughran 1967). Kohlberg (1968), in a twelve-year cross-cultural study of boys in the USA, Great Britain, Canada, Mexico and Turkey, found that although Piaget's stages emerged universally, children in rural societies showed slower progress. Hollingshead (1949), MacRae (1954), J. & E. Newsom (1963) amongst others all claimed to have established social class variations in moral development, where children from higher socio-economic groups were seen to progress more rapidly towards the stage of autonomy. Brennan (1961) showed that progress of E.S.N. children falls far behind those in normal schools and that few, if any, ever reach the final stage.

However, some doubts have also been cast on Piaget's findings, as a result of further investigation. Edwards (1959), for example, in an investigation of the moral judgements of adolescents, found that many of the older adolescent boys in his sample still formed their judgements on the basis of material consequences and paid no more attention to motives or intentions than younger children. Bandura and McDonald (1963) claimed that developmental stages could be readily altered by the provision of adult models who consistently adopted a moral orientation counter to that displayed by the child, even if this resulted in the apparent regression of the child to an earlier stage. Such a claim is in direct contrast to the work of Turiel (1969) who attempts to show that a child's moral thinking can only be changed when he is exposed to reasoning one stage above his own, but that he remains oblivious to arguments presented at a stage below that in which he is established. Furthermore, Rest *et al.* (1969) showed that children judged moral arguments one stage below their own as worse than their own in spite of the fact that they were being presented by an authority figure.

Other workers adopting a Piagetian framework for their research include Kay (1973, 1975) who pursues the stage theory further and suggests an attitudinal model of moral development, laying greater stress on social and environmental influences than Piaget did. Bull (1969) proposed a similar developmental continuum ranging from "anomy" at the very early stage where the infant is amoral, having no regard for others, and passing through stages where he is dependent firstly on authority figures, then upon the decisions of his peer group until he can finally make moral decisions for himself.

The work of Kohlberg

Besides Piaget's work, Kohlberg's can probably be said to have made the most important contribution to the psychology of moral development. Kohlberg, working in the USA, has in his empirical research both complemented and expanded Piaget's ideas. Like Piaget, he too concentrates largely on individuals' moral judgement; that is, the reasoning behind the judgements they make, rather than their actual moral conduct. Kohlberg too (1966) adopts a cognitive theory of moral development and sets out to show that principles of moral judgement gradually develop as children grow older, but that this development is highly dependent on environmental and social conditions. His conviction that external influences can foster children's moral thinking and help them to move onto a further more complex stage leads him to offer a framework for practical moral education (1966) which will be discussed later.

Kohlberg's scheme of moral development takes the form of six main stages, each of which reveals a different kind of motivation for acting morally or for forming moral judgements. At stage one of the premoral level, we find that an individual's motives are oriented primarily towards obedience and punishment. A child at this stage will say that it is wrong to disobey his father because he will be found out and punished or that he must not, for instance, run across the road because his father has said so. At stage two, the actions which are regarded as morally right are those which satisfy the individual's needs. Stages three and four, at the level of what Kohlberg calls conventional role conformity, represent firstly, the "good boy" orientation where the child's actions and judgements are made in order to gain approval from others, while later (at stage four) this gives way to a respect for authority and the given social order. A child will, for example, conform to avoid censure from an authority figure. It is not until the individual reaches stages five and six at the level of self-accepted moral principles that he begins to approach what Kohlberg considers to be moral maturity. At stage five the rights of others are considered and an effort is made to see that these rights are respected and safeguarded. It is rather more a contractual orientation than one involving any feeling for the position of others. At the final stage, probably not attained by the majority of the population, the morally mature person acts according to his own conscience or principles. He is now able to consider universal values involving the rights and feelings of others and his own behaviour towards them.

As in any stage concept, the order of the stages is regarded as invariant; an individual can neither miss out a stage nor take them in a different order. And for Kohlberg, this invariance goes further to include universality under different cultural conditions. This does not mean that in any culture movement through the stages proceeds at the same rate, but rather that the sequence is the same and that, regardless of the nature of the culture, all stages emerge, with the possible exception of the last. Kohlberg's own cross-cultural studies of moral development (1966) compared the moral judgements made by ten to sixteen year olds in Taiwan (urban population), in a Malaysian aboriginal tribal village, and in a Turkish village, with those made by an American sample. The findings suggest a similar sequence of development in all cultures, although stages five and six do not develop clearly in preliterate communities.

He also established (1966) that subcultural differences occur, not in basic moral values but in rate of progress through the stages. At all ages middle-class children tended to be somewhat in advance of their working-class peers. This he attributed to a difference in children's feelings of their participation in a prevailing social order and in their understanding of it. If working-class children find themselves in an authoritarian family set-up (though obviously not all working-class families are of this type) then their individual value as persons is accorded less importance than their position in the family. It would follow then that their moral orientations would lean further towards gaining the approval of others and avoiding censure (stages three and four) than towards a personal autonomous stance as in stages five and six.

Kohlberg's stage theory, like Piaget's, implies a cognitive restructuring and reordering as the individual matures morally. Each stage of development allows a better and more complex cognitive grasp than the one before it; elements of earlier stages are taken account of but are transformed in the light of later understanding and more complex mental structures. Kohlberg attempts to explain how individuals pass from one stage to the next by drawing on the notion of cognitive conflict and introduces the "one stage above" principle, further developed on a practical level by Turiel (1969). His thesis is that when children are presented with arguments one stage above the level they have reached, the conflict or mismatch in the arguments will prompt them to attempt a resolution of the problem and thus help them towards the next stage of moral argument. It is this principle that both Kohlberg and Turiel hope will form a fundamental guideline for any programme of moral education in school.

Although Kohlberg sets out a developmental sequence, showing how children's moral judgements develop and mature as they pass from a premoral level to one where they are capable of making mature moral judgements, his pattern does not only offer an explanation of the child's moral thinking. In addition it goes some way towards furnishing a theory of moral character, suggesting an explanation for individual differences in the moral nature of adults. As we have already mentioned, not everyone reaches the final stage of moral maturity and many of us do not even attain stage five. It is, however, possible to find adults who do not appear to have progressed at all from stage one, those who simply conform to certain standards set up by others because of fear of punishment. If punishment is unlikely, that is, if there is minimal risk of their being found out in their infringement of rules, they have no hesitation in doing just as they like — no inner moral principle appears to operate. Adults are then to be found at any stage, and from this we are able to talk of a character type, if a person's conduct and quality of moral judgement are consistent.

Although research in this area is still in its early stages, findings suggest that it might be possible to account for an individual's fixation at an early stage and therefore, up to a point, for his moral character, by exploring other aspects of his social and moral life. Haan *et al.* (1968), working with college students, found that relatively few came out at the level of self-accepted moral principles on Kohlberg's scale of moral judgements. Those who did were found to be highly independent of their parents, to play an active part in social and political organizations, and to rely very little on religious doctrines for moral guidance, a point which may provide additional support for what we said in Chapter 1 about the essential authoritarianism of a religious morality. Those who came out at the level of conventional morality tended to be generally conservative, to play little part in social or political activities, and to conform to conventional standards set by parents and other authority figures. More will be said about character typology in the next section, but the question to be raised here is whether it is possible to develop the quality of children's moral thinking, so that regardless of parental attitudes or child-rearing techniques, few children do get stuck at the early stages.

Turiel, working with Kohlberg, suggests two interesting and valuable principles derived from the stage theory and designed to form fundamental practical guidelines for those concerned with children's moral development. These are the notions of "one stage above", which we have already discussed, and of stage mixture. Turiel (1969) explains that a moral stage shows how judgements are made rather than whether they coincide with conventional standards or norms. The implication is then that moral stages are concerned firstly with processes of thought rather than with products, and secondly that they reveal qualitative rather than quantitative differences. And since differences are qualitative it would be very difficult to postulate a sudden cut-off point between one stage and the next.

Turiel suggests therefore the notion of stage mixture which he shows to be consonant with the restructuring hypothesis. At any stage in development, children encounter a vast range of experiences, but at any one time they respond more to some aspects of the environment than to others. They respond to those aspects that they can readily understand or, in other words, those at their own developmental stage. But they also experience aspects they do not yet fully comprehend — those at a stage above their own. So although they do not respond directly to these more complex stimuli, many different experiences are jostling in the child's awareness, and it is this variety that Turiel refers to as a stage mixture.

This, he argues, is a necessary part of development through successive structures. Moving from one stage to another is possible only if we admit a basic stage mixture, the practical implications of which are as follows. Slow progress from one stage to another implies little stage mixture — there is little to link one stage to the next; increased stage mixture is therefore conducive to change. Those who do not progress to a mature level of moral judgement show a levelling off of mixture, so there is little stage variability and little chance of progress and stabilization gradually sets in.

These hypotheses were confirmed by detailed analysis of data derived from experimental studies already carried out. It is particularly illuminating in explaining cross-cultural differences: moral development in isolated communities progresses more slowly than in technological societies, for the very reason that there is greater stability, less challenge by new and strange experiences, and altogether less intellectual, social and moral conflict. For anyone hoping to promote children's moral development, the main task then lies in increasing the disparate elements and thus increasing the level of stage mixture and the probability of a move forward. It is here that Turiel's second principle comes into operation.

Turiel and his co-workers found that it was possible to prompt cognitive restructuring of the kind that would help children onto the next stage by confronting them with a cognitive conflict which they were encouraged to resolve. They did this by presenting groups of children with moral arguments at stages other than their own. Arguments presented two stages above the child's own had little or no effect on his subsequent moral reasoning. The conflict was not apparent to children because the gap between the styles of argument was too great. Arguments presented a stage below the child's own similarly had no effect, in fact Rest *et al.* (1969) showed that children considered arguments below their own level to be worse than theirs and therefore rejected them outright. It was only when arguments were presented at one stage above the child's own that any progress was apparent in his subsequent moral judgements. Such children are able to perceive these arguments as contradictory to their own precisely because they function at more than one stage simultaneously. They thus experience cognitive conflict or disequilibrium and are challenged to think in a more complex manner. The practical educational implications of these theoretical notions and empirical findings will be discussed later.

Studies of character development

No account of research in the field of moral development would be complete without some discussion of two major studies of character development, the Character Education Enquiry under the direction of Hartshorne and May (1928-1930) and the *Psychology of Character Development* by Peck and Havighurst (1960). Discussion of these two important projects has been left until now, so that critical reference can be made to the three major approaches to moral development where appropriate.

Hartshorne and May set out to examine the conduct of children of secondary school age in the USA over a five-year period. Their sample consisted of over ten thousand schoolchildren whose resistance to temptation in the absence of an authority figure was measured over a whole series of situations allowing them to cheat, steal or tell lies.

The investigators found a very low and statistically non-significant correlation between the tests, suggesting that, for instance, a high score of cheating in one situation did not point to a tendency to cheat in all circumstances. Similarly, a child found to be honest in one context might easily tell lies in another. They found too that the tendency to cheat depended both upon the risk of detection and the effort they had to make in order to cheat. Non-cheaters were more cautious about being found out, it seemed, rather than being more honest. Honesty seemed to be dictated more by immediate situational factors, such as group norms and group approval, rather than by internal moral principles. Correlations between tests of moral knowledge and experimental tests of moral conduct were low; in other words, knowing the facts associated with moral behaviour was not necessarily reflected in the individual's own moral conduct. Furthermore, direct moral guidance of the kind offered by Sunday school or Bible classes, scout or guide groups, did not appear to have a positive influence upon children's behaviour in relation to lying, stealing and so on. From these data Hartshorne and May concluded firstly that moral traits such as honesty are situation-specific. Children do not show a consistent trait of honesty in their general behaviour, but their moral conduct varies according to the nature of the situation. Secondly, because didactic instruction seemed to have little or no effect, they suggested that moral character is a matter of deep emotional forces operating during the child's formative years—a factor reminiscent of Freud's concept of the development of the super-ego. If moral character is not a matter of consistent moral traits like honesty or generosity, but is rather a matter of emotional tendencies (fear, love, hate, guilt) which are basically affective, then any attempt to develop children's moral natures later on in school is doomed to failure, since the seeds of their moral character have been sown much earlier on.

However the work of Hartshorne and May was essentially an investigation into moral conduct; the nature of their study produced data indicating the products of children's moral thinking, that is, their actual responses or actual behaviour. What this study did not do was to look behind the conduct itself to probe children's reasons for behaving as they did.

Investigations of this sort, that examined the nature of children's thought processes rather than their thought products, were left until a later date, after the establishment of a structural stage theory of moral development worked out by Piaget and later by Kohlberg. As we saw earlier, Kohlberg's stage theory offers a kind of character typology but is based on very different arguments relating to a child's growing understanding of moral situations as he develops intellectually and passes from one stage to the next. Kohlberg attributes the failure of any conventional moral education pro-gramme to have a direct influence on moral character and moral conduct, not to the potency of earlier emotional bonds between parent and child but to a misconception of what form moral education might take in school. Hitherto, he argues, teachers have attempted to train children in "good" moral habits through example, rewards and punishments, rather than matching the level of moral argument they present to children with their stage of moral development. Again, therefore, this supports what we have said earlier about the need for an approach to moral education that is based on the promotion of the pupil's ability to think for himself rather than on any attempt to tell him what to think or how to behave.

There was to be a gap of about thirty years before the second major character development study was carried out, again in the USA, by Peck and Havighurst (1960). Peck and Havighurst themselves attributed the lack of significant research in the intervening years to the rather pessimistic interpretation of the findings in the Hartshorne and May study. These findings seemed to discourage further experimentation and objective study in the field of character education, partly because this area seemed too complex for psychological investigation and partly because the results suggested that even if a typology of moral character could be established there was nothing that could be done in the field of moral education to alter or modify traits so firmly laid down in early childhood. Havighurst and Taba (1949) had reopened research in this area of personality development, thus paving the way for the wide-scale survey published by Peck and Havighurst eleven years later.

These investigators focused not upon the specificity of moral conduct but rather upon its general persistence and the predictability that they detected in earlier research findings. Their basic orientation was a psycho-analytical one which drew upon Freud's view that personality development can be classified according to the orientation a child adopts during his early psycho-sexual development. Thus Freud's personality typology (1905), manifested in oral, anal, phallic and genital types, depending on the area of the body which most involves psycho-sexual and emotional satisfaction, is paralleled by a typology set up by Peck and Havighurst to indicate an individual's orientation towards other people, also in terms of the search to satisfy his own personal needs in a maximally pleasurable way.

They produced what is in effect a motivational theory of morality in psychosocial developmental terms. Five character types were hypothesized. The amoral type is entirely egocentric; he leads a life of self-gratification and pays little or no attention to other people's feelings. The expedient type is basically still egocentric, but acts in an apparently moral way even though he has no internalized moral principles and is still out to satisfy his own needs. The conformist fears disapproval and strives constantly to comply with the requirements of other people. His moral conduct is, as a result, fairly stable, since he always aims to avoid what society would disapprove of. He does not however act on the basis of his own moral principles. The irrational conscientious person begins to show signs of developing his own internal moral code. He has internalized standards of right and wrong but tends to be rather inflexible in his application of them, thus giving an impression of disregarding the feelings and wishes of others. The final type, showing a fully developed sense of moral maturity, is rational-altruistic; he considers the welfare of others and is ready to sacrifice himself to help others.

Peck and Havighurst worked out their scheme on the basis of findings from investigations using large numbers of adolescents between the ages of ten and seventeen, including those in the 1949 study. They suggest three main criteria for identifying moral maturity: firstly, the ability to attend to other people's feelings; secondly, to predict the consequences of one's own actions and the repercussions these might have on others; and thirdly, the ability and willingness to modify the application of one's moral principles according to the demands of a particular situation.

If we examine the typology suggested by Peck and Havighurst, two important points emerge. Firstly, as we have seen, the five main types of moral motivation they propose reflect ways in which individuals tend to behave in a consistent and predictable manner. Thus, if an individual at the age of ten tends to show behaviour that is mainly of the expedient kind, the model suggests that he will still adopt expedient techniques as an adult, even though the specific reasons he gives and moral situations he encounters are relative to his age group. Persistence and stability of behaviour are attributed to early parental influence, as we might expect from theorists adopting a Freudian perspective. Peck and Havighurst suggest, rather pessimistically, that each generation tends to perpetuate its strengths and weaknesses of character largely unchanged. Parents treat their children in a certain way and thus children tend to turn out very much like their parents. Such a conclusion does not offer much hope for a programme of moral education.

The second point of interest, especially in the light of our earlier analysis of developmental stages, is that each type seems to represent a definite stage in a developmental scheme. The amoral type is clearly far less mature morally than the expedient type for instance. However Peck and Havighurst did not themselves propose a developmental sequence showing how children can pass from one stage to another. They were, on the other hand, convinced that moral attitudes learnt in the early years were relatively unmodifiable.

Moral development and moral education

To end this chapter, some observations will be made on the implications of the various approaches discussed for teachers contemplating a programme of moral education and for those conscious of their own responsibility for the moral education of their pupils, even if not in a formal way. The psychoanalytical approach serves to draw our attention to the importance of the emotional aspects of morality. Many teachers, influenced possibly by their understanding of the work of Piaget, who pays little attention to emotional factors, seem to regard the formation of moral judgements and the taking of moral decisions as a largely intellectual matter. But as we shall argue in Chapter 4, morality and the emotions go hand in hand. The affective side of moral behaviour, that is, whether a person really cares about what he is doing and whether he has other people's interests sincerely at heart, is a matter not to be overlooked. Similarly his own emotional response to a situation as well as an understanding of and ability to cope with his own emotions, are important. Feelings of guilt such as Freud postulated in his notions of the conscience and the ego ideal serve to make the individual care about his own conduct to the point of concern even about his intentions, feelings or fantasies. Although Freudian theory cannot offer any positive guidelines to teachers that might help them to deal with the emotional dimension of morality, his case studies illustrate clearly that the effects of fixation at an early stage of development can result in anxiety and uncertainty. These are frequently manifested by a withdrawal from emotional involvement and a retreat into situations which are not emotionally threatening. And although most children do not suffer from the extreme neurotic disturbances such as those described in his case study of little Hans, who developed, amongst other things, a fear that once outside his own house, he would be crushed by a stumbling horse or a falling building, there are nevertheless many children whose emotional responses are lamed, uncontrolled or misdirected.

Learning theorists concentrate mainly on one aspect of moral learning, that of moral training, if such a term is possible, or of moral habits. As we suggested in Chapter 2, some teachers will argue that because young children cannot understand moral reasoning, there is no point in trying to reason with them over moral issues and all that can be done is to inculcate certain standards into them, thus helping them to form moral habits which will guide their behaviour. Others will challenge this view, claiming that any training or habit formation is entirely misplaced in the realm of morality, and make a case either for letting children simply formulate their own moral code, worked out by mutual agreement amongst peer groups, or leave them without adult guidance. Brennan, for example (1965), argues that all children should have the opportunity to live without direct adult supervision. A.S. Neill in his school at Summerhill embraced this basic philosophy. But these extreme viewpoints should surely not be mutually exclusive, as Peters argues when he talks of the paradox of moral education, referring to the need for habits to precede reason. Similarly Oakeshott (1962) argues that in order to cope with the complexities of life in a society such as ours, with its manifold choices and unpredictable moral dilemmas, we cannot always afford the time to stop and consider our moral principles before acting. Instead, where the moral choice is not a new or challenging one, we need habits to fall back on. It becomes a habit, or part of one's nature, for example, to show consideration for others; we do not need to stop to think whether to offer help to a blind man wanting to cross the road. Reflection on moral principles is clearly not necessary in this case. Part of our moral repertory must therefore lie in habits formed in the early years.

But the danger comes when an individual relies too heavily on habits or on what he has been taught by others. It is here that we see the limitations of a learning theory approach. Learning that relies solely on reward and punishment will stultify real moral thinking, simply because it is too inflexible. Such learning will be situation-specific and is not easily modified or generalized to circumstances posing a different problem. Furthermore, once the supporting authority figure is withdrawn, the individual is bound to feel lost, since there is no one present to show approval of what he is doing. Adults in charge of young children may not always be aware of their influence as reinforcing agents in Skinner's sense, or of their potency as examples or models. Bandura's work points to the effects that modelling or imitation can have on children's behaviour and, although he does not offer deliberate guidance on moral education, awareness of his work does serve to draw our attention to some of the unintended outcomes of adult examples.

As we saw earlier in our discussion of indoctrination, it is particularly important for teachers of young children to ensure that they are not merely teaching their pupils a set of habits which they will continue to use unthinkingly. Offering children reasons and explanations appropriate to their level of understanding will go some way towards avoiding the risks of indoctrinating them in this way.

Perhaps one of the most important things teachers can learn from the approaches discussed so far is that much moral learning has taken place before a child enters school. He has not only developed some kind of conscience and internalized some sort of moral standards in his very early years, albeit at an unconscious level, but has also acquired habits and learned conduct as a result of rewards and punishments meted out to him by those in authority. The nature of moral learning of this kind will be discussed more fully in a later chapter. The cognitive developmental theorists seem to offer guidelines suggesting what considerations teachers might take into account in formulating an approach to moral education once the child is in school. As we observed earlier, Piaget did not offer deliberate advice to teachers, but his stage theory nevertheless suggests what it is possible or impossible to achieve at any given level of development. Turiel and Kohlberg go further in outlining deliberate techniques for moral education in schools, based on their own empirical findings. Some of the moral education programmes discussed in Chapter 7 would certainly benefit from the kind of psychological underpinning to be drawn from their work.

Summary and conclusions

This chapter has outlined three of the main psychological approaches to moral development and has attempted to show their relevance to educational practice. The psychoanalytical approach underlines the significance of earlier emotional experiences in the formation of the superego or conscience and draws attention to the unconscious nature of this process. The social learning approach stresses the effects of modelling, rewards and punishments on children's moral conduct, while the cognitive theorists examine ways in which children gradually learn to make moral judgements.

They all draw our attention to the fact that there is an important emotional dimension to morality and to moral development. It is to a consideration of this that we will now turn.

CHAPTER 4

MORAL EDUCATION AND THE EMOTIONS

The reality of moral experience would suggest that the emotions may well be the most important factor in the moral behaviour of most people. Certainly, it would be difficult to imagine a moral dilemma or an occasion requiring a moral choice in which the emotions were not involved in some way and it was for this reason that we stressed in Chapter 1 the importance of including this dimension of human behaviour in any worthwhile discussion of moral education.

Furthermore, as we saw in the preceding chapter, there is some evidence to suggest that moral character is much more a result of deep emotional forces operating during the child's formative years than of any attempts that are made at offering him rational guidance, and the work of psychologists in general on moral behaviour and moral thinking reveals quite clearly the importance of feeling in this area of human experience. There can be no productive discussion, then, of moral education that does not take full account of the part played by the emotions in moral behaviour.

In spite of this, however, the tendency has been for this aspect of human life and experience to be largely ignored by both philosophers and educationists, some because they have felt it to be not in any way their concern, others because they have deplored the very existence of man's emotional life and have regarded it as an obstacle to be overcome rather than as a feature to be given full weight in its own right in any consideration of moral behaviour.

More direct attention has been given to this aspect of human existence in literature, from the time of the Greek tragedians, and even of Homer himself before them, up to the present day. We have already referred to the fact that this conflict between reason and feeling was a major feature of Sophocles' depiction of the dilemma of Antigone. More recently, we have Herman Hesse's account of Joseph Knecht's attempts to resign as Master of the Glass Bead Game because "I have been standing at the frontier where my work as Magister Ludi has become eternal recurrence, an empty exercise and formula. I have been doing it without enthusiasm, sometimes even without faith. It was time to stop." For the most part, however, again, reason and feeling have been regarded as in conflict with each other, as incompatible, the major difference between this approach and that of the philosophers being that when this battle is fought in the arenas of philosophical disquisition it is reason which usually ends the victor, while when it occurs in the pages of literature this result is more often reversed.

Thus, since the beginning of organized thought—certainly in the Western world—there has existed this tension between the intellectual and the emotional dimensions of man's life, the head and the heart, reason and feeling. It is a tension that has never been satisfactorily resolved and it is one that from the beginning has had serious consequences for all aspects of education, as well as having particular import for moral education.

No discussion of moral education could be complete, then, without an attempt to consider what is the proper role of the emotions in moral behaviour or at least the direction in which an answer to this question might be sought. It is the main intention of this chapter, therefore, to suggest some of the areas that need to be explored if we are to begin to look for a solution to this difficulty.

First of all, however, we must familiarize ourselves with the nature of the problem in rather more detail by examining briefly the view of the emotions taken by philosophers and the resultant attitudes that have been adopted to education in general and to moral education in particular. For only when we have seen where the thinking has gone wrong can we hope to discern what form a proper approach might take.

Moral philosophy and the emotions

We have already commented on the remarkable influence Plato has exercised on the thinking of the Western world. That influence can be discerned in so many of our present-day attitudes and practices and this is especially true in the sphere of education. Nowhere has there been a better example of Platonism in practice than in the implementation of his recommendations for the differentiated treatment of children of gold, silver and bronze in the organization of the English system of secondary education for so many years on tripartite lines. Furthermore, this is one aspect of a more general feature of his thinking that has pervaded the thinking and the practice of the Western world in a much more insidious manner, namely the preeminence that he gave to intellectual development in all that he said about education and, indeed, about all other aspects of social living.

He described the soul of man as having three aspects—reason, "spirit" and the appetites. In analogy he likens these respectively to a man, a lion and a beast with many heads. Reason, then, is for him the element which is fully human, even godlike, so that this is the element that he regards as the central concern of education whose task it is to enable us to overcome as effectively as possible the animal life of the passions within us. The appetites, the beast with many heads, must be tamed; "spirit", the lion, must be trained to be the ally of reason; only reason itself, the intellect, the godlike aspect of man's nature, can be educated in the proper sense.

Moral education is central to Plato's scheme. The main goal of his educational system, as we saw in Chapter 1, is the production of moral beings, but this is seen as a purely intellectual matter. The state of being a moral agent is one in which the individual has come to *know* what is right and this knowledge is the culmination, the keystone, the apex of the vast edifice of human knowledge, so that it is only to be attained after a long process of intellectual development. Socrates, Plato's predecessor, had declared that virtue is knowledge of the good. This assertion Plato interpreted in a completely literal manner and he also made the illicit process to its converse, that knowledge is virtue. For not only did he believe that virtue or morality was to be attained purely by intellectual effort (and was thus accessible only to those of high intellectual calibre); he also believed, as perhaps he had to,.that once one had this knowledge, one could not avoid being virtuous. For who could know what was good and right, yet do something else? For Plato this would be analogous to knowing that a straight line is the shortest distance between two points and then setting out on an unnecessarily circuitous route to one's destination. Plato's model for all knowledge was mathematical knowledge and this view of human behaviour followed from that.

This kind of rationalist approach to the problem of human knowledge, then, from the outset created a dichotomy between reason and the passions that has remained with us ever since. Reason is regarded as the supreme factor in moral behaviour; the passions are unfortunate additional features of human life and are to be controlled, subdued, tamed.

Aristotle takes the same basic stance, although, perhaps because his model for human knowledge is biological rather than mathematical, he is more realistic in his view of the strength of the passions. For him, God is "self-thinking thought", pure thought. This, then, is the highest form of existence and man's true happiness consists in sharing this perfect life of God by engaging in this kind of intellectual activity for as long and at as high a level as possible. This activity he calls θεωρία (*theoria*), the godlike, intellectual activity of contemplation.

This is the only truly moral life but it represents a strange view of morality, since of necessity it is a purely private existence that it recommends. It also seems to advise us that this kind of activity is to be chosen always in preference to spending time performing deeds that might be to the advantage of our fellow men. The question must arise, therefore, as to whether in Aristotle's view it would be right to break off from one's contemplation to save a drowning child, for example, a question that many teachers of philosophy have worried their students with. It would seem that Aristotle himself would have to answer that question with a negative, but he does recognize that there has to be another kind of morality and he offers us another, second-order theory of morality, one that focuses on relations between human beings. It is here that he introduces that rather more realistic approach to the passions we mentioned above.

As we saw in Chapter 1, Aristotle, like Socrates and Plato, sees morality as a matter of knowledge, of knowing, in the full sense, what is right, what he calls "the right rule". If one knows the right rule, one will know in every circumstance what the right and moral course of action is. However, unlike Socrates and Plato, he does not believe that acting in the right way will follow automatically from such knowledge. He is well aware of the strength of what he called "pleasure" and of the conflict that arises between what we know to be right and what we recognize as pleasurable. In short, as we also suggested in Chapter 1, he is fully cognisant of the condition that St. Paul was later to refer to when he said, "The evil that I would not that I do and the good I would I do not." This phenomenon Aristotle called ἀκρασία (akrasia) incontinence, lack of self-control or self-discipline.

This can only be overcome, he believes, by the right kind of upbringing. Thus he advocates that, although young children cannot be expected to have the intellectual power to understand and recognize the "right rule" for themselves (for the sorts of reasons we discussed in the last chapter), they must be told how to behave and made to act according to it. Only in this way will they develop the right habits and correct patterns of behaviour, the "settled disposition" that will provide them with the self-discipline they will need when as adults they come to see what is right for themselves if they are to act according to it and not be seduced from the right course by the temptations of pleasure. As Richard Peters expressed it more recently, they "must enter the palace of Reason through the courtyard of Habit and Tradition" (1963, p.55).

Again, therefore, we see the appetites, the passions, the emotions being treated as in conflict with reason, as a serious problem to the would-be moral person and, as a result, as a feature of human character to be deplored, wrestled with and overcome, or at least tamed, in the interests of moral education and moral behaviour.

The Judaeic tradition, as is apparent from the words of St. Paul that we have just quoted, is not dissimilar, nor is the Christian ethic that derived from it. There is little in that tradition that is seriously at odds with Greek philosophy, so that the Christian theology that was developed from a fusion of the Greek and the Judaeic traditions by such men as St. Augustine and St. Thomas Aquinas and which has changed very little in its fundamentals since that time, manifests the same attitude towards the passions. Man's appetites are the domain of Satan, whose machinations with the assistance of Eve led to man's fall from grace in the person of Adam and resulted in all men entering the world carrying from birth the burden of original sin. Thus there has resulted a doctrine and, especially, a view of education which has dominated the thinking of the Western world. At the heart of that doctrine is the notion that original sin is to be overcome by whatever means are necessary, the passions are to be suppressed and man is to be given control over his emotional life, so that he can develop to the full and in an untrammelled manner his capacity for reason, his intellectual potential and especially his ability to attain what Aquinas called "the intellectual love of God".

This dualism, this dichotomy of reason and the passions has dominated Western philosophy ever since. When philosophy reemerged at the time of the Renaissance and freed itself from theology for the first time since the Greek era, it emerged with the same kind of strongly rationalist base, which again led to a view of morality that stressed its intellectual components, usually to the exclusion of all others. Thus, as we mentioned in Chapter 2, Spinoza sets out his *Ethics* in Euclidean form, offering us definitions, hypotheses to be proved, proofs of those hypotheses and conclusions clearly marked QED. Morality continues to be regarded as analogous to mathematics and moral reasoning is seen as the same kind of unemotional deductive process.

Even the advanced form of rationalism that Immanuel Kant developed in response to the challenges offered to the traditional view by the new wave of empiricists such as John Locke and David Hume made no allowance for man's emotional life. In fact, Kant is at some pains to stress that his system of morality is for rational beings rather than for human beings, a distinction whose importance lies in the fact that it reveals a view of human beings as hindered in their search for a rational morality by the unfortunate condition of being lumbered with feelings and emotions. Again, therefore, these are to be overcome so that the individual can behave in that way which is shown to be right by the application of reason. To discover the right course of action is a rational and intellectual activity. One's natural inclinations merely serve to deflect one from putting such right conclusions into practice.

What never seems to be appreciated is that nothing that could be called a moral life would be possible without these same inclinations for the moral will to overcome. Thus there exists a fundamental contradiction in Kant's system. "It has to be allowed that morality is committed both to the destruction of the natural passions and to their preservation: to the former because, in any conflict between reason and the inclinations, it is axiomatic that reason ought to triumph, to the latter because moral reason needs the natural passions both as its antithesis and its instrument." (Walsh 1969, p.30)

Again, therefore, there is the same tension, the same conflict between reason and the emotions, and man's problem is seen as that of achieving control over his natural inclinations, so that he can repress them and attain the self-discipline necessary if he is to be able to live a rational moral life.

Thus rationalism, as we suggested in Chapter 2, offers a moral system more suited to Daleks than to human beings. Certainly it is a system that recommends that in order to achieve morality we should try to become like Daleks and reject those emotions that in a very real sense contribute towards making us human. It is for this reason that rationalism in general has been regarded by many as unsatisfactory and unacceptable. Kant's view of morality in particular has been criticized on these grounds. "The Kantian doctrine which makes practical reason in effect the godlike element in man and writes down the passions as belonging to his animal nature amounts to a form of dualism as objectionable as any to be found in Descartes. The unity of the human being is entirely lost in this account" (Walsh 1969, p.32). Indeed, one might go even further and argue that this dualism is the direct descendant and result of that dualism that Descartes imposed on modern philosophy, the dualism of mind and body, subject and object, consciousness and experienced reality. Again, "The voice of reason in Kant was as remote from the living being as was Jehovah from the ancient Jews" (Walsh 1969, p.38). This was a point made by Hegel, Kant's immediate successor, who recognized this problem and the need to bridge the gap with what he called "a morality of love". His attempts to achieve this, however, perhaps reveal the inevitable limitations of rationalism in this respect. For it was this feature not only of rationalism in general but of Hegelianism in particular that invited the reaction that has followed.

That reaction has taken two main forms, but fundamentally both have accepted the significance of man's emotional responses to the world only by rejecting the possibility of achieving a rational basis to morality. Thus, although rejecting the rationalist solution, they have nevertheless seemed to accept the dichotomy we have described as part of it and have seen reason and the emotions as in conflict.

The empiricist reaction against rationalism is based on the view that knowledge of any aspect of the world and of human experience cannot be attained by the use of reason or the intellect alone but must begin from some kind of empirical observation of how things are. The approach to morals associated with this view does seem initially to have been prompted by an awareness of the need for moral behaviour to involve some kind of caring attitude on the part of the moral agent (early theories, for example, stressed notions such as that of benevolence) and this is one reason why they looked at the role of the emotions in moral behaviour.

However, such an empiricist epistemology led to the conviction that we can only find answers to moral questions by observing how people do in fact behave, what they believe and what they do in moral situations, and that, as a result, no moral position can in any way be "proved". Thus, as we saw in Chapter 2, they produced in various forms an emotivist theory of morals, which, as its name suggests, recognizes the importance of the emotions in moral behaviour but does this by claiming that moral beliefs and behaviour are explicable only in terms of the emotions people have or the way they feel. They suggest, therefore, that moral behaviour is to be assessed in terms of social utility, of what people feel to be right, of maximizing pleasure and minimizing pain, or that all statements of approval or disapproval are to be regarded as mere expressions of the feelings of the individual who utters them, subject in no way to the application of reason. The role of reason here, therefore, is a subordinate one to that of the passions; as Hume said, "reason is, and ought to be, the slave of the passions." Thus the roles are reversed but the dichotomy and much of the tension and conflict remain.

Existentialist philosophy too began as a revolt against rationalism or, at least, the extreme rationalism of Hegel and the German idealist philosophers generally. A central concern here has been with the loss of individualism that must follow from this kind of rationalist view with its emphasis on the general, on universals, that preoccupation with rational beings rather than human beings that we referred to above. Existentialist theories have also been concerned to offer views of existence that will be more than academic, intellectual exercises and will lead to changes in the way the individual organizes his own life. Thus Jean-Paul Sartre tells us, "Existentialism must be lived to be really sincere. To live as an existentialist means to be ready to pay for this view and not merely to lay it down in books."

Again, however, this approach has led to a rejection of reason so that these philosophies are sometimes described as irrationalist. Their claim is that the individual must make his own choices, assert his own unique existence without reference to any universal rules or standards, since adherence to such rules or standards must involve a loss of individuality. They have also come to realize, however, that this creates an insoluble problem for the individual since he cannot refer to any kind of helpful criteria or norms in making these choices so that he experiences what Sartre has called "nausea". It is for this reason that Sartre himself has attempted to develop a more positive theory of the emotions, one that would effect some kind of reconciliation between reason and feeling (1962).

Thus the Western philosophical tradition, having created a dichotomy between man's intellect and his emotions, has for the most part failed to offer any kind of a solution to the problem it has thus presented to us, except to suggest that we reject one or the other. The emotions have either been regarded as unfortunate aspects of humanity which stand in the way of the proper exercise of reason and should be repressed, or they have been seen as the clue to all interpersonal relationships in such a way that those relationships have been regarded as beyond the influence of reasoning of any kind. The same stance has been adopted by those who, as we mentioned earlier, have explored such issues through literature throughout the ages, and its practical expression can be seen still in the celibacy of the Roman Catholic priesthood.

Implications for education

Throughout this time it has been the rationalist tradition that has been predominant in educational theory and practice, perhaps because of the strong influence of the Christian church on the development of education in the Western world. Its effects have been considerable and widespread. In general, it has led to an emphasis on the intellectual development of children at the expense of other aspects of their development, a process whose dangers and potentially disastrous consequences are well portrayed in Herman Hesse's account of the effects of this kind of education on one particular pupil in *The Prodigy*. It has several particular facets that we must note here.

The first of these has a relevance that goes beyond education itself. It is the effects of this view on art itself. For it has led to an intellectualizing of art and to its being given a reduced role in human life and development. Again it was Plato who set things off on this track. For in Plato's society the function of art of all kinds was to assist in the process of holding the society together by promoting those values that were the fabric of the society. It was not to bring to the attention of any citizen the existence of anything evil nor to provide him with examples of bad behaviour. Its role in education and in society as a whole was to promote those qualities of character that were necessary for the stability of society and expressly not to challenge nor do anything that might undermine the norms of society. To this end it was to be subject to the strictest censorship. It is significant and supportive to the view we are arguing here that within the present century this conception of the role of the arts in society has been described as giving to art an important and responsible, even a noble, social role (Nettleship 1935).

As a result of this kind of attitude, a good deal of art over the ages has been the handmaiden of the church or of society, illustrating and decorating, being used to further particular ends but not able to make any significant comment in its own right.

This is one significant feature of that critique of Western art that is offered by the German philosopher, Friedrich Nietzsche, and in particular the distinction he draws between what he calls the Apollonian and the Dionysian cultures. The former is based on a form of art that sees it as its task to gloss over the harsh realities of human existence, to beautify them and thus render them acceptable. The Dionysian culture, on the other hand, is based on a form of art that endeavours to face existence as it really is and to reveal reality to man in its stark and true form. Both of these forms can be seen in Western European culture from the earliest times, says Nietzsche, but it is the former that has been emphasized because the latter involves too open an acceptance of the passionate side of man's nature.

One effect, then, of this divorce of reason and feeling that we are discussing has been this kind of reduction of scope for art in all its forms both in education and in society. And many developments in art in the present century can be seen as the beginning of a movement away from that kind of attempt to intellectualize it or to give it this limited social role towards an acceptance of it on its own terms and as able to offer valuable perspectives on human nature and the human condition.

A second effect of this divorce of feeling and intellect has been the devaluing within education of any activity that has not appeared to have a fully intellectual content and, conversely, an emphasis on those areas of the curriculum that stress the development of the intellect to the almost total exclusion of all else. Thus, again, to an extent that would certainly bring the colour back to Plato's cheeks, the degree to which a subject has found a ready acceptance on the school curriculum has had a very direct relationship to its cognitive content and an inverse relationship to its emotional appeal. Mathematics and science are currently the most well-entrenched subjects on the curriculum, and classics, even without such utilitarian advantages, dominated the curriculum of the public and grammar schools for many years, while art and "handicraft" are still often taught in a shed at the other side of the playground and usually only to those pupils who appear to lack the intellectual capacity for anything apparently more demanding.

However, there are signs that the value of aesthetic and creative activities in education is being increasingly recognized. There is a growing conviction that an education that is concerned with only one dimension of human experience is no education at all. There is still too little appreciation, however, of the implications of this for the intellectual activities, the traditional school subjects, themselves. We are more aware now of the educational value of those activities that have a strong aesthetic or emotional bias, but we have yet to appreciate the existence of this kind of dimension to all educational activities.

For a further result of this emphasis on the intellect in education has been the loss of something of great importance to the intellectual activities themselves, namely a proper concern with the place that feeling must have here too. A lot has been heard in recent educational discussion about the cognitive and the affective dimensions of education. Benjamin Bloom, for example, in his taxonomy of educational objectives, discusses objectives in three separate domains, the main two of which are the cognitive and the affective (1956). One of the most serious criticisms of this approach, however, derives from the impossibility of distinguishing these two elements in practice. It is not possible to set up any educational programme that does not take full account of both of these dimensions. For this reason it is important not only to recognize the value of those areas of the curriculum whose main value lies in their contribution to the education of feeling itself; we must also take full account of and give full weighting to the affective aspects of those subjects which too often have been regarded as purely intellectual. Feeling is an integral part of education.

There are at least two aspects of this. Firstly, it would be difficult to argue that there is any area of human knowledge and experience that does not have its aesthetic dimension. This is true even of a subject like mathematics, which for Plato was the body of knowledge that came closest to being a completely abstract and thus purely intellectual activity. Mathematicians will often speak of the beauty of mathematics and, indeed, they are right to do so. However, because of the emphasis on the intellect that we are discussing, this aesthetic dimension has often been ignored. The same is true even of a subject like music in which the aesthetic dimension is easier to recognize and where, in fact, it might be said to comprise its main, or only, *raison d'être*. For, although this is an art form that in one mode or another is appreciated aesthetically and emotionally by more people than any other, the teaching of it in our schools has often stressed its intellectual content almost to the exclusion of everything else. As a result, there are many people whose instrumental skill is of a very high order and whose understanding of the "mathematics" of notation is supreme but who evince little feeling for the music they are producing. (The converse of this is equally true, of course, since there have been many musicians whose work reveals great "soul", but who lack any kind of intellectual understanding of music.) The same has been too often true of the teaching of literature — classical, foreign and even, unforgiveably, English. Education in any subject area must include an attempt to reveal its beauty and to encourage a recognition and an appreciation of it.

This brings us to the second aspect of the role of feeling in those subjects that have often been regarded as purely cognitive. We referred in Chapter 1 to some of the characteristics that distinguish education from other activities that involve teaching. One of those characteristics is that the educated person must have come to value and appreciate that in which he has been educated. In any truly educational context, therefore, it will be impossible to distinguish the learning of a subject in the intellectual or cognitive sense from being brought to enjoy it, appreciate it, recognize its worth and so on. This remains true even of a subject like mathematics, which for Plato was the subject that came closest to being a completely abstract and thus purely intellectual activity. Furthermore, mathematicians often speak of the beauty of mathematics and, indeed, they are right to do so. Again, however, this implies that any attempt to offer an education in mathematics must be at the same time an attempt to reveal this beauty and encourage a recognition and appreciation of it. Thus there is an affective component even to this most intellectual of activities, which cannot be ignored if we are serious in our efforts to educate people in this area.

The same is true in all areas of knowledge. For it is not possible to conceive of an intelligible concept of education that ignores this dimension. It is not possible even in theory to conceive of claiming that one has educated someone without bringing about in him an attitude of appreciation of what has been the substance of that education. It would be a logical absurdity to say of someone that he is an educated man but that he loves nothing, is interested in nothing, is enthused by nothing. To be educated is to have been brought to care about certain things, whatever those things are. Even in the most abstract of subjects, therefore, we must be constantly aware of this affective dimension, of the "feeling" that is involved in the study of it and of the need to attend to this in all aspects of our teaching. We must promote the enjoyment of education in all its elements. For this is required of us by the notion of education itself.

To ignore this in attempting to educate children is to take a purely rationalist approach, to deny that our pupils have feelings, to deny them their individuality, and to attempt what is fortunately an impossible task, that of turning them into computers, automata, Daleks. This, then, is a further effect of the divorce of feeling and reason in education that we are discussing.

We must finally turn to what is, at least in the context of this book, the most crucial of the implications of this divorce of intellect and feeling for education — its effect on our approach to moral education (or the moral aspects of all education, since, as we saw in Chapter 1, all education is essentially moral education). Whatever view one takes of the role of feeling in activities such as mathematics and science, there can be no denying that it is central to morality. A moral education, therefore, which directs its attention solely towards the cognitive or intellectual aspects of moral behaviour must be a caricature, distorting by the exaggeration of one, not necessarily salient, element.

Worse however is the attempt to recognize the importance of the emotions by recommending devices for their suppression. Yet there is no doubt that until recently this has been the only view of the role of feeling in moral education that has been offered in theory or revealed in practice. The influence of Plato has been total and we have sought for the most effective ways of "taming" the passions, of bringing them under control. Suppression has been the only device that has been discovered and certainly it has been the main result of this kind of practice. Thus the problems of advancing puberty have been tackled in most boys' schools by the simple application of "rugby and cold showers" and the general attitude that has been engendered by this kind of approach is that the feelings one is experiencing at this stage are nasty and people who have been properly brought up don't show them any longer. Any intelligent pupil can, of course, be expected to wonder where he came from if this is really true.

The essence of this process is the denial of one major aspect of man's humanity. It is also an approach that makes it impossible for us to find a proper set of criteria by which we can distinguish between feelings themselves and thus promote and encourage those that most people would agree should be developed. It also makes it impossible to work out a theory of how any of the emotions can be developed. Thus we have often put ourselves into the inconsistent position in which at the same time we have urged pupils to show love and compassion towards their fellow man, but have not been able to help them to distinguish the different contexts in which such feelings might be aroused and the different ways in which they might be displayed.

The most serious aspect of this kind of approach, however, has been revealed to us by those who have explored the dangers and the far-reaching after-effects and side-effects of repression. In broad terms repression is the result of the introjection of the taboos of others, mostly those adults who have access to us, particularly, because of the importance of the early years, our parents, often reinforced by the unpleasant experiences of punishment. It may also result, of course, from unpleasant and frightening experiences that are not deliberately engineered by personal agencies. Thus a child who steals and eats all of his mother's recently baked cakes may have his desire for delicacies as effectively inhibited by the unpleasant experience of vomiting as from any punishment his mother may subsequently mete out to him. As we saw in Chapter 3, this is, of course, part of the development of conscience, of what Freud called the superego or ego-ideal, and of the growth of a self-image. It is no longer realistic to regard conscience as the still, small voice of God, a kind of universal Tannoy system with which we are kitted out prenatally. This is supported not least by the evident fact that, unlike most public address systems, conscience does not offer everyone the same message and advice. We must view it rather, then, as the internalization of the admonishments we receive and the experiences we have, especially in early childhood.

In particular, it is important to realize, again as we pointed out in Chapter 3, that this development is the result of the child's perception of the attitudes of others, especially his parents, towards him and the image of himself he develops as a consequence of this (Williams 1967). In some cases, therefore, it may be based on a misconception of those attitudes, if the adult is not especially careful about the words in which and the behaviour by which those attitudes are communicated.

The other aspect of this that it is important to be clear about is that to a large extent this is an unconscious process. What is internalized affects our attitudes and our behaviour in ways we are not fully conscious of; and the emotions and feelings that are repressed in this process continue to affect our attitudes and behaviour in unconscious and unrecognized ways. This is why in later life we often find ourselves behaving unthinkingly in ways that reveal attitudes the basis of which we are unaware of and quite incapable of explaining to others or even to ourselves. A refusal to imbibe any kind of alcoholic drink under any circumstances, even where the medicinal value is obvious, for example, can often not be explained by the individual concerned and is only explicable through some exploration of early childhood experiences, such as being beaten for getting at the cooking sherry or, worse and unfortunately more likely, witnessing the ill-treatment of one parent by the other when "in drink".

We must be aware, of course, of appearing to assert that this process is totally to be deplored. Some kind of conscience, some kind of ego-ideal, some kind of self-image must be developed by everyone. How else could one make any kind of choice or decision? In some cases, therefore, this process will lead to a proper control of one's emotions and thus of one's behaviour. The dangers of a wrong approach here, however, must be stressed, as must the fact that such a wrong approach is most likely to result from adopting the view that the process is merely one of repression, of subjugation, of "taming the emotions".

At one end of the scale it can be seen to result in an odd, unreasonable, distorted sense of the relative importance of different values and different kinds of behaviour. The example we just offered of the totally unreasoned and unreasonable rejection of alcohol in all its forms is one example of this kind of distortion. For on occasion it will lead to a willingness to die or to see a child or other relative die rather than to break that taboo. Another example is the celebrated case of those young children who, when asked to list in order of seriousness the worst crimes one could commit, placed killing people first and running in the corridors second (Kellmer-Pringle and Edwards 1964). These are prime examples of the effects of the development of an overstrong superego or conscience.

Another aspect of this is that this kind of strong early childhood experience can lead to an overdeveloped conscience even in areas where some reasonable dictates of conscience are to be expected. The strength of the prohibitions placed on some people by their conscience can be such as to make it impossible for them to take a balanced rational view of a particular situation, so that they are led into actions that not only may be disadvantageous to their own lives but may also be detrimental to those whose interests their conscience may bid them to place before their own. Thus a person may attempt to save his marriage in the interests of his children because of the strength of the dictates of his own parents, internalized and thus mediated through his own conscience, and in doing so ill-serve the interests of those very children whose welfare he has most at heart.

At the other extreme, this kind of early experience, as we know only too well, not least from the many films that have been made on this theme, can lead to psychopathic conditions in later life. It would seem that if the early experiences we have been dicussing are too unpleasant or unbearable, then they become in a sense counter-productive; they result not in the development of a strong con-science, ego-ideal or self-image, but in the development of none of these at all. The same also seems to be the result of being deprived of the love of a mother or mother-substitute in the very early years (Bowlby 1973), or, as we saw in Chapter 3, of lacking the kind of close attachment to parents that inhibits the expression of feelings of aggression or hostility. For, without involving ourselves in the technical aspects of psychopathology, we can recognize that what characterizes psychopathic behaviour above all else is the lack of any conscience. The behaviour of the psychopath is not so much immoral and antisocial as amoral and asocial; he reveals a complete indifference to the effects of his behaviour on other people or on society. He is often described as the "affectionless character". "He appears to be without any sense of guilt. Every action is assessed in terms of personal advantage, and the world is seen as a place where jungle law operates. As one might expect from this description, the psychopath may be frequently observed in prisons, for he is often a habitual offender, who seems to be untouched by punishment. In short, he appears to be the very antithesis of the morally developed person" (Williams 1967, p.272).

This deficiency of moral development that is revealed by the behaviour of the psychopath illustrates dramatically the importance of achieving a view of moral development which takes a proper account of the role of the emotions within it. What we have said in general about this process by which conscience is developed also highlights the need for such a view. For the central feature of this process, as we have seen, is that it is unconscious. As such, it leads to a loss of control over behaviour. In the last analysis, this is the major criticism that we must offer of any attempt to approach the moral development of children that stresses the repression of feelings or of certain kinds of feeling. For such an unconscious process cannot be regarded as in any sense educational, since by definition it is not open to conscious appraisal. This is the central message of Freudian psychology, which attempts to offer us advice on how to make these processes conscious, precisely in order that we may begin to exercise control over them.

This is also a further and very important criticism of those traditional attempts to attend to moral upbringing by means of religious training. For the emphasis there has often been on the repression of feelings, usually reinforced by fear of eternal punishment, and thus, as we suggested in Chapter 1, represents a quite deliberate attempt to develop a form of morality that is completely authoritarian and does not invite the conscious thought of the individual.

This is why this kind of approach is unacceptable as a form of moral education. To be brought up to act on the dictates of others, especially when these are internalized in this unconscious form, is not to be morally educated at all. As we saw in Chapter 2, it is a kind of moral conditioning or indoctrination, since it denies the individual his right as a human being to think for himself. It is not only, therefore, an unsophisticated version of moral education. It is no version at all. We cannot begin to plan moral education as we have defined it on the basis of establishing unconscious motivation for behaviour. It is for this reason that we need to begin the search for a more positive theory of the role of the emotions in moral behaviour and thus in moral education, not only in the interests of moral education itself but also in the interests of mental health.

The emotions in moral education   ·

We have suggested in what has gone before that morality has been seen too much as a matter for rational beings and that we need to consider it in the context of the behaviour of human beings. We argued in Chapter 2 that behaving morally is not the completely rational process that people such as Plato and Kant seemed to think; we have been arguing further in this current chapter that it is not even enough to note and recognize the tension that exists between feeling and reason, whether this leads us to try to suppress the former or to abandon the latter. What is needed is a positive examination of the role the emotions play in moral behaviour, of the links between feeling and reason. "A satisfactory moral philosophy must give an altogether different account from that found in Kant of the relationship of moral reason and the inclinations" (Walsh 1969, p.32). Furthermore, in the context of this book, we need to explore some of the ways in which moral education might be approached in order to take full account of the need for such a philosophy. We must develop a more constructive theory of the affective aspects of moral education. It is to this issue that we must now turn.

The first step towards such a theory must be to recognize that the distinction between reason and feeling is itself a false distinction and encourages a wrong view of the relation of the emotions to the intellect. For it suggests that they are usually in conflict, each one tugging us in a different direction, that we must choose whether to act according to the one or the other, that in practice what each will lead to can be separated out, and that, while the one offers us a rational solution, the other is always and by definition irrational. Each of these features of this view of the emotions we must look at in turn.

A moment's reflection will reveal that our inclinations do not always push us towards behaviour that is at odds with rationality. Sometimes our inclinations and reason are in agreement. Kant himself recognized the truth of this and it seemed to worry him that in such situations one would enjoy doing one's duty, a fact that seemed to him somehow to make it less than fully moral. For example, it is our duty at certain times of the week to meet groups of students who have gathered together for educational purposes and to use such skills as we possess to the best of our ability to forward those purposes. Only occasionally do our inclinations favour spending such times differently. Quite often, therefore, reason and feeling are in harmony. There is no inevitable conflict.

Secondly, seldom if ever in practice are we faced by two quite discrete courses of possible action, one dictated by reason, the other offered enticingly by the passions. Moral behaviour is not as simple as that, nor are moral choices. Even if the rational course of action is clear enough, what the passions offer is always a confused and confusing jumble of conscience, desire, pleasure, concern for the feelings of others and many other emotions clamouring for our attention. Just as it is impossible in any practical educational context to separate cognitive from affective goals, so it is impossible to distinguish these two aspects of any practical moral issue.

Lastly, and perhaps most importantly, it is not the case that the passions are irrational and can thus be held in this kind of contrast with reason. The etymology of the word "passion" may suggest that we are concerned here with things we suffer (Peters 1973b) and that they are not as a result susceptible to reason, but other words such as "emotion" do not have this kind of connotation and it is clear on reflection that there are such things as rational passions and that "although manifestly these terms relate in some way to our feelings, they are also intimately connected with cognition, that is, with our ways of understanding situations" (Peters 1973b, p.81).

Some emotions, for example, are the result of the way in which we view certain situations; they result from what reason tells us about the world. A feeling of fear is often prompted by a rational appraisal of a situation in which one is faced, say, by a man-eating tiger. The small child who lacks such reasoning powers and the knowledge and experience on which they must be based might not feel fear in such circumstances. Conversely, our emotions sometimes affect the way in which we perceive situations. This is the essence of the phenomenological viewpoint which asserts that every man's perceptions are unique and individual since they are intimately intertwined with his emotions and his personality. It is not necessary to go that far, however, in order to recognize the influence of emotion on perception. We all see different things in a painting, a photograph, a poster since we all respond emotionally in different ways to the content. It is also a well-known feature of the condition known clinically as paranoia that the paranoid perceives a good deal of his world as threatening and hostile, sees persecution in relatively trivial and innocent acts of others, experiences unreasonable sexual jealousy and in general has a view of the world which has been considerably influenced by his emotions.

Furthermore, not only may reason influence the kinds of feeling we have; it often also affects the way in which we give expression to those feelings. It may reveal, for example, that we have two or more feelings that are incompatible with one another and suggest ways in which such conflict can be resolved in our actions. It may also indicate that a particular feeling, say, to punch one's boss on the nose, may best be dealt with by some method other than the actual behaviour it is urging, by violently abusing him from a safe and private place, by hammering a ball around a squash court, or even by thinking through his problems and trying to see things from his point of view. Again, however, the converse is also true. For it is not just a matter of reason guiding the emotions. It will itself in turn be influenced by them and take full account of their presence and their strength. Thus, if we are lucky, it may on occasion recommend that the only solution to our problem is to punch the boss on the nose. The desire and the need may have gone beyond the point where sublimation is possible.

The relation of feeling and reason in human experience, then, is one of reciprocity rather than conflict. The conflict model is unsatisfactory. The fact/value distinction is difficult, if not impossible to maintain at any level. The interaction is of a much more subtle kind.

It is the presence of this element of cognition in the emotions that has encouraged some people to accept that the emotions can be educated rather than merely tamed. From what we have said so far it would appear that, at least in respect of their cognitive element, this ought to be the case. We must also, however, explore the question of whether the education of the emotions has to be limited to their cognitive aspects. Certainly, it would seem that an exploration of the role of the emotions in moral education might be forwarded by a consideration of the kind of education the emotions in general might be susceptible to.

The first thing we must note is the role of education in relation to that element of cognition in the emotions that we have already drawn attention to. If we are to understand and deal adequately with our emotions a lot of knowledge is required, some of it of a largely "factual" kind. The feeling of fear, for example, can only be dealt with by learning more about the object of our fear. When we do this we either find we have dispelled the fear or we have a clearer idea of precisely what there is to be reasonably afraid of and thus of whatever necessary action should be taken to protect ourselves. It is not true that fear is always the result of ignorance, but often it is. We need, therefore, to know both what we should be afraid of and what we need not be afraid of. Feelings of jealousy and envy, and even desires and wishes, can be dispelled or brought into clearer focus in the same way. In short, we need to be able to make a realistic appraisal of situations and to understand them in order to be able to act appropriately. To do this involves learning of a clearly cognitive kind. It is information about the world we need in order to make such appraisals. It is plain, then, that in this respect at least the emotions are susceptible to the influence of education (Peters 1973b).

This is why we must avoid the divorce of reason and feeling that we referred to earlier in all aspects of education. The only way in which we can attend to the education of the emotions even in relation to their cognitive element is by taking full account, in all of our teaching, of their impact. As we said above, it is impossible to separate the cognitive and the affective dimensions of any educational experience.

Furthermore, if we do not take full account of the emotional aspects of all our teaching, it may be detrimental even to the purely cognitive learning we are seeking to ensure. Children have feelings, whether we acknowledge them or not, and they do react emotively to what is offered them. Children's emotions and fantasies can also obstruct their learning, but this happens only when those emotions and fantasies are uncontrolled (Jones 1968). If we do not help pupils to control these emotions, then, the learning we are seeking to promote may well be impaired. On the other hand, it can only be enhanced if we recognize the existence of these emotions and endeavour to harness them to our educational purposes. Again it is not a matter of creating conditions of control in order to repress or of offering cathartic opportunities for letting off steam and thus getting their emotions out of the way. Emotion and fantasy are substantive elements in most kinds of learning.

This is one of the most interesting points to emerge from the experiences of those who have been concerned with that major curriculum project, Man—A Course of Study (MACOS). For the early experiments with this project revealed not only the need to recognize the emotions that were aroused in children by the project materials but also some of the ways in which they could be used to further their education on both the cognitive and the affective fronts. Thus Richard M. Jones, in describing and analysing the early experience of the project, tells us, "The first claim on our attention should be that many teachers...will jump at a chance to make these films part of their routine stock of teaching tools and will get out of them only a portion of the teaching power that is in them" (1972, p.26). He goes on to say, "The crux of this issue is not obscure. Only in the vicinities of schoolrooms do we make it so. Normally, the human mind and the human heart go together. If not normally, may we say optimally? We are witnessing a revolution in pedagogy which is committed to honest dealings with the minds of children. It follows, therefore, that we may also enjoy more honest dealings with the hearts of children. Not that this *necessarily* follows, nor that it should always be made to follow. Admittedly, there are times for *dis*passion in schoolrooms, but teachers need no reminding of this. They do, however, need reminding that there are also times for passion in schoolrooms" (*ibid*).

Nowhere is this more important than in moral education. For here the education of feeling and reason in harness is crucial since it is intimately concerned with the life, the values and the behaviour of the individual. In fact, this serves merely to highlight a point we have made several times, namely that there is a moral dimension to all education and that moral education is the concern of every teacher. Certainly, it is by this kind of approach to most of what we offer pupils in schools that we stand our best chance of providing them with the kind of education of their emotions we are claiming is crucial to a proper moral education.

This attempt to take full account of the emotions in education has several further aspects that we must briefly pick out as being of special relevance to moral education. In the first place, we have said a good deal in this chapter about the control of the emotions. We must not let it appear that we are saying here that this is to be avoided. We have tried to argue that it is dangerous to regard this as the only way of approaching emotional development, so that we are accepting by implication that it is one aspect of the problem. Certainly, children need to learn to control their emotions. They need discipline. They need to be able to avoid that problem of ἀκρασία (akrasia) that Aristotle drew our attention to. They need, therefore, to develop what John Wilson has called KRAT (1967), the ability to translate moral principles into action. It may well be true also that the best way in which we can help children, especially younger children, to develop this ability is, as Aristotle advised, to help them to develop certain habits of "good" behaviour when they are young. It is for this reason, as we saw in Chapter 2, that some people have claimed that the moral education of young children must always be indoctrination.

However, there are different kinds of control and discipline and the only kind of discipline that can be accepted as part of the educational process is self-discipline and, whatever devices we use, the goal must be to produce a person who is in control of his own emotions and can thus prevent them from getting in the way of his executing his own moral decisions. Thus, while control is important, we must work to ensure that it is truly self-control and that it is not the kind of unconscious repression of the emotions we discussed earlier. It is, then, a matter of giving pupils, or helping them to attain, control of their feelings rather than controlling them for them or establishing unconscious control mechanisms within them. This, as we saw earlier, is the process that Freud was concerned to assist us with, the bringing to the level of consciousness of those unconscious urges that result from repression. Education, then, must help us to understand our emotions in order to give us this kind of conscious control of them.

However, control of the emotions is only half of the story. It is also necessary to help children to understand their feelings in order to accept them. This is a major feature of the value of those areas of the curriculum such as dance and drama which allow and encourage pupils to express their feelings in socially acceptable ways and thus enable them to come to terms with them. Again, we must beware of seeing their function as merely cathartic, a letting off of steam. To take that view is to do scant justice to the valuable work that many sensitive teachers are doing in these fields. It is far more a matter of enabling pupils — especially those who lack the facility to use other more formal media such as the written or even the spoken word — to face their emotions, recognize them for what they are and thus come to terms with them, developing understanding and acceptance as well as control.

This kind of experience will provide them with an understanding of the feelings of others too. This is another important aspect of the work that is done in these areas of the curriculum. The role-play that is part of some work in drama and dance clearly has as one of its central concerns the development of the ability to see things from someone else's point of view, to put oneself "in their shoes". This kind of insight into the feelings of others is a central feature of the teaching of literature too. What we must not fail to recognize is that again its main point and purpose is moral and that this is another element in a proper and comprehensive moral education. For this reason, it is another of the components of moral education that John Wilson has identified. "EMP refers to awareness or insight into one's own and other people's feelings, i.e. the ability to know what those feelings are and describe them correctly. A distinction might be drawn between self-awareness (AUTEMP) and awareness of others (ALLEMP)" (1967, pp.192-193).

Again, however, we must beware of assigning this task to teachers in certain subject areas and assuming it is not a legitimate concern of those of us who are involved in teaching other subjects. The experience of those associated with MACOS is relevant here too. For it is precisely this kind of understanding of one's feelings and those of others — especially through considering the feelings, attitudes, values and so on of human beings living in a totally different environment — that they have suggested can and should be developed by adopting a new approach to teaching, certainly in the areas of the social studies and the humanities and possibly every-where. By studying the life-style of the Netsilik Eskimoes, for example, not merely at a descriptive level but by means of filmed material specially designed to highlight the starkness of some aspects of their existence, the harsh decisions they have to take—like infanticide and the abandonment of older folk—the moral prob-lems they face, the solutions they come up with and so on, it is hoped that children will "deepen their comprehension of their species, of what makes all humans human" (Jones 1972, p.22). They should also in this way gain a deeper understanding of their own feelings of a kind that will give them more than a mere control of them.

What is important here, of course, is not only the content of our teaching but its approach, its manner and its method; and there is no doubt, as the MACOS team also discovered, that the crucial element, as always, is the quality of the teacher.

There is a final point we must note that some people would want to make about the education of the emotions that is especially relevant to moral education. Some would want to claim that there are some emotions that we need not to control, nor even merely to understand but rather to welcome, embrace and promote. Some feelings are not generally regarded as bad, are not seen as inclinations or impulses to be controlled or repressed but are felt to be the motivating force for behaviour that would be acclaimed as good and positively encou-raged. We mentioned earlier Kant's doubts about the moral value of an action that is done for the sake of duty but at the same time in accordance with one's inclinations. Many people have been as worried about the converse of this, those actions that are performed because they accord with duty but are done in a mechanical, loveless and almost grudging manner. It would seem that to be fully moral an action should not only conform to certain standards of rationality, it should also be performed with certain kinds of motivation. It is not for nothing that the basic tenet of Christianity bids us to love our neighbour. Kant's completely rationalist approach makes no allowance for this and perhaps to that extent may be felt to be more realistic. Certainly one will find it easier when dealing with a filthy tramp to recognize and even to fulfil any duty one may have to feed or clothe him than one will to embrace and love him in any sense of those terms. Yet there would seem to be something beyond this cold performance of duty in most people's concept of moral behaviour and the Christian doctrine of universal love lays emphasis on this. As we saw in Chapter 1, Kant stressed the centrality of the will to truly moral behaviour and Aristotle too suggested that it is not enough for an action to be performed "not unwillingly", but that to be moral it must be done, in the full sense, "willingly". However, it is perhaps also not enough to regard this as a purely intellectual or cognitive matter. Questions of motivation, again as etymology would suggest, cannot ignore the emotional state of the individual whose action is under discussion. There are two ways in which one can "go through the motions" of behaving morally. One can do what seems to be expected without oneself understanding or accepting the reasons for such behaviour or intending it in the full sense. But one can also do it for the right reasons but with the wrong emotions, or worse, with no emotions at all.

Thus there are those who would claim that moral education should also concern itself with the promotion of certain kinds of feeling in pupils. John Wilson, for example, offers us a further component of moral education. "PHIL refers to the degree to which one can identify with other people, in the sense of being such that other people's feelings and interests actually count or weigh with one, or are accepted as of equal validity to one's own" (1967, p.192).

However, he speaks of these components, both EMP and PHIL, in a manner that suggests that he sees them largely as kinds of cognition, recognizing the feelings of others and understanding them rather than feeling for them and with them. Thus he also says of PHIL, "Like the other components, this is a matter of whether, in principle, one accepts others as equals; not a matter of how far one loves them, feels for them, etc." (1967, p.192). Many would want to go beyond this and argue that the moral educator must be concerned to develop in his pupils the ability not only to recognize the importance of other people's feelings or to understand them, important as these abilities are, but to sympathize with them, to feel for them, to have empathy with them, even to love them. This represents a more positive development of, or education of, certain of the feelings and the emotions of our pupils, an attempt to enable them to become people who not only know and recognize what is right at the intellectual level, who not only can make reasoned moral choices in an autonomous manner, but can also recognize the importance of so doing not merely because it fits some rational scheme that may appeal to their minds but because it also involves a response to their fellow man that comes from their hearts. It is not merely a matter of controlling those feelings that are at odds with our reasoned moral decisions, however we set about that; it is also a matter of promoting those that will support and enhance them.

Thus there are a number of levels at which the emotional life of our pupils may be seen as of legitimate concern to the moral educator. Children will need help with the task of developing control of their feelings. Furthermore, such control is better based on understanding and self-discipline than on authoritarianism and suppression. It may also be argued that they need an understanding of the feelings of other people. Lastly, however, it might be claimed that such understanding is of limited value in its contribution to the moral life if it is not accompanied by appropriate feelings in the individual himself.

Finally, we must note that this kind of feeling for others can best be developed by certain kinds of curriculum subject or educational experience. Here again dance and drama have a major part to play. Here too the kind of outdoor pursuits and "outward bound" activities that many teachers of physical education and others now engage their pupils in has a lot to offer. For there is probably no better way of developing this kind of feeling for others than by learning to live with them, to work with them and even to face and share hazards with them. This again must be one of the goals of those community service projects that have come to be a feature of the work of some schools with older adolescent pupils. Again, however, we must stress that, while certain areas of the curriculum may have more to contribute to this process than others, opportunities for pupils to work together exist in every subject. Conversely, every teacher can allow the opposite kinds of feeling to develop by encouraging too much competition between children and perhaps also a resultant intolerance of the slow worker. Thus again we note that moral education runs right across the curriculum and no teacher can evade his share of responsibility for it.

Summary and conclusions

We have tried in this chapter to outline briefly the divorce of reason and feeling that has characterized most of our thinking in the Western world since the time of the ancient Greeks. We have also tried to identify some of the implications of this for education in general and for moral education in particular. We then went on to suggest some of the directions in which we might begin to search for a more positive theory of the role of the emotions in moral education. In doing so, we acknowledged the need to assist children to develop control over their emotions but stressed the advantages of the kind of control that comes from an understanding of them; we suggested too that an understanding of the feelings of other people is important; and, finally, we considered the suggestion that certain kinds of emotion, such as respect, and even love, for others might need to be positively promoted and encouraged. In considering these issues, we discovered again that it is difficult to divorce moral education from education itself and impossible, as a result, not to acknowledge that every teacher must accept his share of the responsibility for moral education.

However, it is not only teachers who contribute to the moral development of chidlren. The teacher's responsibility derives not only from the content of his teaching but also from the fact that every act of teaching involves interaction between him and his pupils and every act of human interaction is an act of moral interaction. For this reason all adults play a part in the moral development of the young—parents, other relatives, neighbours, passing strangers and especially those who interact with children via the media, television, radio, magazines, comics and so on.

It is this that makes for one of the peculiar difficulties of moral education. For, unlike the teaching of French or Latin or even, for the most part, science and mathematics, history, geography and so on, moral education has to be directed at pupils who come to school with a good deal of moral learning already behind them and further moral learning goes on continuously, out of school as much as, if not more than, within it. Thus teachers cannot regard themselves as offering moral education from scratch or developing it in the isolation of the school. Their contribution is only one of many contributions and often not even the most important. What is important, however, is for every teacher to ensure that what he is offering is moral education in the full sense rather than further moral learning of an uncritical kind, that he is in fact helping to transform that moral learning that goes on elsewhere into something truly educational in the sense we have defined.

It is to the problems of that task that we must turn in our next chapter.

CHAPTER 5

MORAL EDUCATION AND MORAL LEARNING

In the earlier chapters of this book we have attempted to consider some of the major dimensions of both moral behaviour and moral education, looking in particular at the part that both rationality and feeling must play in both. We have examined some of the psychological and developmental factors that we must bear in mind as we plan the moral education of the young. And we have stressed the inevitable responsibility of all teachers for the moral development of their pupils. In the final chapters we shall explore some of the ways in which teachers can and do attempt to meet this responsibility through the curriculum in general and special provision for moral education in particular.

Before we turn to that, however, we must give some attention to a feature of moral education that makes it a particularly difficult area of responsibility for the teacher, the fact that children do not wait until they come to school to begin their moral development nor is their moral learning restricted to what they are offered in school. They bring a good deal of moral learning with them and they continue to acquire moral attitudes, to adopt moral beliefs and to develop patterns of moral behaviour as much, or even more, as a result of their experiences outside the school as from any deliberate provision that may be made for them within it. Furthermore, throughout their time at school, they need to make moral decisions and thus need a code of values to base these on. The teacher of French can assume that most of his pupils will know no French when they first come to him; he can also advise them not to chance a visit to France until they have reached a reasonable level of proficiency. But the moral educator faces pupils who have already done a good deal of moral learning and he cannot advise them not to make moral decisions until they have had the benefit of all he has to offer. In this respect, moral development is again like language development. For not only is it the concern of every teacher; it is also the product of many different kinds of interaction between pupils and many "significant others" both inside and outside the school, and moral decisions have to be made while moral learning is still going on. No provision that we make for the moral education of pupils, therefore, will be or can be adequate unless it takes full account of this feature of moral development and it is to a consideration of both the major characteristics of this phenomenon and its implications for the teacher's task that we must now turn.

As we approach these questions, it is worth noting that this is a place where the distinction between education and other kinds of teaching and learning is again of crucial significance. For the problem we have identified really boils down to a question of converting moral learning into moral education, of accepting that our pupils will already have acquired many moral attitudes, beliefs and habits, and exploring how we can convert that learning into moral education of the kind we have defined.

There would seem to be three main aspects of this problem and we must look at all of them in turn. In the first place pupils acquire and go on acquiring moral attitudes, beliefs and habits from many sources other than their teachers. Secondly, we must note that the school itself is also a source of this kind of incidental moral learning and, as we have noted before, such learning is as much a result of the way in which the school is organized as of the behaviour of the teachers in it. Thirdly, as we try to convert this kind of moral learning into moral education in the full sense, we must not deplore the presence of previously learned moral attitudes in pupils; we must acknowledge and accept this. For we must recognize the need for pupils from the beginning to have a system of values to guide their behaviour, a content to their morality, and the resultant obligation on teachers to see the development of such a content as an important part of what it means to offer them a moral education.

At all stages, therefore, we must accept that pupils will have moral attitudes and beliefs, held with different degrees of both consciousness and intensity and at all stages we must recognize that it is the task of the moral educator to guide pupils in the acquisition of such values as well as to help them to become more reflective, more thoughtful and overtly conscious both of the values they hold and their reasons for holding them.

In order to gain a clearer view of the factors to be borne in mind as we set about this task, we must first of all look in a little more detail at the sources of such moral learning outside the school, then at some of its hidden sources within the school and finally at the problem of how we can use this learning to provide a content for a moral education of the form we have earlier defined.

Sources of moral learning outside the school.

One of the major factors in the recent questioning of the assumption that there is any one absolute system of values has undoubtedly been the growing awareness of the many variations in moral beliefs that are to be observed in different societies. The recent rapid development of communications of all kinds has brought with it a greater familiarity with the customs and habits of other societies and other cultures, as has the cultural mix that has occurred in many societies in recent times. We cannot now fail to be aware that in some societies polygamy is accepted, that some societies practice euthanasia, that others permit abortion, that some even accept infanticide, while others regard all or some of these practices as immoral and in some cases even render them illegal. Furthermore, it is no longer possible for anyone who claims to be rational and reasonably objective in looking at such issues too readily to assume that those societies that do things differently from his own are necessarily primitive or misguided or evil. The range of value positions that can be observed in any one advanced society make it clear that many different viewpoints can be taken, in a perfectly reasoned and sincere manner, on any of these issues.

This has important implications for the status of judgements of moral value and for moral education, some of which we have examined elsewhere. Its particular relevance for this discussion, however, derives from the fact that it highlights the central role that society plays in the development of moral attitudes and values. If a person believes in monogamy, it is as likely that that belief will be explicable in terms of his having grown up in a monogamous society as that he has come to the view through a rational and objective appraisal of its advantages and disadvantages. Different societies will be both the result of and productive of different social norms and a large share of the work of sociologists has been directed over the years towards questions of the relationships between the economic and political aspects of societies and the social norms that characterize those societies or, perhaps more importantly, between economic, political and technological change and changes in value structures. This indicates, then, that society has to be seen as a prime source of that moral learning that we are suggesting here is the foundation on which moral education has to be built or the raw material with which it has to work. Moral values are the very fabric of any society and it is from society, in the broadest connotation of the word, that children absorb most of their values, attitudes and beliefs.

In considering some of the agencies that contribute to this process, we must begin by distinguishing those deliberate attempts to manipulate people's attitudes and beliefs from those that happen in a "hidden", implicit, incidental manner. For children are subjected to quite explicit efforts from many quarters outside the school to promote in them certain attitudes and standards of behaviour as well as imbibing such values unconsciously from the infra-structure, as it were, of experiences not overtly or specifically designed to have that kind of effect. In practice, of course, the same agencies are likely to be involved in both processes, but it is important to be aware of and to distinguish the explicit and the implicit sources of moral learning.

The most obvious source of explicit attempts to affect children's values is, of course, the parents. There are those parents who think that they can leave this to the school, but most parents recognize that they have a responsibility to bring their children up "proper" and none in any case can escape the moral training that is endemic to the necessity to exercise some sort of control over their children's behaviour from the earliest age.

There are several points arising from this that are of importance for the teacher. In the first place, the practice of parents will vary enormously both in the degree and the kind of attention they give to this aspect of their role. Their approaches will reflect all shades of the spectrum from the authoritarian through the democratic to the laissez-faire. Child-rearing practices will vary from the immediate gratification of the quick slap or the silencing dummy or sweet to the long drawn-out attempt at reasoned debate and persuasion. The range here can be quickly appreciated by a half-hour's observation of the different methods of control used by parents on a trip around any supermarket on a Saturday morning.

Evidence shows that there are in fact social class differences in child-rearing practices that affect children's moral development. Studies by Sears *et al.* (1957), Kohn (1958), Kohlberg (1966), Kay (1968) and Bull (1969), to mention but a few, all suggest that children from families of higher social status show greater maturity in moral judgement than those from lower social class backgrounds.

There are several possible reasons for these differences. Firstly, it has been suggested that children from higher status families tend to be future-oriented. Parents offer them guidance in advance so that they are encouraged to consider the consequences of their actions. Conversely, parents of lower social status tend to punish after a misdemeanour, so that their children are more likely to be concerned with the immediate present. Linked with this is the practice in higher status families of defering gratification; children are thus further helped to consider long-term consequences and, it is claimed, are less likely to break promises, tell lies or steal out of pure expediency and a consideration only of present circumstances. Furthermore, as Henderson and Bernstein (1969) demonstrate, middle class parents spend more time answering children's questions, giving them reasons why they are expected to behave in certain ways and explaining why they consider some behaviour morally unacceptable. Children from such families are thus more likely to understand reasons offered them and to formulate their own at an early age than those from lower status families where "because I say so" takes the place of a reasoned explanation.

William Kay (1975) also stresses the importance of personalism in child-rearing practices. Parents who treat their children as persons worthy of consideration and respect rather than merely as occupants of an inferior status are more likely to help them to learn to respect others and show consideration for them.

Rigidity and flexibility in thinking are also reflected in children's moral conduct. Those accustomed to an authoritarian background are used to being told what to do and feel insecure outside such a framework. They seem to prefer authority to autonomy and are reluctant to make their own moral choices because of the degree of uncertainty involved. They are more concerned with particular instances than children who have learnt to be flexible in their moral thinking and to look for a general principle underlying particular rules and regulations.

Studies by Sears *et al.* (1957), Kohlberg (1966) and Sugarman (1967) all offer similar explanations for these differences. Middle-class children usually have more say in family decision making from an early age, are encouraged to consider the motives and intentions of others and to develop some sort of inner self-control.

Kay (1975) stresses the importance of moral flexibility, the ability to consider particular circumstances and special considerations surrounding a moral action or choice rather than applying blindly a rule that one has been taught. He suggests that it is only by being morally flexible that children can develop what he calls moral dynamism or creativity—something akin to what we have referred to earlier as moral autonomy.

We noted in Chapter 3 how strongly attitudes and values are affected by early social experiences of this kind, so that we can appreciate how this degree of difference will lead to a similarly wide variety of levels of moral learning in pupils when they come to school. Some will be used to attempts to reason with them and will thus perhaps be some way on the road to moral education and to moral autonomy; others will be used only to the quick authoritarian reaction and will thus be still very firmly at the heteronomous stage. Indeed, one might even borrow the terminology of the language experts and speak of "restricted" and "elaborated" codes of morality. This is just as likely to be a function of social class too. This wide variety of experience will create as great difficulties for the teacher as a moral educator as the equally wide range of language experience creates for him or her in other aspects of their work.

Secondly, there will be a similar variety in the content of the moral learning that has taken place. Not all parents will, either through their overt attempts at moral training or the incidental effects of their own behaviour, offer the same kind of moral guidance. For example, reactions of parents when their child has been physically attacked by another range from "Never mind, dear. I expect he was upset at something" through "What had you done to him first?" to "Next time he does it you make sure you hit him back harder". Other problems arise too from those differences of belief and practice that derive from the cultural differences to be found in a multi-ethnic school or classroom, such as the unwillingness of Pakistani girls to discard clothing in public for P.E. or games lessons. It is not for teachers to involve themselves in conflict with parents over the content of their pupils' moral beliefs, since, as we have suggested elsewhere, such conflict must be non-productive. It is important, however, for teachers to recognize that the variety of attitudes to be found amongst any group of pupils again creates very real difficulties for the conversion of such moral learning into moral education.

Further, we must note that a good deal will have been learnt unconsciously from parents — perhaps more than is learnt from their deliberate efforts at moral upbringing, since children are more likely to learn to do as their parents do than as their parents say, to pay more attention to what they practice than to what they preach. This means that they will have acquired, probably uncritically, most of the attitudes of their parents. The unthinking racial prejudice of some young children would seem certainly to derive from this source.

It also means that in those situations where their parents' practices and precepts are divergent, the children's moral attitudes are likely to be highly confused. This is a major source of those double standards of moral behaviour that are to be observed throughout society, the inconsistency of "one rule for myself and another for the rest of the world" that we suggested in Chapter 2 was incompatible with the notion of a rational morality. Young people are likely to be highly confused by parents who steal quite unashamedly from their places of employment but punish their children for behaving in what appears to them to be the same way, by parents whose attitude to sexual matters generally is liberal but who try to insist on firm sexual discipline in their own children, just as they will be bewildered by a society which condones and even encourages acquisitiveness but condemns greed or by a church which proclaims "Thou shalt not kill!" and blesses the troops before battle.

All of these factors create problems for the moral educator.

Nor is it only parents who are a source of moral learning of this kind. Siblings, other immediate family members and many other adults will play their part too, from the archetypal grannie of Giles cartoon fame who expresses stern disapproval of almost all childish behaviour to the equally archetypal jovial Uncle Fred who encourages every kind of horseplay and seems to regard it as his mission in life to undermine all the restrictive practices of the most dutiful parents. Other adults too, either by accident or design, will influence children and young people morally through any kind of contact they have with them, so-called "charismatic" personalities being particular influential. For the most part, attitudes will be caught from such sources rather than taught by them and we noted in Chapter 3 some of the evidence for the importance in moral development of imitation and modelling.

The peer group too is a particularly fruitful source of values, expecially at adolescence, and will play a major part in determining the value positions young people adopt and the behaviour patterns they come to feel they ought to conform to, a point which a visit to any first-class Association Football ground on any winter's Saturday afternoon will quickly and deafeningly confirm. This source of learning will give rise again to conflicts of values which are particularly difficult for the young person to resolve without the sensitive help of the teacher or another adult. Nor should we assume that, because the peer group is particular influential at adolescence, it is not important at other ages and stages; at the "gang" stage of the seven and eight year old it is perhaps equally important. We noted too in Chapter 3 Piaget's claims that not only does moral learning derive from this source but that also cooperative activities and mutual understanding between peers are necessary conditions for the development of autonomy. On the other hand, we should not forget, as Kohlberg points out, that isolates can be as morally developed as other children.

It is also worth noting that in some societies the influence of the peer group is far greater than it is in others. Bronfenbrenner's comparative study (1970) of child-rearing practices in the USA and USSR demonstrates some of these differences clearly. Because of the nature of Soviet society, children are brought up in a collective atmosphere from the time they enter nursery school. Rather than being encouraged to act as individuals, they have stressed to them the importance of the group, so that they grow up learning to act in the interests of the group, to conform to its standards and norms and to accept responsibility for the behaviour of group members. Using observational and experimental methods, Bronfenbrenner found that Soviet children were less willing to engage in antisocial behaviour than their peers in the USA, England and Germany, mainly because they are held in check by other group members — not by adults. However, such practices tend to produce children who are obedient and conformist and who perhaps remain at Kohlberg's stage 3 or 4 in terms of their moral development. But, as Bronfenbrenner points out, Soviet society is slowly changing and patterns of upbringing are showing signs of greater flexibility, with a shift away from features which foster dependency and conformity to those conducive to individuality and independence.

Similarly, children brought up in Kibbutzim, the Israeli collective setting, were found to display values which were more peer group oriented than those brought up in ordinary families (Luria *et al.* 1963). Spiro (1958), however, had shown that adults who had lived in a Kibbutz as children nevertheless reached a stage of moral responsibility similar to that of those brought up in their own homes.

Another major source of moral learning is the many forms of mass media to which children are exposed — radio, newspapers, comics and, especially, television. We noted in Chapter 3 in discussing the importance of imitation and modelling for moral development the influence of symbolic models observed on film and television or in books.

Again some of the learning here is the result of deliberate attempts to foster particular moral attitudes, while some is the result of the same kind of unconscious absorption that we have just spoken of. Those television programmes and novels, for example, that are produced or written expressly for children usually offer a positive moral message. The triumph of "good" over "evil" is the theme of a good deal of children's literature, a point particularly well illustrated by C.S. Lewis's tales of Narnia, and it is clear that the community of Camberwick Green displays what Durkheim would have called a mechanical solidarity, a social cohesion that is based on the thoughtfulness and altruism of every one of its inhabitants.

Other values, however, of a kind that one might not regard with so ready an acceptance or with equanimity are implicit in programmes and other offerings that do not make any explicit attempt to promote them. This is true even of those that are specifically devised for children. Whatever toys Andy Pandy and Teddy choose to play with and whatever mess they make in playing with them, they can enjoy in an untrammelled manner and in the full knowledge that faithful and subservient Looby Loo will come along later and tidy everything up. This kind of programme is a major source of that learning of sex roles that must infuriate any liberated woman. Nor are the values implicit in the comments of those who present some of the magazine programmes directed at children always of a kind that one could believe the presenters themselves would accept if they were fully conscious of them. Items that are not specifically designed for children, of course, are likely to present even more serious problems of this kind. The violence of many of the most popular of television programmes, the attitude to sexual relationships evinced by such programmes, by some of the offerings of the popular press and by many other publications are but the more obvious examples of this. Less obvious, but perhaps of equal importance, are the effects of those many quiz programmes whose appeal is based on the monetary or material rewards they offer their contestants and over which an acquisitive audience drools.

Advertisements too, which scream at us from television, radio, newspapers, magazines and, sometimes it seems, every available blank space in the environment, contribute to the same process. The fundamental values of advertising itself are such that many people would want to question, based as they are for the most part on a morality of acquisitiveness, materialism and sometimes downright greed. Some advertisements that are directed specifically at children, however, are particularly questionable, such as that which in promoting the sale of a certain kind of confectionery based its appeal to children on the philosophy of "Wot a lot I got", or that which drew children's attention to the fact that the lucky child was the one that had two bars of a certain brand of chocolate rather than one.

Other agencies too, such as organized religion in its various forms, which will attempt in a quite overt, explicit and deliberate way to influence children and young people morally, will contribute both by accident and design to this process of moral learning and each child's system of values will be the product of these many forces acting upon him with varying degrees of strength and impact.

The relative influence of each of these agencies and sources of moral learning will vary also according to the kind of society in which they are experienced. In some societies, for example, the influence of the family is greater than in others. The same can be true of different groups or communities in the same society. In our own society, for instance, the family unit plays a more dominant role in the moral upbringing of Jewish children than it does in that of other children, a fact that has been appealed to as an explanation of the lower level of juvenile delinquency among Jewish adolescents. The relative influence will also vary according to the age of the children. Parental influence is usually very great in the case of young children, while, as we have noted several times, the peer group comes into the ascendant at adolescence. All combine, however, in varying degrees of strength and influence to create the moral content of each child's value system upon which the moral educator must work. They present him with three major problems. For, firstly, they lead to a great variety of learning, attitudes, beliefs and values. Secondly, there is a similar variety in the manner in which pupils will have come to hold these beliefs. And thirdly, in all cases, much of this learning and many of these attitudes, beliefs and values are unconscious or, at least, are held uncritically. For either they are the result of unconscious influence and absorption that will entail uncritical acceptance or, as in the case of an authoritarian approach by, say, organized religion or parents of particularly strong and dogmatic convictions, they are the result of deliberate attempts to secure uncritical acceptance.

Because of this they are often in conflict with each other and lead to double standards of behaviour of a kind that we suggested in Chapter 2 cannot be accepted as rational nor, therefore, as constituting a moral education. Thus, the unreflective and uncritical nature of this learning makes the moral educator's task an especially difficult one, since he must help his pupils to become conscious of them before he can encourage them to reflect critically on them and to make a reasoned appraisal of them.

The school as a source of moral learning

It would be a mistake to assume from what we have said so far that all the moral learning that goes on outside the school is unreflective and uncritical while all of that which goes on inside it is always educational in the full sense. Clearly, a lot of the experience and direct tutelage that children have outside the school will be of such a kind as to encourage them to think about the issues involved — certainly some parents will actively work at promoting this. The converse, however, is also true and it is to this that we must direct some attention here. For a moment's reflection will reveal that the school itself also contributes in a number of ways to this process of unreflective learning that we are describing. A lot of learning of this kind goes on as a result of the experiences pupils have at school, even though those experiences are not always acknowledged by teachers as having this kind of moral import. It is not only when teachers are deliberately setting up projects in moral education or extracting moral lessons from their work in literature or history that moral learning is going on. As much, if not more, is learnt from the way in which they organize the work of their pupils, react to the behaviour of individuals, use punishment, exercise discipline, achieve control and, in general, approach their pupils, handle their classes and manage their classrooms. Moral attitudes are caught from every interaction of teacher and pupil since these again, like all human interactions, are moral interactions.

It will be apparent that the school will contribute to this kind of unreflective moral learning both by its deliberate attempts to ensure the acceptance by children of certain values and through this kind of unconscious absorption of the values implicit in its patterns of working and its structures, in short, through what has been called the "hidden curriculum".

For, in the first place, teachers will often for a variety of reasons attempt to establish certain habits of behaviour or attitudes in their pupils without concerning themselves too much or at all with the question of whether their pupils come to hold these attitudes or adhere to these habits reflectively or unreflectively. In other words, they will actively work to promote moral learning without considering whether at the same time they are forwarding the task of moral education. This is particularly likely to be the practice of teachers of young children, especially if they take too seriously or too naively the suggestion of the developmental psychologists that at this age children cannot be expected to be critical or reflective on such issues.

The reason for such behaviour may often be a quite legitimate concern to establish and maintain order or to protect some pupils from the excesses of others, so that "Be quiet when I tell you to!" or "We mustn't talk when we're in the classroom" or any other such straight injunction may be justified in such utilitarian and pragmatic terms. Or they might be prompted by a genuine, if misguided, urge to promote "good" habits, as is true of a good many new-style school assemblies. But all such injunctions provide the wrong kind of basis for morality, since they all suggest that the prime reason for adopting such habits or beliefs is respect for, or even fear of, the authority of a superior. To that extent, therefore, they are not conducive to moral education and, as we have seen, may even, if they are too strong, positively inhibit it. It is this kind of moral teaching that, as we saw in Chapter 2, has been described as indoctrinatory and, as we also saw there, it can only be avoided by offering reasons for any injunction so that, even if the precise reason is not understood at the time, the relevance of reasons to behaviour is always made clear (Hare 1964). If teachers are not aware of the dangers, therefore, they can in this way through their own deliberate attempts at moral teaching contribute to the kind of unreflective moral learning we are discussing here and thus perhaps effectively inhibit moral education. On the other hand, if teachers are conscious of the potential dangers, the way to avoid them is not difficult to find and they can very easily use such situations to lay the right kinds of foundation for moral education.

Much less easy to deal with are the hidden sources of moral learning in the school, those values, attitudes and resultant habits of behaviour that are assimilated by the pupils in a largely unconscious manner. There are several sources of such learning and it will be helpful if we can look at each of them in turn.

We shall see in Chapter 6 that there is a moral dimension to most, if not all, areas of the curriculum. In many cases, as, for example, in the teaching of history, literature and the humanities generally, this moral dimension is explicit or at least can and should for the most part be made so. One cannot go very far in introducing pupils to the plays of Shakespeare without recognizing that one is presenting them with important moral dilemmas and thus contributing to their moral education. This is also true, as we have seen, of the kind of literature that we might introduce quite young pupils to, so that he or she would be a strangely insensitive teacher who did not appreciate that at any age there exists this dimension to the work children do in school in these areas of the curriculum.

What is less readily apparent is that similar value positions are implicit in other material that we present to children in contexts where it is not our intention to encourage such critical reflection and response, and that not all the values residing in such material can be made explicit in this way. Some are woven into the very fabric of the material and this creates especially difficult problems when our concern is not to promote debate and discussion but to achieve rather more mundane goals. Thus those texts which are used as basic readers for young children and whose prime purpose is to effect a fluent and steady development of reading skills must have a content and that content will inevitably be based on some kind of value structure. This is why many such reading schemes are currently under attack as sexist, as promoting a hidden and unconscious acceptance of sex roles, or as reflecting a middle-class ethos—Janet in the kitchen helping Mummy, John in the garage helping Father to clean the car (and Rover, good dog, Rover, coming and going between them). Indeed, attempts have been made to use this phenomenon of unconscious assimilation of values to promote particular kinds of attitude, political, religious or social. The readers written for use by young children in some countries have a content that is quite overtly and blatantly political and/or religious, for example, and several attempts have been made recently to produce reading schemes for use in the USA and the UK that would by this method promote such social virtues as racial and social harmony and tolerance. Much moral learning, then, takes place in this largely unconscious manner through the content of materials that teachers might regard as having no such wide-reaching purpose, function or significance.

Secondly, there is no way in which children can avoid "catching" moral attitudes, beliefs and habits from their teachers. This is a further implication of that claim of the Newsom Report with which we began, that "teachers can only escape from their influence over the moral and spiritual development of their pupils by closing their schools" (1963, §160). The moral views that teachers hold and the manner in which they hold them will be communicated to their pupils whether they wish it to be so or not. As we noted above in considering the role of the parents in moral development, moral learning comes from every kind of human interaction, the interaction between teacher and pupil no less than any other. The individual teacher's values will be plain from the way in which he sets about his business in the classroom, the kinds of relationship he develops with his pupils, the way he organizes their learning, the way he reacts to their mistakes and misdemeanours, his use or abuse of punishment and in general his whole approach to the job of teaching. The teacher who without question or explanation requires a pupil who has not done his homework to write it out ten times by the next day is clearly promoting a different kind of moral learning from the one who asks whether any circumstances at home made it difficult for him to do it. (He is also, incidentally, fostering a very strange notion of education.) Similarly, the teacher who was once heard telling a class of boys to take particular care of a set of books because they had paid for them themselves was encouraging a moral attitude that he himself, one suspects, would have been horrified by if he had thought seriously about it. Which of us has not been guilty of the same kind of thoughtless remark? A good deal of unreflective moral learning, then, goes on through the ordinary day-to-day business of every teacher's classroom.

Furthermore, pupils will also learn from the manner in which teachers hold their value positions and this is a more serious problem because it has direct implications for their moral education as well as their moral learning. If it is apparent from what a teacher says or does that many of his moral beliefs are held unreflectively or have been accepted uncritically from other sources, if, in short, he reveals that he is not himself morally educated and morally autonomous, then pupils are likely themselves to settle for an authoritarian form of morality and remain at the stage of heteronomy or socionomy, so that their moral education will in this way be impaired and retarded. To absorb in this unreflective way an attitude from someone who himself holds that attitude as a prejudice, unreflectively, is likely to be more detrimental to moral education than to imbibe it from someone who holds the view because he has thought it out. What we are discussing in general here is that accidental indoctrination or miseducation we examined in Chapter 2. However, we are now taking the issue a step further and suggesting that it is likely that our influence will be more seriously miseducative or indoctrinatory if we ourselves hold views in such a manner as to indicate a response to moral issues at the level of heteronomy or even socionomy.

Thus both the matter and the manner of every teacher's moral code, its content and its form, will be communicated to his pupils through all of his contacts with them and will contribute, for good or ill, to their moral development.

Lastly, we must note that the organization of the school is a further source of moral learning. Just as the way in which the individual teacher organizes his class will reveal certain values that he holds, so the way in which the school as a whole or even the school system is organized will display the same kind of hidden value structure. For implicit in any kind of organization is a set of values and those values will be absorbed, for the most part unconsciously, by those who are the objects, even the victims, of that organization or system. Moral learning, then, is as much a function of the way in which we organize our schools as of any deliberate provision we make for it within them. It has become apparent in recent years that the way in which the school is organized will determine to a large extent the kinds of relationship that are possible within it; it will also govern the kind of moral learning that goes on and, indeed, the kind of moral education that is possible.

Again, this can be used quite deliberately to promote moral education. The use by many schools of "councils" of staff and pupils is not only a device to ensure the smooth running of the school, it is also an attempt to create an organizational structure that will itself contribute to the moral education of its pupils. Again, however, it is what happens in an unrecognized and unacknowledged way that is more important, since its effects, because they are "hidden", are more influential and difficult to control and those effects may well be positively inimical to moral education. It is for this reason that many people have condemned all forms of selection in education, secondary school selection and streaming in particular, because it reveals attitudes of mind that children exposed to such a system will absorb, attitudes that are based on a competitive ethos and a notion of differential human worth and which are felt by many to be as reprehensible when they lead some pupils to regard themselves as members of a superior race of human beings as when they lead others to develop feelings of inferior value. Conversely, it is this that in part explains why the introduction of mixed-ability grouping with its corresponding assumptions of human equality and collaboration has invariably led to improved social relationships in the school (Barker-Lunn 1970, Ferri 1972, Newbold 1977). For it represents a change in the infrastructure of values within the school, a different kind of "hidden curriculum".

It is also worth noting that in some cases, where the ethos of the school is in too direct an opposition to that of the homes from which the pupils come, the effect can be not only detrimental to moral education but also to education of any kind. This was, for example, posited as a major factor in the failure of pupils from "working-class" homes to achieve the success they seemed capable of in the school system, especially after they had obtained admission to grammar schools (Jackson and Marsden 1962). The values, the ethos of the grammar school were too much at variance with those of the homes they came from. The notion of a corporate school spirit, for example, is not one to which children and young people from such backgrounds too readily respond. Nor is this phenomenon confined to grammar schools, as Barry Hines in *Kes* reveals plainly and sensitively.

We must again note, therefore, the many kinds of danger and threat to moral education that reside in the kind of moral learning that is promoted by the way in which the school is organized. We must note too that it is not just a matter of getting the "right" kind of organization. What is important is to realize that, whatever kind of organization we adopt, this kind of hidden learning will result, so that again we need to take account of it in considering what steps we should take to further the moral education of our pupils. It is probably true that a looser, more fluid, more flexible, "democratic" form of organization will ensure that pupils are encouraged to think more deeply about such matters, but the important thing is that they should be so encouraged and that again unreflective learning should not be allowed to inhibit or impair their moral education. If we were concerned only with socialization, in the structural-functionalist sense of coming to accept the social values of the group, it might be enough merely to ensure that our organizational structure reflected the value structure of our society (if, indeed, any one such structure could be identified). But, since we are concerned with education, this is not sufficient.

From all of these sources, then, both inside and outside the school, children will acquire moral attitudes, beliefs and habits of behaviour. All of this moral learning must be converted into moral education. Indeed, this is the only realistic way in which we can approach moral education. We must accept that every pupil will have a content to his moral learning and that we must ourselves contribute to that content as well as being concerned with the form of moral education. It is to some of the problems of providing that kind of content and building a moral education on that kind of foundation that we must now finally turn.

Providing a content to moral education

Let us first of all remind ourselves why we need to provide a content for the developing morality of our children. There seem to be at least three reasons for this. The first of these is that children from the earliest age need rules, norms, criteria of choice, standards of behaviour, since from the beginning they need to make choices. They may not yet for the most part be faced with the big moral issues that come with adolescence and that widening awareness of the world that accompanies that stage of human development, but moral choices still have to be made. Should I, to avoid being punished, tell mother I have not been at the jam? Should I eat my friend's sweets while he or she isn't looking? Should I use my greater size and strength to bully someone smaller and weaker? Should I tell lies about someone or, in circumstances where it will get them into trouble, should I tell the truth about them? And so on. We must not see moral problems as always being on the grand scale. For most of us they are usually much more mundane.

From the earliest age, then, children need criteria to appeal to in making such choices. This is probably one of the reasons why they do absorb values, norms and standards from all aspects of their environment in the ways we have just tried to outline. For this reason, then, teachers must not only recognize that they do acquire their values in these ways, they must also acknowledge the need to help them to acquire the "right" kinds of value.

Secondly, as we noted in Chapter 4, children need to develop settled habits and patterns of behaviour if they are to have the self-discipline to carry out the rational moral choices they may later come to make. They can only develop such settled dispositions if they are provided with or helped to acquire some standards and norms of behaviour from earliest times. As Aristotle said, we become virtuous by acting virtuously. This raises the problem of what Richard Peters, echoing Aristotle, has called the paradox of moral education. We shall shortly be suggesting that this is not a paradox but rather the very essence of moral education, although we must consider some of the difficulties it raises for teachers.

For, thirdly, children need a content of this kind to provide the raw material of their moral education. Even if our concern is primarily with form or manner, this can only be taught, as Kohlberg argues, through content. Moral education, as we have had cause to note on several occasions, cannot be planned or practised in a vacuum. There is a content on which it must work and, in turn, it needs such a content to work on. It is essentially the process of converting moral learning or even moral training into moral education. It is not, therefore, something different from moral learning; it is something more than moral learning. It must start with moral learning and go on to something very much more sophisticated. We have to accept that there is a continuous interaction between moral behaviour and moral education at all stages and that, in the end, moral education will be the product of the individual's moral experiences as well as those deliberate attempts that we are suggesting teachers should make to promote his moral education. To put it differently, before a moral education that has the *form* we described in Chapter 1 can be achieved, the individual will need and, indeed, will possess a *content* to his morality, a system of values of some kind, however acquired. Not only, then, can we not, as moral educators, ignore the existence of this kind of moral learning, we must also recognize and accept its necessity both for the individual's continuing behaviour and actions and as the raw material of the education we are hoping to offer. Moral education — again perhaps like all education — can only be effective if it starts from what the child brings to school with him and every child needs to be helped to develop moral values and not merely to be able to reflect rationally about them. In short, the moral educator must be concerned with the content as well as the form of morality, a truth that much that has been written on the subject of moral education has been inclined to ignore.

The existence of moral learning acquired in these informal ways, therefore, provides the teacher with a basis for moral education. It also, however, creates a problem for him, since essentially the moral educator is in a business where his pupils must use the tools and skills he is trying to help them to acquire long before they have acquired them. It is as though we were trying to give driving lessons to pupils who travel to and from school in their own cars or train fighter pilots who, in between lessons, take up their planes and engage in dog-fights, or give lessons in the use of a lathe to pupils who are endeavouring, outside school hours, to make a living as machine-tool operators — a crazy and seemingly impossible task.

This problem manifests itself in different ways according to the age-range of pupils we are concerned with. In the case of the younger child, for example, it is this feature of moral development that gives rise to those fears of indoctrination that we mentioned in Chapter 2. For it appears that children are acquiring a content to their moral beliefs, a content to which their teachers themselves, as we have just seen, must contribute, and are requiring guidance from their teachers in the development of such content, long before they appear to have the mental and intellectual capacity to achieve the level of understanding necessary for them to think for themselves on such issues. It would be a mistake, however, to assume that this problem does not arise with older pupils. Certainly, the onset of puberty does bring more important moral problems for the individual to resolve; it also brings with it a greater awareness of moral issues, a greater consciousness of their importance and a wider view of their significance, so that it is at this age that the horizons widen and the young person suddenly takes an interest in the cares of the world and adopts all kinds of idealistic views on them. He is thus at his most impressionable and, therefore, at his most vulnerable stage. It cannot be assumed, however, that, unlike the younger child, he has now the understanding to think for himself and to be autonomous, that his moral education is almost complete. Certainly he should be further on in his moral development but he is still highly susceptible to influence, as the incidence of religious "conversions" at this age indicates, and, as we suggested in Chapter 2, we are flirting with danger as moral educators if we assume that indoctrination is a problem that only the teacher of young children need be concerned with.

For all of these reasons children need to be helped to acquire moral values and all teachers must accept that they have a share in the responsibility for offering them such assistance. We must now turn to a consideration of what this implies for the practice of moral education and some of the ways in which teachers might aim to fulfil this responsibility.

The first problem we face in approaching the task of providing a content to the moral education of pupils is that which we discussed at some length in Chapter 2, the impossibility of establishing a universally valid or acceptable basis for any particular set of moral precepts. However, this problem is not peculiar to moral education. For judgements of value are as difficult to substantiate in other spheres too and the problem that we are identifying is one that is common to all education, the problem of finding the middle road between leaving children entirely alone and imposing our views and values on them. This is well brought out in the words of John Dewey, "There are those who see no alternative between forcing the child from without, or leaving him entirely alone. Seeing no alternative, some choose one mode, some another."

The solution Dewey himself suggests here is summed up by the word "guidance". "Guidance is not external imposition. It is freeing the life-process for its own most adequate fulfilment." It is precisely this kind of guidance that the child needs in the sphere of morality. Children and young people need and have a right to expect guidance with the day-to-day choices they must make. Like most education, moral education is best forwarded when it begins from the first-hand experience of the individual pupil. Opportunities for discussing far-reaching moral issues of the kind the Schools Council's Humanities Curriculum Project has directed its attention to, as we shall see in Chapter 7, have a great deal to offer to moral education, but they do not always have the direct personal relevance that the most effective moral education will require. It is for this reason that the teacher in the context of this kind of discussion can remain neutral and get away with it. He cannot, on the other hand, take a detached view of the real problems children and young people are endeavouring to solve. This is why the development of counselling services in schools has to be seen as one aspect of moral education, a point we must return to in the next chapter.

The difficulty, however, remains. For even if we see it as our task as teachers to guide pupils rather than to impose upon them, we still have to resolve the problem of attaining acceptable criteria upon which to base such guidance. There are two points to be made that have a bearing on this problem, the first of which can be dealt with quite briefly; the second will require the rest of the chapter to answer.

A good deal of basic, commonsense guidance can be offered to pupils in a largely uncontroversial manner. There are certain broadly accepted social norms concerning such matters as respect for human life, for truth, for honesty, upon the basis of which one can suggest that pupils should not kill, steal, lie, cheat, harm or hurt other people and a lot more besides. The more one looks into this question the more it appears analogous to questions of freedom in education generally. There is a lot of "interference" in the lives of pupils that we can justify in terms of protection of others, to use J.S. Mill's famous criterion, and there is a good deal more that we can justify if we are prepared to appeal to the concept of education as embodying respect for persons, for knowledge, for truth, for freedom of thought and so on. Furthermore, if there is any value in what we said at the end of Chapter 4 about the need to promote in our pupils a feeling of concern, empathy, even love for others, then that will take us some way towards establishing a positive content to the moral advice we can offer. We must not assume because there are no valid or universally accepted arguments for ultimate moral value positions, that our hands are tied as moral educators and that we must not be positive in the moral guidance we offer our pupils.

The second point that needs to be made here is a little more complex and one that we must be careful to explain clearly to avoid misunderstanding. It is important that we provide moral guidance but, in a sense, the exact content of our moral teaching or moral guidance does not matter overmuch if the manner of it is right. If our approach to moral teaching and guidance is always such as to be conducive to moral education, if our concern is that pupils should be brought as soon as possible to think for themselves and to make their own minds up on these issues, if we are concerned always that they should be developing self-control and so on, then, within reason, the exact advice we offer, the precise precepts we encourage them to adopt are not as crucial as they would be if our approach was an intentionally authoritarian one and we were aiming to implant certain beliefs unshakeably. John Dewey's solution to the problem of finding a basis for educational guidance generally was the notion of the "experiential continuum"; that experience is to be encouraged which appears of all the possible alternatives to be likely to be productive of the most fruitful further experiences. It is a notion that would appear to be at least as useful in the sphere of moral education, since it would suggest that our approach should always be such as to promote the continuing moral education of the individual or, perhaps more importantly and more usefully, such as not to block this continuing development. In other words, we must have constantly before our minds the basic principles of moral education if moral learning is to be converted into moral education, however slow a process that might be, and if pupils are to be brought to the inside of this form of life. This is not perhaps so different here from other subjects.

Nor is it necessary to assume that if we get out pupils' moral thinking onto a sound and autonomous basis they will go off in all directions when it comes to establishing their own moral principles. In fact, the reverse is the more likely. Just as an education in English literature is unlikely to result in a preference for the *Beano* above all other works and an education in music will seldom produce an addict of the bagpipes, so a moral education is unlikely to lead to a rejection of all human values. It is probable that a concern for the manner of moral education will lead to that respect for persons, that belief in the importance of treating others as ends in themselves and never as merely a means to the satisfaction of our wants and desires, that Kant and others have seen as the supreme principle of human morality.

To say that, however, is not to say that there is a rational or logical connection between the two nor is it to argue that anyone who did, after due and proper reflection, reject this principle would not be entitled to do so or would be behaving in an irrational way. The connection we are arguing for here between a proper form of moral thinking and human values is contingent rather than necessary, but it is perhaps sufficiently firm ground upon which to base the positive guidance that our pupils will need. Provided that we do not lose sight of the crucial importance of manner, both the manner of our pupils' moral thinking and the manner in which they come to hold their moral beliefs, a content can be established upon which real moral guidance can be given.

In the end, however, as is the case in education generally, the teacher's main task as so often may be to avoid doing positive harm. It may be more important for him to recognize the ways in which he can inhibit the moral education of his pupils than to seek for ways in which he can positively further it. What are the main dangers here?

Undoubtedly, the first of these is that which derives from an over-dogmatic approach on the part of teachers or, indeed, of any adult. If it is to be possible for a child to think for himself at some later stage about any particular moral issue, the guidance he is offered at an earlier stage must not be too heavy-handed or dogmatic. A light and easy touch is essential if autonomy is ever to be possible. For if any moral precept has been forced upon us in early childhood in an aggressive manner, perhaps accompanied by severe punishment for any misdemeanour in this area, it is unlikely that we will ever be able to come to a detached, objective view of it. Whether it remains embedded in our value system or we later kick against it and reject it, a proper appraisal of this particular attitude will always be very difficult, if not impossible, since either of these reactions will give a "twist" to our moral thinking and will involve our emotions in the wrong way. Thus the child whose infantile explorations of sex are dubbed as "dirty" by his parents, and perhaps accompanied by severe punishment, will always find it difficult to divest himself of such an attitude, no matter how hard he might try to hold the issue up to the subsequent test of rationality.

For the dangers of fixation here are immense. This is exactly the kind of experience we suggested earlier might lead to such fixation and thus cause the individual to "get stuck" at an early stage of moral development. Most of us are so stuck in relation to some aspect of our behaviour. We all have our "hang-ups". Too dogmatic an attitude on the part of teachers or parents, too severe a reaction to certain kinds of behaviour will be likely to lead to such fixations and will thus be counter-productive to the cause of moral education, since they will make subsequent rational, objective appraisal very difficult, if not impossible.

Furthermore, they will imply an authoritarianism that will be equally detrimental to moral education as we have defined it. To be dogmatic on any issue is to suggest to pupils that, whether they understand the reasons or not, they must accept our direction simply because we insist upon it. It is thus to imply that the important thing is to behave in certain ways rather than to understand the reasons for our behaviour. It suggests, therefore, that the authority of others is acceptable as a basis for moral behaviour, that a heteronomous form of morality is acceptable. In so far as it does this, then, it is not only not conducive to the notion of autonomy as a central element in morality, it is also positively counter-productive to moral education. It will not encourage progress beyond the heteronomous stage.

This in turn highlights the need for teachers themselves to be morally educated, autonomous persons. For only then will they find it easy to be non-dogmatic and non-authoritarian in their approach to moral issues, since only if they have given a good deal of thought to the matter themselves will they realize how little basis there is for being dogmatic about anything and how slender are the grounds for any kind of moral authoritarianism. If, on the other hand, they themselves have fixations and "hang-ups", if the basis of most or all of their moral views is heteronomous rather than autonomous, they will convey this to their pupils and will thus make it very difficult for their pupils to get beyond that stage themselves. As we suggested earlier, if pupils "catch" not only the matter but the manner of such beliefs from their teachers, their hopes of becoming morally educated may have gone beyond recall. Just as it is difficult, if not impossible, for a teacher of mathematics to take pupils beyond the level of his own attainment in mathematics, so is it impossible for the teacher to help his pupils towards a morally educated state if he has not reached such a state himself.

Moral education is essentially a matter of accepting the moral views that pupils already have and helping them to become conscious of what these are and to subject them to some kind of critical evaluation in order to raise and improve the quality of their thinking. This is one of the things that the Humanities Curriculum Project sets out to achieve, as we shall see in Chapter 7. In offering pupils help and guidance with what to believe, we must always stress and establish within them respect for the quality of their opinions. We must remain always aware of the need for them to appreciate that they must take full account of all relevant information, that they must be objective, rather than selective, in their interpretation of such information, that they must attain the highest possible level of understanding, that their views must be rational in the sense of being coherent, consistent and so on and that they must avoid double standards. Whatever content we offer, whatever particular views they have or are encouraged by us to have, the most important thing is that our approach to their moral upbringing must be such as to further, and certainly not to inhibit, the ultimate attainment of moral autonomy.

Particular problems are raised here, of course, for the teacher of very young children. For at this age children are particularly malleable and susceptible to the influence of adults as well as being at a stage when it is unlikely that they can attain the conceptual level of thinking necessary if they are to make their own minds up on moral issues. There would seem to be at least three things for the teacher of young children to bear in mind in this connection. The first of these is that some children from a very early age do reveal the beginnings of really critical thinking about morals. Comments like "That's not fair, miss" are indications of this. We must not too readily assume that stages of development are closely linked to chronological age. Secondly, as we have suggested before, it will help towards the ultimate achievement of moral education if, even when children cannot understand the reasons for certain moral precepts, we still give the reasons so that they begin to get the idea that morality is not a matter of the authority of those with greater power than oneself but of reasoned consideration and argument, that reasons are relevant to moral decisions. In particular, as we noted in Chapter 3, if their moral education is to be forwarded, we must offer them moral advice and guidance couched in terms "one stage above" the stage at which they are currently operating. Lastly, if reasons do have little effect at this early age, as it has been suggested, this is all the more reason for trying to adopt a light and easy touch with young children, for not being too dogmatic or authoritarian. What Freud has told us about fixation, about unconscious motivation and the resultant loss of control and autonomy suggests that it is in the earliest years of life that we are most at risk in this respect. The message thus seems to be clear. At this stage, more than at any other, teachers should be concerned to avoid doing positive harm. If they can achieve that, they may have contributed more to moral education than by any positive steps they might take.

The crucial thing is that whatever content there is to our pupils' moral learning and wherever it comes from, our own contribution to it as teachers should be such as to forward its conversion into moral education. In other words, we should, on the one hand, avoid doing anything that will militate against that process and, on the other, we must do all we can to raise their attitudes and beliefs from the almost unconscious level of unreflective acceptance to that of fully conscious critical awareness, to encourage a fully rational approach to morality and to help our pupils in their progress from anomy to autonomy. This we must do in respect of values they acquire from sources outside the school. We must also, therefore, see to it that from the outset the values they acquire from us and from the school as a whole are of such a kind and are presented in such a manner that they at least do not inhibit this process but rather promote and forward it.

Summary and conclusions

In this chapter, we have tried to suggest that no attempt at moral education can be successful unless it begins from a realization that a good deal of moral learning goes on in many informal ways both inside and outside the school. We have discussed some of the sources of such moral learning outside the school, considering in particular the contribution of parents, the peer group and the media. We then examined some of the "hidden" ways in which the school through its organization and the teacher through his approach to the day-to-day business of the classroom can also contribute to this kind of learning. We also noted that as well as being a factor to be considered by the moral educator, this is also a necessary part of moral development since pupils need to make moral choices from the earliest age, that, in fact, such moral learning is the very "stuff", the raw material, of moral education. We finally looked at some of the problems that face the teacher in his attempt to make a reasonable contribution to this learning and to convert it into moral education. In doing so, we recognized the importance of providing positive moral guidance but suggested that it is not so much the matter as the manner of what we have to offer here that is crucial and that, as so often in education, the important thing is for us to avoid doing positive damage.

It is one thing for all teachers to be aware in general of what harm they can do in this area or of what positive steps they should be taking to promote moral education. There are also, however, very specific contributions that can be made by teachers in particular subject areas and there are projects in moral education that have been specially designed to help us to meet some or all of the problems we have considered here and in the earlier chapters of this book. It is to a consideration of these that we must now turn.

CHAPTER 6

MORAL EDUCATION AND THE CURRICULUM

Most people would agree nowadays that moral education not only is one of the important concerns of the school but that it should play an ever-increasing part in the life of the school. One survey (N.O.P. 1969) showed that 22% of a random sample of the population saw moral training as the most important aspect of the education of pupils over the age of twelve, while a further 26% saw it as the second most important aspect. The Schools Council Report *Young School Leavers* (1968) showed that around 70% of fifteen-year-old school-leavers expected help from their schools in deciding what constitutes a good or bad action and would have welcomed guidance in interpersonal matters. Yet again May (1971) found that around 70% of pupils in his survey in the Durham area expected their schools to offer some kind of moral education.

There must be few if any teachers in this country who do not acknowledge their responsibility for the moral education of pupils. Indeed, as we have pointed out, since moral issues permeate the whole of school life, it is impossible not to be involved in some way, unless one ceased to be a teacher. But to point out that morality is to be found in all aspects of school life does not necessarily mean that pupils, merely by being in school, are being morally educated. Moral learning is undoubtedly going on, just as it is in the home, on the playground or at the sports club, and in fact, wherever people meet to engage in social activities. As we saw in the last chapter however, moral education is not the same as moral learning. And if the majority of teachers, older pupils, parents, as well as a considerable proportion of the population at large, regard it as such an important part of education as a whole, we need to ask what place it has on the school curriculum.

Among the important questions we shall discuss in this chapter are the following: is morality a subject to be taught in the secondary school like any other or should it be dealt with through other subjects? Should time be allocated formally on the timetable to some kind of moral education programme? Should the aims of moral education be reflected in the organization of the school? Are there to be specialist teachers in charge of the moral education work or is every teacher to participate in it? What contribution to moral education can or should be made by other curriculum subjects? What are the problems of ensuring that in our planning we match the content of what is being taught to children's developmental stages? These are the issues that arise when we begin to consider the kind of practical provision for moral education that schools and teachers can and should make.

Moral education as a subject

There seems to be little doubt that moral education in some form will find a place in the curriculum of the future both at primary and secondary level, but what form it will take is still a matter for enquiry, deliberation and possibly action research.

One of the major problems encountered in attempting to find a place for moral education in its own right on the school curriculum is that of what to include or exclude. Moral problems arise in many other areas—for example, history, literature, science, health education—so if we want to make a claim for moral education as a separate independent area, we need to justify its uniqueness.

John Wilson (1975), basing his argument on Hirst's theory of forms of knowledge (1965), claims that moral knowledge constitutes a distinct form of thought and therefore needs to have its own peculiar concepts, methodology and procedures highlighted. He argues on two grounds against the claim that morality is all around us and therefore needs no special singling out. Firstly, there are choices we have to make which do not include a moral element, and secondly, those that do have to be recognized and brought to the attention of children. Just as no teacher would expect a child to be able to work out the principles and methods of mathematics for himself we should not expect him to do so in the realm of moral thinking. He in fact goes so far as to suggest that, in secondary schools, at least two periods per week should be set aside for work on "Moral Thinking" where material is provided which the teacher goes through step by step, using direct instructional teaching methods and even testing pupils' knowledge informally from time to time to make sure that they have properly grasped the tools of moral thought. He and his associates are currently preparing such material for use in schools under the title of "First Steps in Morality". Material may of course be drawn from other areas, for example, literature or religion, but must remain illustrative and supportive. It cannot, in Wilson's view, take the place of basic teaching in moral thinking. Wilson's own moral education project, developed with the Farmington Trust team will be discussed further in the next chapter.

We noted in Chapter 3 that earlier studies had shown attempts at direct moral teaching to result in failure. Hartshorne and May (1928) had found that attempts to inculcate in children moral traits such as honesty, truthfulness, consideration did not have long-lasting effects. Those who had received such moral instruction at Sunday school or in other kinds of youth organization had proved no more honest or truthful than those who had not received such guidance. But probably, as Kohlberg (1966) suggests, this was because the aims of the programmes were misguided and adults were trying to teach habits rather than helping children to under-stand moral issues and to develop the skills necessary to make their own moral choices. This distinction between teaching a certain content, which earlier programmes tried to do, and developing in children the ability to reason is of crucial importance and is one we have discussed at greater length in Chapter 2. Baier (1975), discussing the importance of moral autonomy as an aim of moral education, would agree with Wilson's claim that instruction in moral reasoning should be a necessary part of any programme of moral education and suggests that it might also include instruction in legal reasoning since, in spite of their differences, moral and legal reasoning have many characteristics in common.

J.P. White (1975), although not altogether in agreement with Wilson that morality must necessarily be taught as a separate component, concedes that if it can be shown that there are elements that cannot be dealt with in other curriculum areas, there might be a case for moral education as a distinct subject area. He certainly agrees that the school curriculum should include ethics, especially for older pupils who need to be able to distinguish moral considerations from prudential ones. One of the compulsory elements in his curriculum is a study of the humanities which in his view provide a suitable niche for moral education. Hirst (1974) argues strongly for the inclusion of moral education as a separate component in the curriculum, since in his view it is too important to be left to the general influence of the school, even though the school structure may be such as to allow children to form moral judgements of their own. Similarly, he argues, it is not enough to hope that children will learn what is morally important while they are learning about something else, whether it be history, literature or religion. The overwhelming case for bringing together the knowledge and skills germane to moral thinking, reasoning and behaviour lies in the fact that making moral judgements involves learning to ask particular kinds of question and to reason in particular ways. It is the responsibility of the teacher to see that the appropriate knowledge is acquired by pupils and also that they learn to master the logic of moral discourse and acquire a basic understanding of fundamental moral principles. As we shall see later, Wilson (1967, 1973) attempts to put these principles into practice in his project designed for teachers faced with the task of providing moral education at any age level.

Apart from attempts to justify or refute the claims for moral education as a separate element in the curriculum, at any rate in secondary schools, attention must be drawn to some of the practical difficulties that are likely to be encountered both from the pupils' and teachers' points of view. In spite of the apparent demand for some moral guidance by large numbers of adolescents, there are some pupils who are likely to be resistant to any direct teaching in moral reasoning, claiming, quite rightly in some respects, that they already have to cope with their own personal problems and that after all, morality is a personal matter. They are of course assuming that they already know best how to do this, can do it without help and have already reached moral maturity. There are others who will expect teachers to offer right answers and will regard the teacher as an authority in moral matters just as they do in matters of history, science and so on. It is for this reason that Stenhouse (Schools Council 1970) advocated that the teacher should act as a neutral chairman in discussions of controversial issues so as to avoid appearing to give right answers.

A further difficulty stems from the nature of our achievement-oriented society. Many pupils feel impelled to collect a respectable number of O-level or C.S.E. passes at the end of their school career and attribute far less value to work in school that does not lead to a publicly recognized examination at the end of the course. Many schools, as we have seen, have tended to include moral education on the curriculum of only the less able pupils, thus indicating to them and others that it is not considered important enough to be justified for all pupils. A subject that by its very nature is non-examinable, at any rate in a formal sense, could easily become a low-status subject in the eyes of pupils, if not teachers.

Singling out moral education for a separate place on the curriculum might furthermore lead some pupils to assume that matters of morality belong only to the moral education period, resulting in a failure to generalize moral thinking to practical real-life situations or to see the moral significance of material they are introduced to elsewhere. And surely one of the aims of any moral education programme, formally timetabled or otherwise, is to help pupils to develop their moral reasoning and judgement so that it guides their moral conduct. In this area, of all places, theory and practice must not remain separate.

Problems too arise from a teacher's point of view. Firstly, who is to be responsible for moral education if it appears as a separate entity on the curriculum? Are there to be moral education experts or specialists? If so, what are their qualifications to be? Are they likely to be regarded as "more moral" than their colleagues or will the implication that they are morally superior have unfortunate reper-cussions on their image as teachers? If there are certain teachers in charge of moral education, does this mean that the rest will feel relieved of their own responsibility in this area?

There are practical solutions to these problems, but they too present difficulties yet to be resolved. Moral education programmes could be assigned to a team of teachers working on courses for which they accept joint responsibility, just as in integrated studies programmes. School counsellors could be called on to participate as members of the team — in fact, this might be a very appropriate area in which they could make a teaching contribution. On the other hand, if we argue that all teachers must play some part, even in a school where moral education is run as a separate element, then it might be possible for class teachers or tutors in charge of mixed age tutor groups to assume responsibility for this work. Clearly this would call for some kind of in-service guidance, possibly from local teachers' centres or from a central research team working on a specific moral education project.

Alan Harris (1976) claims that the teacher in charge has to be an authority on morality, just as the teacher of any other subject does. That is, he needs to know more about morality than his pupils and to keep up to date with new developments in this area. What this means, however, is that he must have a full understanding of the nature of moral problems, of methods of arriving at possible solutions and know how moral judgements are formed. He must be aware of the distinction between moral content and the ability to reason morally. Hirst too (1974) makes a strong case for specialist teachers who have studied the nature of morality and have been trained to teach in this area. Teachers of the evangelist type who think they know how to deal with moral issues with young people are, in his view, very often the worst equipped to do so.

But whether the task of teaching in the area of morality falls to specialists or to all teachers, it must be emphasized again that anyone concerned with the moral education of children needs to understand the notion of developmental stages as propounded by Piaget (1932) and Kohlberg (1963) and outlined in Chapter 3. Any school-based curriculum project in moral education needs to take developmental stages into account in compiling short-term objectives, selecting material and deciding on appropriate teaching techniques. If the development of moral judgement is one aim of moral education, then it is supremely important to recognize the level of understanding a child has reached. Kohlberg talks of moral readiness, that is, readiness to proceed to a more advanced stage of reasoning. The fundamental implication here is that an understanding of moral development should be an integral and important part of any programme of teacher education.

Alternative approaches to moral education

If we agree with Kerr (1968) that the curriculum involves "all the learning that is planned and guided by the school, whether it is carried on in groups or outside the school", we are encouraged to consider not only what children learn through curriculum content, but also what they learn as a result of being in a particular kind of school, organized in a particular way. We discussed in the last chapter the learning that results from the way in which a school is planned and organized, the "hidden curriculum", hidden either because pupils are not aware of what teachers intend them to learn as a result of working within a particular school organization or because the values and attitudes learned via the hidden curriculum are not directly intended by teachers but are merely a by-product of what is planned. Barnes (1976) contends that whether such learning is intended or not, teachers should be aware of what is going on and accept responsibility for it and this is a point we have made ourselves in relation to the particular problems of moral education.

Some educationists who reject the idea of introducing moral education as a separate entity would indeed prefer to tackle it via the school organization, through such devices as school councils and so on. This is, on the one hand, a more indirect way into the problems of moral education. It avoids direct teaching or instruction and evades the problem of selecting suitable content. On the other, it is a more down-to-earth, practical approach in that children are given the opportunity and encouraged to put certain moral principles into practice. Whether this is in fact possible, without having the moral knowledge to do so, is a debatable point. John Wilson certainly argues that the two should go hand in hand, being mutually supportive.

Blackham (1975) suggests a fourfold approach to moral education in schools, including some direct teaching but having three further elements deliberately built in to complement this. These, he suggests, should take firstly the form of diversity within a broad curriculum so that each pupil is able to choose some of those areas in which he can succeed. He points out that if a child is offered only what he cannot succeed at, he never feels respected or valued by others and so does not learn to respect himself. He comes to feel a failure within the school community and eventually becomes alienated from it. Studies of the effects of streaming in secondary schools (Hargreaves 1967, Lacey 1970) have shown that this is the case. Pupils who fail in school achievement and who are thus labelled as failures tend to reject what the school has to offer and often form some sort of deviant subculture. Blackham argues that since the school community is one of the main influences on a child's moral education it must inevitably fail to exert such an influence, or at any rate, a positive one, on those who feel thus alienated from it. One might further argue that its effects are likely to be morally miseducative. Diversity of choice within the curriculum is then one of his remedies, provided that pupils do not sense that some choices they might make count as low status areas in the eyes of the teachers.

The other two built-in areas he recommends are closely related: guidance and orientation throughout a child's school career, from primary school onwards. Guidance should serve to make the pupil familiar with the range of choices open to him and should provide room for discussion and negotiation so that the pupil's real interests and needs are met. Orientation is that part of the guidance programme that makes clear to pupils the consequences of the choices they might make and the implications of these choices in their immediate and long-term future. Such an approach towards moral education has as its cornerstone respect for the individual as a person capable of developing as an autonomous being.

McPhail: "Our School"

Although McPhail and Wilson are both responsible for developing moral education projects for use by teachers, they each advocate a supportive element which really amounts to putting into practice the principles learned in a more theoretical context. In addition to his Lifeline programme (1972), McPhail suggests the most appropriate means of providing pupils with the opportunity of practising a considerate life style upon which his Lifeline project is based, is the introduction into the school of structures which encourage the practice of democracy. In his view, moral development is most likely to be encouraged by organizational structures which promote communication between teachers and pupils, since by communicating with others we learn to understand and respect them as persons and are thus able to consider their feelings, needs and intentions.

McPhail analyses communication in this sense in terms of four main abilities: reception, interpretation, response and message. Reception involves the skills of not only listening to others in order to understand the full impact of what they have to say but also being aware of what they convey implicitly through changes of intonation and so on. In addition, it involves watching others and becoming aware of the significance of their gestures, bodily posture and other aspects of non-verbal communication. Interpretation involves skills in making sense of what has been communicated by others — no easy task for young people. After all, how many of us who are more experienced in interpersonal communication fail to understand others and hurt their feelings by such misunderstandings? Message ability involves the skill of making what one says clear and unambiguous, so that other peoples' interpretations are not unnecessarily confused. Response ability is regarded by McPhail as the most important of the four sets of skills. It concerns itself with the ability to take decisions and accept responsibility for them. Taking decisions inevitably has moral consequences for oneself and for others, since whatever course one person decides to adopt almost always has repercussions for other people. Pupils need to learn how to make independent decisions that show their respect for other individuals, as well as their concern for the community, McPhail argues.

He suggests that the most appropriate way of enabling pupils to acquire these skills is to organize the school on democratic lines so that all pupils have the opportunity of participating in the running of certain aspects of school life for which they are mainly responsible, under teacher guidance but not teacher direction. Such democratic practice in schools must however remain an educational process and not become the centre of a political issue, as some teachers might fear.

In his practical handbook (1973) on democratic practices in schools, McPhail discusses the functions and workings of class and tutor groups, clubs and other interest groups, school councils and school meetings. He offers practical guidelines on electoral procedures, the organization and running of such groups and pupils' responsibilities within them, such as keeping records, taking minutes and so on. All pupils, regardless of their educational status—that is, pupils of all ages and abilities—should have the chance to take part. Educational status, he comments, should not be equated with a child's moral status, an important point which we discussed in Chapter 2. In such a democratic set-up, there should be no élite to whose lot the major part of responsibilities and duties falls. Allowing, and indeed expecting, all pupils to participate, implies that they are all to be respected as persons capable of learning to accept responsibility and to take autonomous decisions which will affect not only their own lives, but also those of other people.

In many secondary schools, the kinds of activity that would lend themselves to democratic pupil participation are already in existence. Clubs and societies catering for a variety of interests such as chess, athletics and sports of various kinds, music, debating and so on are usually run by senior pupils. Being responsible for their own election of club officers, arranging for visiting speakers or visits to other schools, providing refreshments and coping with financial arrangements all afford pupils the kind of opportunity we have been discussing. They learn not only to assume responsibility but also to consider the consequences of their own doings for other people. A debating society is a particularly useful channel for learning to consider the viewpoints of others and to listen to opinions that are different from one's own.

School councils can provide an arena where pupils of all ages can discuss and contribute towards the running of the school, especially in such matters as rules, punishments, the wearing of uniform and so on. To be run on truly democratic lines, however, must necessarily mean that pupils' ideas must carry equal weight with those of their teachers; a situation where a teacher's vote counts for more than that of a pupil is not to be countenanced.

It is clear from the start however that such a system will only work if the teachers concerned are supportive and are willing to make a

positive contribution. Studies of streaming and mixed-ability grouping (Barker-Lunn 1970, Ferri 1972) have shown that where teachers
are unfavourably disposed towards a method they are required to
adopt, success is unlikely. Furthermore, since democratic procedures by implication allow every participant to voice his opinions
through appropriate channels, teachers may feel threatened if they
find themselves openly criticized by their pupils. The Ford Teaching
Project (Elliott and Adelman 1975) has shown that some teachers are
resistant to criticism by pupils of their teaching methods and that
many are very surprised to find that pupils interpret their behaviour
in a way different from that which they had intended. Thus teachers
who think that they are acting in a democratic way towards their
pupils may still be perceived as dictatorial or authoritarian by them.
The democratic organization that McPhail recommends can only
hope to succeed if there is some room for open debate and negotiation
between teachers and pupils.

Wilson: The School Community

John Wilson, as we have already seen, is firmly convinced that direct
teaching should play the most important part in pupils' moral
education, but like McPhail, he also advocates a supportive social
context within the school, reflected in its organization, in which
pupils can put into practice what they have learned in an academic
context. In Wilson's view, the mere opportunity of mixing with
others does not teach children how to understand them or why they
should act considerately towards them any more than the acquisition of moral knowledge guarantees them the skills to put it into
practice. If attempts at moral education are to have a chance of
success, three kinds of practical provision must be made. Firstly,
there must be a constant process of cross-reference between the
theoretical elements of the moral education course and the social
context of living with others. For example, understanding why old
people have difficulties in coping alone and getting to know how
they live must be paralleled by opportunities to help them. Secondly,
the social context of learning must fit the content and methods
being advocated. Open discussion groups, for example, cannot take
place in a traditional classroom where all pupils are sitting facing
the teacher. Instead, seating arrangements must be made so that
multi-channel communication can go on. We mentioned in Chapter

2 the importance of language for moral behaviour and Wilson, as we have seen, lays great emphasis on language and communication as part of his moral education programme. He believes that without language there can be no real morality and advises the practice of language and communication games designed to help children not only to use words precisely and to think about their meaning, but also to listen to what others have to say without interrupting, giving irrelevant answers or merely responding with an anecdote of their own. It is clear that such communication needs appropriate seating and grouping arrangements so that face to face interaction is possible. We know from the work of Argyle (1969) the importance of non-verbal communication such as gestures, facial expression, eye contact, bodily posture as an adjunct to language in conveying meanings implicitly to others. Wilson's third and possibly most important suggestion is that the school should adopt a "traditional family" model as a means of grouping pupils, since ideally it is within the traditional family that we first learn to live with other people of different ages in a small group setting. He would like to see a house system adopted where each school house has its own house parents and a home base. Each house should consist of not more than eighty boys and girls (but ideally fewer) of all ages and abilities, so that just as in an ordinary family, interests and rituals could be shared. Cooperation within the house would be an important element in fostering love for and consideration of others and would also provide pupils with a sense of security and an awareness of being wanted, essential to their feelings of worth as persons. Such a system would allow for collective responsibility for such matters as catering, planning extra-curricular activities, financial arrangements, matters of discipline and so on.

Wilson's suggestions have far-reaching implications for the reorganization of the structure within an individual school, since they involve not only personal but also physical features, such as buildings and the use of accommodation. It is easy to follow his rationale for suggesting such an organizational set-up, but any head contemplating adopting it would surely want to have some indication of its possible efficacy. Public schools have long since been run along the lines advocated by Wilson but there is no hard evidence to suggest that such a system does have a positive and beneficial effect upon pupils' moral development. In any case, evaluation of the effects of a particular system would be very difficult. Not only are the marks of a morally educated person difficult to recognize, but even if we could say with some measure of agreement what it means to be morally educated, we should not know precisely the influences responsible. Teachers' attitudes must clearly play a major part, regardless of any deliberately organized structures within the school.

Sugarman: "The School and Moral Development"

Sugarman worked with John Wilson in the early stages of the Farmington Trust research, but unlike Wilson does not support direct teaching of moral issues. Accepting the broad definitions provided by Wilson of a morally educated person (and these will be discussed at greater length in the next chapter), he sees the school as having a significant part to play in the development of such qualities, but perhaps not as the most important influence. However, since the school can and does contribute towards children's moral development he claims that certain kinds of school structure can be more or less effective in moral education or even in some cases detrimental to it. The school, he suggests, occupies a bridging position between the home, where children are treated in a personal fashion, and the broader social environment, where they tend to be treated more impersonally, as members of categories. And, since this is the case, the school can provide a gradually broadening framework within which pupils can proceed from an early stage of living with others where they learn to consider individuals' interests, to a more mature one where they learn concern and consideration for their fellow members at large, most of whom are anonymous, for example, minority or underprivileged groups.

Rather than advocating a particular type of school structure, as Wilson and McPhail both do, Sugarman (1973) points to particular qualities within the school and particular opportunities that can be provided in the interests of moral education. Three areas of concern are discussed — teacher-pupil relationships, the rule system and the nature of learning situations.

One mark of the morally educated person, as we have seen, is to learn to care about others and to take their interests into consideration. Sugarman suggests that the most important contributory factor here is the experience of feeling cared for and respected oneself. In the early years of schooling, when the teacher is usually in charge of one class of children for most of their work during the school year, he has the chance to build up a relationship with each of his pupils from what he knows of them over a broad range of activities — a relationship which can form the basis of care and consideration in later years. As pupils move to the secondary school, their relationship with teachers is usually a narrower one, formed during the the pursuit of a subject specialism, but concern and respect for pupils can nevertheless continue to promote their feelings of self-respect and consideration for others.

Since any definition of a morally educated person is multi-faceted, it is unlikely that any one kind of learning situation will contain all the basic requirements for fostering and developing the qualities we hope to find eventually in a morally mature person. Group work provides opportunities for pupils to develop consideration and concern for their fellows in an intimate face-to-face situation. It can also help them to develop communication skills which are important in conveying their feelings to others. Group discussions too provide the occasions for pupils to show consideration to others by allowing all members to have a say, by showing respect for what others contribute even if they are not in agreement with their opinions. Discussions with teacher intervention or with mixed-age groups can afford invaluable opportunities for presenting less mature pupils with moral arguments one stage above their own, in the way that Kohlberg suggests. Yet again, and here Sugarman reminds us of the stress laid by Kohlberg (1966) upon role taking as a means of promoting moral development, group work can help children to see the role of others or even, through drama or simulation techniques, to adopt the role of other people. These suggestions, with others, all point to an open and flexible school organization, and since most schools are now neither completely closed nor completely open, as Bernstein's analysis (1967) might lead us to expect, most if not all, in Sugarman's view, should be able to provide the variety of learning situations conducive to moral learning.

The rule system of the school, in contributing towards pupils' growing moral autonomy, should again reflect an open, flexible approach. Sugarman compares the school as a rule-governed institution with certain therapeutic communities he is familiar with, concerned with the treatment of delinquents and drug addicts. Individuals, on first entering one of these institutions, have to agree to abide by the rules and do as others tell them, although they have an opportunity to question the rules during group sessions. As they show that they understand the rule system and can gradually assume greater responsibility for themselves and others, so they are allowed greater freedom. Similarly, Sugarman suggests, children on entering a secondary school should have a firm framework of rules and regulations to guide them, while at the same time having access to some kind of organized system, such as a class or school council, for questioning the framework of rules. It is important that a delicate balance is maintained and a rule system achieved that is firm enough to provide guidance, yet not rigid enough to retain control beyond a limit compatible with the growing autonomy and responsibility of older pupils. If this point is reached, any rule system can be inimical to moral education, in Sugarman's eyes, because it undermines the ability of pupils to think for themselves, and to make moral decisions of their own.

Although Sugarman puts forward these suggestions for ways in which the structure of the school can play a part in moral education, he finds little empirical evidence so far to indicate the superiority of any one type of school or learning situation over any other. The problems of evaluating the effects of a school on moral development are of course enormous, not least in the task of reaching agreement on the specific attributes of a morally educated person.

The school climate

Our discussion of the part that could be played by the nature of the school organization towards children's moral education has repeatedly suggested the importance of the social climate of the school in general terms, since it is through this that the moral character of the school is reflected. The nature of personal relationships within the school, whether we are concerned with relationships between staff or between teachers and pupils, is very often set by the head. If the head is the sort of person who sets high store by his own status, he is likely to remain aloof from the rest of the staff, to be unapproachable by colleagues and pupils and very often to be feared as an authority figure rather than respected as a person. Under this kind of head, the rest of the staff is likely to be hierarchically structured, with heads of departments ranking higher than the rest of the teachers, so that position or status is all-important. If relationships within the school are coloured by this sort of authority structure, there is little opportunity for the kind of social interaction that would lead to respect and consideration for others out of a feeling of concern or care for them. A hierarchy of this kind where social order and rank take priority over the individual is likely to imply categorization of its members, so that children are seen not as persons in their own right, with their own characteristics, interests and idiosyncracies, but as members of a group. Groups are very often then evaluated differentially with A-stream pupils ranking higher than those in lower streams (Downey 1977). If the creation of an élite implies that others are of lesser value as persons, as it very often does, then respect for persons, one of the cornerstones of morality, is likely to be sacrificed.

Furthermore, if children are not respected as individuals, they do not come to have the positive self-concept or high self-esteem essential to their development as social and moral beings. Children with a negative self-concept, as Kagan (Mussen *et al.* 1967) showed, have difficulty in making friends and in establishing relationships with others. They have little confidence in themselves or in their own judgements and opinions and therefore tend to remain spectators rather than to participate in joint activities with others. We have argued earlier that part of what it means to be morally educated is to learn to become social beings, to communicate with others and show consideration for them. A school whose social or moral climate does not recognize the uniqueness of the individual but labels or typifies him in some way is not consonant with any kind of moral education programme. The need to provide pupils with a secure framework within which their personal identity can develop and where they feel wanted, respected and useful cannot be stressed too much. Personal contact with teachers (who in Mead's terms play the part of "significant others" in the formation of a child's self-concept) is of paramount importance.

Schools that have a rigid hierarchical structure tend also to have inflexible rule systems, backed by ritual and tradition. While a firm authority structure is essential, especially for younger pupils, its rules, principles and forms of punishment must be clear, defensible and justifiable on rational grounds. As Hirst argues (1974) the maintenance of rules, traditions and rituals for which there is no apparent rationale, together with a similarly irrelevant use of status is not conducive to moral development. Pupils need the sort of framework where they can see that moral rules are not to be justified either by the personal whims of an adult authority figure, by private beliefs of a group or by mere tradition, since these conditions do not promote autonomous moral thinking of the kind we have discussed. The main reason for this apparent digression into a discussion of the atmosphere of the school is to underline the fact that wherever there is an intention to make deliberate provision for moral education within the school, whether by the introduction of moral education as a separate component on the school curriculum or by providing opportunities for the practice of democracy by pupils or through existing curriculum areas, it must be backed by a corresponding climate within the school where justice, fairness, autonomy and respect for persons are recognized and practised. An atmosphere at odds with the goals of moral education not only fails to lend it support but in effect militates against it.

Moral education through existing curriculum areas

Some educationalists, amongst them J.P. White (1975), argue that the curriculum already affords ample opportunities for dealing with moral issues in school within the context of other studies, so that there is no need to introduce any kind of moral education programme as a separate element. Whether we accept that this obviates the need for separate provision for moral education or not, it is impossible to deny that many, if not all, areas of the curriculum do have an important moral dimension. Most curriculum areas, such as history, environmental or social studies, the study of literature, health and sex education, the study of religion, offer obvious occasions for the discussion of moral problems. The expressive and creative arts too can provide opportunities for the development of the emotional or affective components of morality. To illustrate some of the possible contributions that could be made by other areas of the curriculum to moral education, we shall look briefly at three existing areas: the study of literature, history and religion.

Literature and morality

It is interesting to look back on some of the early books written specifically for children, as opposed to those thought to be good for them, although written for adults (such as, perhaps, *Pilgrim's Progress*). We find that very many had a marked didactic, moralistic element. Some of the well-loved children's classics of the second half of the nineteenth century set out to teach their young readers that to do wrong led to disaster of some kind, whereas the virtuous were always rewarded, if not in this life, then in the next. The theme of Kingsley's *Water Babies* (1862), for example, is redemption for one's sins. Similarly, that of Farrar's *Eric or Little by Little* (1858) unfolds the fate of Eric, who gradually treads further along the path of sin by inattention in chapel, then swearing, lying, drinking and stealing. The message conveyed here to its innocent readers was that even to tell a white lie put one on the road to moral ruin. Thomas Hughes' *Tom Brown's Schooldays* (1857) provides an example of the virtuous rewarded. Tom submits to bullying, tormenting and cruelty at Rugby only to emerge as an example of moral fortitude at the end, as a result of bearing his trials bravely and showing loyalty to his peers through a sense of team spirit.

While few today would set out deliberately to inculcate moral values or standards into children by the choice of such literature, there are nevertheless moral aspects to any human situation portrayed in novels, drama or poetry. Books written over the past two decades for children up to early adolescence include realistic family and social situations which help to expand children's experience and heighten their awareness of social and moral dilemmas. Such realism is found, for example, in Townsend's *Gumble's Yard* (1961) or *Widdershins Crescent* (1965), both of which portray a family of four children, neglected and at one stage abandoned by their feckless parents. It is left to the two eldest to keep the family together and to try to keep their dishonest father out of trouble. Southall, an Australian writer, presents his readers with moral problems of such enormity that one is left wondering whether those for whom they are intended can cope, so great is the emotional impact. In *Ash Road* (1966), for example, a group of boys out on a day's hike light a fire against all prohibitions and are ultimately responsible for a vast bush fire which destroys thousands of homes and brings about the death of hundreds of people. Many other modern children's stories deal with problems of handicapped children, racial conflict and broken families. All of these provide good narratives and readily absorb children's interest and sympathies. But they also provide material for discussion at a deeper level in relation to current social and moral dilemmas, if teachers so wish.

In fact, few thoughtful adults who read great literature of the past will be left untouched by the social and moral questions raised, whether by the inner conflict of Hamlet, Macbeth or Raskolnikov or the social injustices raised by Dickens, Gaskell or Balzac. Teachers concerned with any great literature cannot avoid discussing the motives, intentions and conflicts of the characters with their pupils, thus raising issues of a controversial and ethical nature.

But to regard the study of literature merely as a means of raising moral and ethical questions would surely be to debase both literature and morality. Novels, plays or poetry are read for their intrinsic value as literary works, for their richness of language, their structure, and perhaps their reflection of the author's personality or social background. Literature should surely not be used purely instrumentally, as a means to some other end beyond itself. Similarly, if morality is considered of such importance that it needs a place at all in children's education, then some deliberate attention must be paid to the nature of morality with its own peculiar concepts, methodology and truth criteria. It cannot then be regarded merely as a by-product of some other area of study. However, it is important for teachers of literature to be aware of the contribution that they cannot avoid making to the moral development of their pupils.

History and morality

Similar claims could be made for the teaching of moral concepts through history. Children learning about wars arising from religious conflicts, about uprisings, revolts or protest marches, about the treatment in the past of the underprivileged are not normally left with a mere collection of factual information. If they are taught to think historically, their attention must be drawn to the social and moral climate of the period they are concerned with. They must be encouraged to reflect on the motives, aims and intentions of the great figures of the past. And to do this, they become inevitably involved with questions of moral attitudes, feelings and conduct.

It may not be possible and it is certainly not easy to judge the morality of another age. But this should not deter teachers from considering the moral implications of a political or military event or a social phenomenon, partly for the light they throw on our own attitudes. This after all is one of the reasons for learning history. It is often impossible to assess a political or military event in terms of individual motives because the sources simply do not reveal what these were. To take one of the most obvious examples: the events of 1066. We can attempt to assess the personal aims of William and Harold in terms of the spirit of the age. This was an age of warfare in which the most prized possession was land, and the ultimate achievement was to win a kingdom. At the simplest level, William and Harold were rivals for the most distinguished throne and kingdom in northern Europe. As we go into the story in greater detail with older pupils, we reveal both greater historical complexity and a greater scope for raising moral questions. The Normans claimed that Edward the Confessor had nominated William as his heir and had later sent Harold to confirm the bequest and that Harold had bound himself by oath to support William's succession. Moral implications are raised firstly by the suspicion that both points were fabricated and secondly by the binding power of oaths. The English view was that Harold had received Edward's dying bequest, was duly consecrated king and acclaimed by the English. Again, we can consider this expression of the will of the people and the role of representatives of the state and the church.

With such political and military events, it is harder to make the move from purely historical considerations to moral issues than it is with the recurring social issues in history. Slavery is one example. Here we can examine the attitudes of ancient and classical civilizations to an institution on which their economy was totally dependent. Aristotle, for example, writes of the justification and acceptance of slavery in the *Politics*. We can compare classical attitudes with those of the 16th-18th centuries, when trade based on slavery flourished, but without the total dependence of classical times. This would lead to the growth of the movement for abolition and the attitudes that led up to this—all of which throws light on our changing views of man and respect for the individual.

But again we must reiterate that although the contribution of history to moral education is considerable, the concepts and methodology of history are not those of morality. Similar objections could be raised here in relation to moral education via history as were made in our previous discussion of literature, although again teachers must be aware of the moral dimensions of their work in this field.

Religious education and morality

Amongst all the possible curriculum areas which could be used as a basis for moral education, religion is the one claiming most attention, since it is here that greatest confusion has prevailed. In a society like ours, which for many centuries was a predominantly Christian society, where religious institutions were of central importance, morality tended to derive its character and potency from Christian doctrines. In addition, the church played an important part in providing education, so that its legacy still remains in the minds of many educators. Many people today attribute the alleged decline in moral standards amongst the younger generation to the decreasing influence of the church and other religious bodies, thus implying that without faith in a deity, moral values have no firm basis. There are, admittedly, similarities between religion and morality. Both are concerned with attitudes, intentions and questions of value; both appeal to the emotions — guilt, remorse, respect in the case of morality; awe and wonder in the case of religion.

However, as we stressed at the beginning of Chapter 1, to pick out features shared by religion and morality does not mean to say that they are mutually dependent. Hirst (1965b) sees them as two distinct forms of knowledge, with their own concepts, truth criteria and methodology. Dearden too (1968) claims that morality must be independent of religion. Both offer a similar kind of argument to support the case for the autonomy of ethics, namely that to rely on the existence of an omniscient, omnipotent being to tell us what is right or wrong is unjustified, since to obey the commands of such a being without questioning the morality of his commands would be mere compliance or obedience. The moral status of a rule or command does not depend on its source, whether that source be a legal, traditional or religious authority. It has to have its own moral justification. If we therefore talk of the moral nature of God, we must be able to judge and recognize this nature in moral terms. If we have no prior knowledge of what it means to be moral, how can we recognize the moral nature of a deity or of his commands? In other words, morality must be logically prior to any religious claims about the goodness of a deity, as we pointed out in Chapter 1.

Such arguments about the autonomous nature of religion and morality as forms of knowledge can help us to unravel some of the problems of moral and religious education. Hirst (1974) defends the view that because of the very nature of religious claims, all matters of religion should, in a society such as ours which nowadays is very much a religiously pluralist society, be regarded as private. He sees our society as a predominantly secular one because there is no one religious faith adhered to by the majority of people. Because of this pluralism of faith then, every man's faith must be respected. But every man's faith is his own private concern or the concern of his parents, in the case of young children. He does not subscribe to the view that the school should accept the responsibility for providing religious education in the sense that it teaches children a particular faith, and would certainly not accept religious teaching as the vehicle for moral education. In his view, any act of worship at a school assembly is out of place because the tacit assumption is made that children already accept the existence of a deity. However, the school assembly as such provides an occasion where all teachers and pupils meet together. It is one of the rituals of school life and as such exemplifies the values of the school. Provided that the head does not take the opportunity to preach or moralize, this occasion could provide a backcloth for moral education where, for instance, pupils are acquainted with local and community affairs which raise moral issues, are invited to think about them and perhaps to participate in them.

The Schools Council's report on religious education in the primary school entitled *Discovering an Approach* (1977) makes clear that the aims of religious education outlined in the report are geared essentially towards teaching young children about religion, not about morality. The report reminds us that much of our earlier thinking about religion was in terms of making children good, unselfish and considerate towards others. In fact, this seems to be the sentiment expressed in that quotation from the Plowden Report (1967) with which we opened Chapter 1, that spiritual and moral values go hand in hand, a view that we cannot support. The authors of the 1977 report agree that there is morality inside religion in that every religion has its own moral code and that this is part of what children learn in religious studies. But they also point out that morality exists outside religion, that moral beliefs can be held or must be justified without appealing to religion. But just as moral education is freed from religion by this kind of argument, so also is religion freed from morality. In other words, it is or should no longer be shackled with the task of making children good, but rather should have its own intrinsic aim, that of developing in children an understanding of the nature of religion.

This understanding, just as the understanding of literature or history, will in part be developed by an explanation of ethical and moral considerations within the overall framework of that particular curriculum area. This in turn may have an influence on children's moral development and life style, but just as we argued earlier that we should not teach history or literature merely in order to further children's moral understanding, so we should not see religious education as a vehicle for this purpose.

It is possible to go on to discuss further curriculum areas and to show how these might contribute towards moral education. However, it is to be hoped that these few examples suffice to illustrate our basic argument, namely that nearly all subjects can be used for moral education purposes and that, even more important, their morally educative aspects are unavoidable. Again, our contention that moral education is the responsibility of all teachers is underlined.

Counselling and pastoral care

As we saw earlier in considering some alternative ways of making provision for moral education other than introducing it onto the school curriculum as a separate component, Blackham (1974) stressed the importance of guidance within the school. This raises issues about the nature of pastoral care and counselling, both of which have in this country been traditionally part of the task of teachers already in the school rather than the job of a specialist. But recently a need has been felt, especially in larger secondary schools, for specialists with teaching experience to be appointed to the school as counsellors. However, although counselling courses have been running now for more than a decade and many larger schools have counsellors working on the staff either in a full- or part-time capacity, the role of the counsellor is far from clear, as are the major aims of a counselling system. Gill (1967), one of the organizers of the counselling course for experienced teachers at Keele University, sees the development of a pupil's self-concept as one of the important aims of counselling. The assumption behind this is that the individual is of supreme worth in and for himself and that through counselling he can be helped to understand himself, to clarify his self-image and realize the value of his own qualities. This, it could be argued, might provide a valuable first step towards understanding other people, appreciating their feelings and gaining insight into their motives, intentions and sympathies.

Some teachers in this country have been reluctant to see a counselling system introduced into schools, partly because they consider themselves capable of doing this work as part of their normal teaching duties. Still others accept a counsellor, albeit reluctantly, onto the staff, provided his work does not interfere or overlap much with their own, and that he deals only with pupils who are referred to him because of special difficulties. But if counselling is to play an appreciable part in the moral education of pupils, then clearly it must be provided for everyone and be an integral part of their curriculum.

Howden and Dowson (1973) consider that educational and vocational guidance should play an essential part in the school curriculum in that they offer opportunities for taking pupils into partnership in the educational endeavour, making clear to them what choices are open to them so that they can understand the likely consequences of the choices they make. Such guidance programmes may begin in the primary school to help children transfer to secondary level and continue by regular sessions throughout the secondary school. They have worked out a five-year course which has been running now for some years at Earl Marshall School, Sheffield, under the direction of a guidance team. The guidance department, created within the school, has an experienced teacher as head of department, and enlists the services of year and house tutors, the school counsellor, the careers teacher and the local careers officer. The earlier part of the course, designed for first- and second-year pupils, deals largely with factual matters concerning health, community life, school life and so on. The later part, designed for the more senior pupils, includes ethical and moral aspects of life at school, home and work; personal relationships, worthwhile leisure pursuits; responsibilities and obligations and so on.

Schofield (1977) outlines an attempt to introduce an element of guidance and counselling as part of pupils' moral education at a comprehensive school in Berkshire. All senior pupils spend some time learning about their environment, the occupational choices available to them and the likely consequences of the choices they might make. In this way it is hoped that by the time they leave school they will have developed a degree of self-esteem which will enable them to feel valued as individuals capable of making an informed choice rather than simply being directed by teachers, a careers officer or counsellor.

Summary and conclusions

We have argued in this chapter that moral education is the concern and responsibility of every teacher and that all teacher-pupil interaction contributes inevitably towards pupils' moral learning and can be geared to contribute towards their moral education. We have shown how moral education can be treated as an independent element in its own right and have also pointed out the contribution that can be made to it by other curriculum areas as well as being reflected through the social climate and organization of the school. Since moral issues are by nature controversial, many teachers may fear that by deliberately undertaking any work in this area, they will run the risk of indoctrinating their pupils, perhaps even unwittingly. The unfortunate and undesirable implications of indoctrination are not to be denied, as we have already seen, and it is therefore of utmost importance that the teacher accepts all content as provisional, and that, as well as encouraging pupils to hold up their values and beliefs to rational scrutiny, he is prepared to do the same himself.

However we choose to cater for children's moral education, we must remember that some coherence and harmony must exist between the various channels open to us. The structure and social climate of the school must reflect the aims of any teaching programme whether it be through existing curriculum areas, through counselling or guidance programmes, or through moral education as a curriculum subject in its own right. It is to a consideration of several projects in moral education currently in operation in schools that we shall turn in the next chapter.

CHAPTER 7

CURRICULUM PROJECTS IN MORAL EDUCATION

Although many secondary schools are still making provision through some kind of humanities programme or through already established curriculum areas, there are some teachers who, like John Wilson, see a place for moral education in its own right on the curriculum. It was to meet this need that three major projects in moral education have been developed and it is to a discussion of these that we now turn.

The work of the Farmington Trust

The Farmington Trust Research Unit, with John Wilson as its director, was set up in 1965 to conduct research into moral education. Since its first publication in 1967, several more works have been produced for the guidance of teachers, educators and researchers. So far no material has been made available for use by pupils in schools though Wilson is currently working on an introductory textbook, *First Steps in Morality*, which should be available shortly.

As we have already seen, Wilson makes strong claims for teaching morality as a subject in its own right, for "to treat morality as a kind of addendum or fringe topic is to court disaster". He argues forcefully that there are right answers to moral problems and right ways of arriving at them. In other words, it is evading the issue and being irresponsible to suggest that all moral solutions are up to the individual and that one view is as good as another. We must instead give pupils a clear idea that appropriate and valid solutions can be reached by the use of a coherent methodology. But this cannot be picked up incidentally; pupils need to be taught how to think morally just as they have to be helped to think mathematically or scientifically. And this is too important and complex a matter to be left to chance; we cannot hope that children will learn to think morally while they are studying literature or history, or even while they are being encouraged to think seriously about social or personal problems of a controversial nature which stimulate an interest in ethical and moral issues. While such material and methods are useful, in Wilson's view, they fall short of offering a rational methodology for settling the controversial issues under discussion. Since teachers cannot give their pupils right answers to moral issues, they are bound to provide them with the skills to do the job themselves, that is, to equip them with the appropriate powers of reasoning so that in later life they do not find themselves in a moral vacuum and have to turn to authority to make decisions for them.

Wilson's main aim is to develop in pupils the kind of moral autonomy that we discussed earlier in this book, that is, one which enables them to use a rational methodology for arriving at moral decisions and making moral choices of their own. To achieve this end, there are several things he believes we should try to do. We must aim firstly at helping pupils understand that moral thinking is a subject in its own right and that there are appropriate ways of arriving at solutions to moral issues. Secondly we need to initiate pupils into skills and techniques which they can adopt and use independently to cope with real-life situations. In doing this we must further wean them away from inappropriate methods, such as reliance on authority, on majority decisions or group pressures. In order to achieve all this we must finally try to ensure that they have every opportunity to understand fully and to use particular moral qualities and skills that in Wilson's view go to make up the truly morally educated person.

Direct teaching methods appear to Wilson to be the most appropriate means of achieving these aims, but clearly in the interests of variety they need to be supplemented by other methods, such as drama, discussion, role playing, participation in practical class activities, provided that these methods retain their supporting role.

One of the merits of the methods Wilson recommends is that they are practical and easily adopted by any experienced teacher; there is no need for any extensive retraining. They can be practised in all types of educational institution from primary schools to sixth-form colleges or institutes of further education. Wilson himself claims to have used them over an age range of nine to twenty-one.

In attempting to produce an operational definition of what it means to be a morally educated person, Wilson has drawn up a list of moral components, some of which we have considered already, those qualities, skills and attitudes typical of someone who is morally educated. Global terms such as "sensitivity", "maturity" and so on he regards as too vague to give teachers any specific guidelines, so instead he breaks down the complex term "morality" into more specific components, each of which is given a technical label, derived from classical Greek, and represents specific moral attributes, as Wilson sees them.

The following is a brief descriptive summary of his scheme. PHIL is an attitude denoting concern for other people, including showing respect for others, treating them fairly and according them equal rights (PHIL 1), as well as showing benevolence towards them and being able to make their interests part of one's own (PHIL 2). PHIL encompasses four main elements — having the concept of a person; believing that others are worthy of respect; feeling respect towards them; and finally acting with respect and benevolence towards them. EMP signifies the ability to be aware of feelings and emotions in others (EMP 1) and in oneself (EMP 2). GIG refers to factual knowledge about moral issues, for instance, knowing that alcohol or drugs are likely to impair driving performance and to cloud judgement and thus possibly to cause harm to others (GIG 1). A further aspect of this kind of moral knowledge is knowing how to do certain things, for example how to sympathize with, console or assist others (GIG 2).

In order to bring to bear one's respect for others (PHIL), one's awareness of their feelings (EMP) and one's knowledge of the facts relevant to a particular situation (GIG), we need to develop a further set of skills—KRAT. This implies firstly being alert to a situation, thinking seriously and thoroughly about it and committing oneself to a particular course of action which one thinks ought to be taken (KRAT 1). But since it is possible, of course, for a person to decide how he ought to act but to be too frightened, embarrassed or inhibited to do so, a further necessary aspect is to translate one's decisions into courses of action (KRAT 2).

Two additional concepts must be mentioned before we can describe Wilson's "moral equation", his formula representing what is logically required for morally educated behaviour. DIK, the ability to formulate principles relating to other people's interests and PHRON, relating to personal prudence and ideals, represent stages reached at which a person can make a firm moral decision. The formula is represented as follows:

$$\left. \begin{array}{l} \text{PHIL 1 \& 2} \\ \text{EMP 1 \& 2} \\ \text{GIG 1 \& 2} \end{array} \right\} + \text{KRAT 1 lead to DIK/PHRON;}$$

DIK/PHRON + KRAT 2 lead to right action.

Thus a morally educated person is one who has regard for other people's interests and is sensitive to their feelings; he is logically consistent, knows the facts relevant to specific moral cases and is able to translate his skills into appropriate action.

Wilson recommends that teachers work through the components, explaining them to pupils with constant reference to examples from everyday life and drawing where possible on material brought in by the pupils. Pupils' grasp of the concepts should be tested periodically to try to ensure that they are not merely learning by rote. Rather than worldwide political or social situations, familiar everyday examples should be used to illustrate the various components, since pupils are more likely to be personally involved in such matters and thus to be more emotionally committed to solving moral problems raised by them.

One useful technique suggested by Wilson, once the whole range of moral components has been worked through, is to discuss cases of "moral misdoing", to see which particular components were missing and were responsible for the unfortunate outcome. Such an approach would help to consolidate pupils' understanding of the moral components as well as encouraging them to consider how they themselves might have acted or thought they ought to have acted in a comparable situation. Such examples will inevitably contain instances of unreasonable or inappropriate ways of thinking about morality, such as reference to an outside authority, to one's own personal preferences or intuition or to expediency. Discussing the validity of these inappropriate ways of moral thinking, with reference to the moral components, is likely to show pupils the inadequacy of their own reasoning and, it is hoped, guide them towards more adequate methods. This is reminiscent of Kohlberg's practice of presenting children with arguments one stage above their own in the hope that they will recognize the illogicality of their previous moral reasoning.

As we have already said, direct teaching methods play a major part in Wilson's scheme, supported by group discussion, drama, role playing and simulation techniques as well as the practical application of what pupils have learnt in the form of organizing group activities and sharing responsibility for them. But whatever method is adopted, language is seen as of essential importance in communication. As we suggested in Chapter 2, language is logically bound up with rational thinking, with working out reasons for our behaviour on the one hand (particularly important for KRAT 1) and also for conveying our intentions to others and showing sympathy for them (EMP 1, GIG 2). Language assumes such central importance for Wilson that, as we have noted earlier, he goes so far as to claim that without language there could be no such thing as morality. He insists that particular attention be devoted to developing children's language skills so that they can express themselves accurately and precisely and can discuss sensibly with others without interrupting or introducing irrelevant, facetious or sarcastic remarks. Appropriate discussion techniques which have their own constitutive and guiding rules should become part of every child's repertory of social skills. In fact real discussion where participants listen to others, respect their right to express opinion and wait their turn to contribute gives a valid and useful opportunity for applying the moral components they have learnt elsewhere, for instance PHIL, EMP and GIG.

We discussed in the last chapter how Wilson sees the structure of the school complementing a programme of direct teaching of morality and saw that by implication a democratically run school was considered conducive to moral learning and moral autonomy. In order now to link what has been said here about the nature of moral components with the democratic running of a school we need to consider the nature of rules and contracts, since any society must be rule-governed.

All societies must have rules and contracts although the difference between societies is reflected in the function of these rules. A liberal society, like a democratically run school, has a framework of rules to protect individuals and to give them enough security and freedom to learn to think for themselves. A totalitarian society, like an authoritarian school, has a rigid set of rules designed to direct and dictate to individuals at every step so that their minds are made up for them. Within a democratic framework, rules have no ends in themselves; there is always a reason behind them and if this becomes outdated or irrelevant, the rule no longer applies and should be dispensed with. School rules referring to running in corridors or walking on the right on staircases clearly have a point whereas rules about dress or hairstyle are more debatable and it is often difficult, if not impossible, to justify them. Adherence to rules in school, for which reasons must be made clear to pupils, is demanded by concern for the interests of other people (PHIL)—we avoid running indoors for fear of harming others. Awareness of what might follow if rules are infringed involves anticipating the consequences of one's actions (GIG). In a democratically run school, pupils need to learn the distinction between a person being in authority to see that rationally based rules are adhered to, and one exercising power to enforce rules, whether or not they have a point. But they also need the opportunity to voice their dissatisfaction with rules and the chance to discuss and perhaps change them by appropriate methods. All this is in keeping with what is taught about moral components — a way of translating theory into practice, in fact.

Wilson's project is undoubtedly to be commended for its stress on the importance of helping children to form their own moral code as a result of rational thought and consideration. Moral autonomy is particularly important, as we have emphasized throughout this book, in a society where the young are at the mercy of group pressures, the power of fashion and various influences of the mass media. His notion of a morally educated person (sometimes referred to as the Farmington Man) is in accord with our outline discussed earlier, although perhaps its emphasis on certain components is a little different. The view of a morally educated person that emerges from our discussion and from Wilson's account encompasses three broad areas: intellectual factors concerned with rational thinking, knowledge of facts relevant to a moral situation and awareness of alternatives and consequences of an act; social skills required to put such knowledge into practice with due regard for others; and the emotional or affective component involving not only a knowledge and understanding of others' feelings but also care and concern for them and the ability to respond emotionally oneself to moral issues.

It is this last area that we should want to draw more attention to than Wilson appears to do. He has been criticized (Woods 1969) for propounding his own idea of a morally educated person rather than *the* morally educated person, but this comment could surely be made of any ideal picture. No writer seriously engaged in a discussion of what it means to be morally educated sets out to put forward a definitive view — and this Wilson and his co-workers do not claim to do. After all, to claim to have found a definitive view would imply that there is some end point or destination that could be reached. And if this were the case, moral education and moral development would, theoretically at some point, be completed — a view we have already shown to be misguided.

We have argued elsewhere that any programme of moral education must be planned with due regard to stages of children's moral development, and it is here surely that the main shortcoming of the Farmington Trust project lies. Nowhere does Wilson mention the importance for teachers to link the complexity of moral concepts and the nature of moral argument with developmental stages such as those outlined by Kohlberg (1966) and discussed in an earlier chapter. Perhaps Wilson envisages in practice some sort of spiral moral education programme in the manner of Bruner's spiral curriculum (1960) where moral components are dealt with on a cyclical basis with examples and arguments appropriate to children's level of moral thinking, but this is not made explicit. Admittedly, Wilson declares that his objective is to give the teacher "a set of concepts, categories and lines which he alone can know best how to apply to his particular task". This leaves teachers free to plan the use of the material offered as they think appropriate but, nevertheless, more specific guidance would surely be welcome.

A further difficulty in the use of such project material, and one of which Wilson is very well aware, lies in the assessment of children's progress. We can, as he suggests, periodically test their understanding of moral concepts, but to assess the effect of any such programme on progress or development in morality and moral conduct is a totally different and far more complicated matter. More recently (1973) Wilson has outlined some of the problems of assessing morality but so far has few guidelines to offer the practising teacher.

To point out the difficulties and limitations of a project such as this, however, is not to deny its value. If its main impact on those who become familiar with the material is to stimulate further thought and debate in such a significant area, then it must be recognized as a valid contribution to our thinking about moral education.

Schools Council Project in Moral Education: Lifeline

The Lifeline material and accompanying books were prepared by McPhail, Ungoed-Thomas and Chapman and first published in 1972. The overall general aim of the programme is to help pupils to adopt a considerate style of life. McPhail argues (1972) that an exclusively philosophical approach to moral education, consisting largely of an analytical approach to moral concepts, is too far removed from practice and in addition neglects the problem of motivation. That is, it fails to probe into what disposes, moves or drives an individual to act in the way that he does. Instead, he claims that the kind of moral education we need to provide, particularly for adolescents, is that which is concerned with how people live their lives, how they see themselves and treat others. They need to understand their own behaviour, its consequences and the effects it may have on other people.

The objectives of the preliminary work before the project was finally formulated were fourfold: .

1   To establish a basic criterion of relevance of approach and materials in order to meet the needs of adolescents.

2   To find out from pupils what these needs are.

3   To decide what adolescents mean by "good" and "bad" as

applied to behaviour and personal relationships and to proceed from these findings to establish what *ought* to be done.

4   To explore the motivation behind pupils' behaviour and to build this into the project material and methods.

The preliminary work itself consisted of three major pilot studies carried out to establish the views of secondary school pupils on several crucial issues. The first took the form of a survey amongst 800 boys and girls in the thirteen to eighteen age range who were each asked to give one example of a situation where an adult had treated them well and one where they had felt badly treated by an adult. An analysis of their replies showed that "good" behaviour on the part of an adult most frequently denoted a readiness to allow adolescents a reasonable degree of freedom; to help them with problems or difficulties; to listen to them and try to understand what they had to say; to show a sense of humour; to set a good example themselves and, most important, to show consideration for others. Adults who treated young people badly were typified as those who imposed unreasonable restrictions on them, who made unreasonable or impossible demands and inflicted punishment unjustly. Furthermore adults like this were seen to behave in a hostile or superior manner, to be constantly finding fault and to be insincere, by not living up to the standards they propose for younger people.

The second survey, like the first, was carried out with the help of Argyle, and involved 458 boys and girls, again from the thirteen to eighteen age range. They were asked to complete a questionnaire showing categories of good and bad adult behaviour derived from the first study and to show which examples they had personally experienced and how frequently. The overall conclusion derived from an analysis of replies from these two surveys was that there was general agreement amongst adolescents about what constituted good or bad behaviour on the part of adults and that treatment by others during the formative years was likely to have a profound influence on the adolescent's own behaviour.

The third survey explored the way in which adolescents perceived the behaviour of their peers and these results reflected a similar finding to those in the first survey. That is, good peer behaviour consisted mainly in showing consideration for others and vice versa.

It was on the basis of these findings that the framework of the Lifeline Project was built. McPhail had claimed that to construct a moral education programme starting from what is known about the needs of adolescents is far more appropriate than setting up an ideal picture of a morally educated person and teaching pupils to understand the moral components involved. His approach is then the reverse of that adopted by Wilson in the Farmington Trust Project. McPhail tries to show how we can arrive at some idea of what ought to be done or what the good or moral life should consist of from an understanding of what people want. In other words, he sets out to show how an "ought" can be derived from an "is", arguing that we ought to treat others with consideration for their needs, interests and feelings, but in order to do so, we must identify these by empirical enquiry.

The philosophy underlying the Lifeline Project is that the basic form of moral motivation lies in treating others with consideration which will not only prove intrinsically rewarding but will also result in one's being treated similarly by others, the kind of prudential approach to ethics that we criticized in Chapter 1.

The practical implementation of the programme is derived from the view that moral education cannot be taught as a separate entity, since living the considerate life is a matter concerning the whole life of the school. The programme is thus conceived as one which spans a five-year course and is strongly backed by the organization and structure of the school, making for its democratic running, as described earlier in this book. The materials provided for use with pupils are graded according to the needs of pupils of different ages, thus showing how teachers can use and build on the immediate personal needs of younger pupils and gradually work outwards to deal with wider social and moral issues, less intimately related to the individual pupil.

The material, together with teachers' handbooks, published in the form of three sets of discussion cards which all depict a moral situation or dilemma, is based upon the findings from the three surveys showing the main areas of adolescent concern in the field of interpersonal and moral issues. The first set of materials, "In Other People's Shoes", presents personal and intimate situations involving two or three people, set usually in the home or immediate neighbourhood, thus providing younger secondary school pupils with the kind of problem they must inevitably have encountered in their own everyday lives. "Proving the Rule", the next set of materials, also depicts situations set in the immediate surroundings but involving more people, so that problems of group conflict, relationships within groups and personal identity can arise. Finally, the third part, "What Would You Have Done?", deals with actual incidents that occurred during the period 1900 to 1970. These present much broader social and moral problems than those encountered in the first two sets, for example, problems of racial conflict and discrimination, drug addiction and vandalism. The material is thus graded so that it can be used progressively to match the needs of pupils and their level of understanding. The first set of materials begins by getting younger pupils involved in thinking about situations and problems already real to them, thus attempting to capitalize on existing motivation. As pupils gain more experience in thinking about situations from other people's points of view, they are gradually introduced to material demanding a broader perspective, but nevertheless the overall aim remains the same—to help pupils to adopt a considerate life style.

Although the material is thus graded in order to enable teachers to begin with younger pupils' needs and concerns, it is not intended that "In Other People's Shoes" should be disregarded completely after the first two years. It can continue to be used alongside the other material to support and reinforce it. It is left to teachers to select appropriate materials from all three sets, as they think appropriate, as is also the choice of teaching technique. A variety of techniques is suggested: discussion, role play, socio-drama, writing plays, dialogues, stories and even painting or drawing. McPhail stresses the importance of responding emotionally to situations; and since some pupils would feel restricted in their responses if these were permitted only in verbal form, other modes of expression are to be encouraged. Not only must pupils be allowed to choose the medium they prefer but teachers also should feel free to adopt the technique they feel most at home with. The only approach which is not in keeping with the aims of the project is a didactic authoritarian one where teachers attempt to provide pupils with right or wrong answers to moral problems and try to direct them to adopt these answers to guide their own way of living.

Although clearly it is quite incompatible with the aims of any moral education programme for teachers to force their views onto pupils, McPhail is firmly convinced that pupils should be able to identify clearly teachers' value positions. Adolescents in the preliminary survey had claimed that for a person to refuse to state what he thinks about an issue while expecting others to do so is to adopt a superior position in which the others are not treated with due respect as persons. In any case, if teachers do not give some indication of their own values, children are being deprived of the opportunity to experience value positions different from those they have already met. Parents' values may differ from those of teachers, but far from being undesirable, this may well be a stimulus to productive moral thinking. For these reasons, then, McPhail is opposed to complete teacher neutrality although he admits that to be a short-term neutral chairman may work to good advantage in certain contexts.

In addition to the overall aim of helping pupils to lead a considerate life, McPhail points out several other advantages which might follow from the adoption of a programme such as Lifeline. If some attempt is made to meet the personal needs of pupils, they are likely to be relieved to a degree of some of the strain and anxiety inevitably engendered in a large secondary school. Further, if pupils feel that an attempt is being made to meet their needs, they are likely to be more highly motivated and thus present fewer problems of behaviour for the teacher. Thirdly, developing the social skills implicit in such a programme can be a sophisticated intellectual matter and highly satisfying on that account.

Unlike John Wilson, McPhail is opposed to providing a place for moral education as a separate subject mainly because he sees it as the concern of every teacher as well as those few chosen and specially trained experts. Since all teachers, whatever their specialization, have an inescapable responsibility in the field of moral education, so all teachers should have the right to participate in a programme if they so wish.

His suggestion for the implementation of the Lifeline Project is essentially school-based. All teachers within a school who are interested and wish to take part should meet together to establish first of all which departments will be involved and then to plan in detail who will be responsible for each part of the programme. To do this, each member of the team must fully understand how the separate elements of the programme are related and what the unifying themes and principles are. Their planning would include selecting material appropriate to the needs and interests of different age groups as well as relating it to the other areas of the curriculum with which they are concerned. A team approach of this nature would be able to make full use of the variety of teaching skills and techniques of those involved. Furthermore, when teachers are collaborating and cooperating as a team rather than working as individuals, which most teachers do most of the time, pupils have the opportunity to see them showing consideration for one another, sharing responsibilities and offering one another support. Thus they are in a way showing living examples of the moral qualities they hope their pupils will eventually learn to practise. McPhail has in fact worked out an example of a five-year plan showing how the Lifeline programme can be slotted into a school timetable without unduly disrupting or intruding on existing subject provision.

As we saw in the previous chapter, McPhail argues in addition that no programme of moral education would be complete if it did not consider ways in which the life of the school in general can help to promote moral development. We have already discussed his suggestions for running a school along democratic lines in order to allow pupils the opportunity for working with others, understanding them and communicating with them — in short creating a context in which they can learn to live a considerate life.

In his introductory chapter, McPhail states "moral education is a field of study in its own right, with its own concepts, skills and techniques", yet later on he argues strongly against timetabling moral education as a separate curriculum component. These views seem perhaps at first contradictory, since it is difficult to see how the unique concepts and techniques typical of an area of study or form of experience can be singled out if that area is not regarded as an independent area on the curriculum. Wilson's method of teaching children what moral thinking implies is, as we have seen, to analyse systematically the qualities that he considers to be characteristic of and essential to a morally educated person. McPhail's approach, by its very nature, rules out this method, since he set out to discover what adolescents considered to be examples of good or bad behaviour and thus attempted to deduce from those findings what, in the eyes of young people, characterized a good person (morally good, it is assumed). And it is here that two of the main weaknesses of the project lie. Firstly, the findings showed that adolescents preferred adults who lead a considerate life, but the jump made from this empirical finding is considerable. Leading a considerate life is then equated with being morally mature and the assumption made on the basis of this reasoning is that to educate children morally means to teach them to lead a considerate life. But on what grounds can it be argued that a considerate style of life does involve a set of ideals that guide moral conduct and moral actions? McPhail offers a detailed *description* of the qualities a considerate adult shows, but gives no analysis of the moral components a pupil needs to understand in order to distinguish between, for example, considerate behaviour that is truly moral and that which is merely expedient. We stressed in Chapter 1 the importance of a person's intentions to the morality of an act; this approach appears to ignore them. In addition, as Richard Peters (1973a) points out, consideration for others is emphasized at the expense of other aspects of morality, such as courage, determination, justice, impartiality—all qualities which the authors tend to ignore.

Secondly, to try to arrive at what *ought* to be done from what *is* the case is to fall into the trap of the naturalistic fallacy. To derive an "ought" from an "is" is not possible, as we saw in Chapter 2. As it happened, the adolescents in McPhail's survey tended to agree on what characterized a considerate type of adult and presumably few people would want to argue against cultivating the qualities they found desirable and sympathetic. But that still does not mean that simply because adolescents find certain qualities desirable, we ought to teach them to emulate these qualities. Majority decisions merely tell us what is the case, not what ought to be. If for example, the findings had indicated that young people prefer a strictly authoritarian adult who directs other people's lives, does not allow them any freedom of choice and forces them to conform to certain immutable patterns of behaviour, would it still follow that these characteristics *ought* to be fostered in pupils? The example should serve to make clear the illogicality in such reasoning. The approach adopted by the authors of this project is reminiscent of that of empiricist epistemology, discussed earlier in this book, namely, that to find answers to moral questions, we have to observe how people behave. The shortcomings of this approach are, we hope, obvious by now.

On the other hand, one of the main attractions of the Lifeline Project is that it attempts to provide secondary teachers with the sort of framework within which to work out a five-year programme, based on pupils' stages of development. McPhail claims that one of the major criteria to be employed in deciding which material to use with pupils is the stage of development they have reached rather than their chronological age. Accordingly the material is made available in such a way that teachers can select from all three sets that which is most appropriate to a class or group of pupils within a specific school. We have already seen how the problems and situations posed range from those which are near to a younger pupil's experience to those which have worldwide implications.

However, the research team gives no guidance at all on how teachers can recognize a pupil's stage of development or readiness for certain types of moral argument. Moreover, McPhail seems to be confident that moral development will follow from group discussion, role playing and so on. Unlike Kohlberg, he does not make clear how important the quality of the moral argument used is, if it is to lead to progress towards a later stage of moral reasoning. It seems a great pity that the wealth of research material on stages of moral development has been neglected. To have linked a programme such as this with Kohlberg's findings, for example, would have given the whole project the firm psychological basis that it needs.

Although it is nowhere explicitly stated, McPhail's project seems to rest on a social learning theory approach to moral development. His argument that children learn considerate behaviour by being treated with consideration by others is reminiscent of the work on modelling carried out by Bandura and others (1963) and discussed in an earlier chapter. The suggestion that much moral behaviour is caught rather than taught is apparent in McPhail's discussion of the importance of teacher cooperation. As we have already mentioned, McPhail regrets that the model of adult behaviour presented to pupils by their teachers is normally one of solitary self-reliance, and he stresses the importance of team cooperation as a means of presenting another kind of model. In discussing forms of motivation for moral behaviour, he makes quite clear the importance of a second characteristic feature of the social learning approach, namely that of reward or reinforcement. One of the main motives for treating others with consideration, he argues, is that "such behaviour is pleasant in itself and can be rewarding". We also tend to receive general social approval and to be treated by others in the way that we should wish. On the other hand, failure to treat others with consideration may result in unpleasant consequences for ourselves; we therefore adopt a considerate approach towards others in order to avoid an unpleasant outcome. However to base a theory of moral learning or moral education upon the notion of reward raises serious questions. Are children merely learning to conform to certain standards out of expediency or because moral conduct has become a habit rather than because they have understood what it means to act morally and have worked out their own principles? In all, the Lifeline Project seems to concentrate on moral behaviour and conduct and pays insufficient attention to other elements which, as we have argued earlier, are of supreme importance, namely moral reasoning and moral feeling. It is possible to act considerately towards others without really caring about why one is doing so or really respecting other people's feelings. EMP seems to be a very meagre ingredient in the whole project though perhaps this judgement is a little harsh.

Assessment of the success or effectiveness of the project, as always, presents problems. After a three-month trial period, 300 boys and girls using the "sensitivity" items from the first set of materials showed a 50% increase in responses to questions referring to other people's needs and feelings in a written test, when compared with a control group who had not used the material.

But this would be a naive way of claiming any advance in their moral education. Morality cannot be assessed in this way, since it is so complex; answers to written questions might merely be revealing what pupils think their teachers want them to say or, at best, indicate that teachers have been successful in making them interested in moral and social issues.

To criticize such an ambitious project, perfectly sincere in its aims, with concern for adolescents as its cornerstone, does not mean however to reject it. Research and evaluation go hand in hand and if no feedback were offered in the form of criticism, no advance would be possible. If at the moment the Lifeline Project has succeeded in stimulating teachers' interest and arousing their concern for the moral education of their pupils, its value is not to be underestimated.

Schools Council Moral Education 8-13 Project: Startline

The Schools Council Moral Education Project team, also under the directorship of McPhail, is currently working on materials for use with children in the middle years of schooling. Experience with the Lifeline Project had convinced the team that social and moral education should form an important and essential part of education for all children and should ideally begin in the early years.

As with the Lifeline Project, the Startline materials are not intended for use in separate moral education lessons, but are seen as a potential stimulus for work in English, drama, environmental and social studies, and religious education. It provides a basic structure for several years' work and can be extended and adapted to suit the needs of particular classes and particular schools.

Startline, a handbook of moral education in the middle years, is due for publication early in 1978. Further materials, including six illustrated booklets of short stories with suggested activities, a series of photographs and posters and other illustrated cards are being prepared for publication in April 1978.

The Humanities Curriculum Project

The Humanities Curriculum Project, sponsored by the Schools' Council and the Nuffield Foundation, and set up in 1967 under the directorship of Lawrence Stenhouse, differs from the other two projects discussed in this chapter in that it was not designed as a moral education programme as such. We find therefore no analysis of what it means to be a morally educated person and no discussion of the place of moral education on the curriculum. Stenhouse (1970) refers to the subject of the project as "values education" which is the term used in some American programmes where we should perhaps normally refer to moral education (Kuhmerker 1974). However, the very aim of the project, "to develop an understanding of social situations and human acts and of the controversial value issues which they raise" (Stenhouse 1970) reveals its concern with the kind of moral reasoning we have been discussing throughout this book.

The project was initially designed for teachers working in the field of humanities with adolescents of average and below-average ability and aimed to extend the range of choice of teaching methods open to teachers by offering them materials, training and research support. The project was in fact initiated in anticipation of the raising of the school-leaving age when secondary teachers would for the first time be facing full classes of fifth-year pupils, many of whom were at school not from choice but rather against their will. Since many such pupils would already be rejecting traditional school subjects, the project team set out to select material that would be educationally worthwhile and that would be seen by pupils as relevant to their own lives. It was with these criteria in mind that the idea of human issues of universal concern was arrived at. Stenhouse (1970) explains that the criterion for selection of material was not that pupils were already interested in such issues (though of course they might be) but that they ought to be interested. McPhail, we remember, tackled the problem of content from a different perspective, selecting issues which adolescents in his surveys claimed already to be concerned with and to consider important in their own lives.

One of the major premises of the Humanities Curriculum Project was that controversial issues should be handled in the classroom with adolescents. If issues are controversial, there are clearly no right answers, clear-cut solutions or undivided attitudes that can be reached. In fact the definition used of the term controversial was that it was concerned with issues that involve problems about which different individuals or groups suggest different courses of action, an issue for which there can be no universally accepted solution. The issues selected by the project team clearly meet these criteria; for example, "law and order" or "relationships between the sexes". The other major premises stated were as follows:

1   That the teacher accepts the need to submit his teaching in controversial areas to the criterion of neutrality, that is, that he regards it as part of his responsibility not to promote his own view.

2   That the mode of enquiry in controversial areas should have discussion rather than instruction as its core.

3   That the discussion should protect divergence of view among participants, rather than try to achieve consensus.

4   That the teacher as chairman of the discussion should have responsibility for quality and standards in learning.

The team suggested that discussion groups should ideally consist of half classes of about fifteen to sixteen pupils and that about four to six hours per week should be devoted to the project. The materials supplied in packs are meant to provide foundation collections in each of nine areas: War and Society; Education; The Family; Relationships between the Sexes; People and Work; Poverty; Law and Order; Living in Cities; Race. Each pack contains a selection of materials relevant to the particular issue, such as newspaper cuttings, short stories, poems, pictures, film material and so on, designed to provide evidence around which discussion can be centred. Clearly such materials do not act as evidence in an empirical sense — they cannot settle a value issue, since ethical problems are not resolved by reference to what is the case. To call such material evidence means in this context that it provides illustration of matters under discussion; the analogy, as we suggested earlier, is with legal rather than scientific evidence. It serves to present controversial issues in concrete, everyday terms and calls for judgement and interpretation on the part of those using it. Teachers can add their own materials to extend these collections and to ensure that there is always something of current impact available. Humanities teachers must of course be familiar with the contents of their resource packs so that they can select something appropriate if the discussion is becoming arid or irrelevant or to provide another side to the argument that pupils might have overlooked, or merely to provide information that they need in order to take a proper view of the issue.

The role of the teacher, which will be discussed in greater depth later in this chapter, is very different from a traditional one where instruction or class teaching are the principal pedagogical styles. Since enquiry and discussion methods replace direct teaching, learning should take on a more active nature, with the teacher acting as neutral chairman in the discussion group. The nature of the teacher's authority is thrown into relief; he can see himself no longer as an authority on certain subject content who can in the end provide answers. Instead his authority rests on his skill in guiding the discussion, maintaining standards of learning and in his sensitivity to the atmosphere of the group. Some teachers in fact, who have been used to the traditional role of subject specialist and who have derived security from subject identity, may feel threatened and insecure as a result of the changing demands made upon them, as Bernstein suggests (1971). Stenhouse, however, hoped that teachers would regard the whole area of values education as the opportunity to acquire a new identity, since the area itself is quite new as a formal category and does not in fact usurp any existing subject areas.

The major responsibility of the teacher as discussion group chairman is twofold. Firstly, he must create conditions and opportunities which encourage pupils to develop their own understanding of value issues relevant to human behaviour and experience. Secondly, his task is to see that the rules and procedures of discussion are observed so that pupils listen to one another without interrupting, in order that the enquiry may be not only orderly but fruitful. He must encourage pupils to express their views freely so that divergence of views is protected. As neutral chairman, he refrains from expressing his own views, but instead listens, introduces new evidence when appropriate and summarizes at the end of a discussion. He controls interruptions and encourages pupils to concentrate on interpreting the materials and discussing with one another rather than addressing their remarks to him.

Inevitably, the role of the pupil changes from one where, in much class teaching, he is the more or less passive recipient of teacher-selected information. Pupils working on the Humanities Curriculum Project have to learn to take responsibility for their own participation; this implies a far more active part than they have perhaps been used to. It involves relying not on the teacher's authority to reach a solution but in weighing and interpreting evidence relevant to the issue under discussion and in tolerating an outcome that does not produce consensus. This is in fact for many pupils a difficult procedure to learn, but what they do learn eventually is that they are regarded as people who have a right to express their views and that these views are respected. This aspect of the work is particularly important for the group of pupils for whom the project was originally intended — fourteen to sixteen year olds of average and below-average ability — since these are people who often tended to be labelled unfavourably, for example, "Newsom Children", "early leavers", "the less bright". To label or typify pupils in this way is to treat them collectively, rather than as individuals who are important for their own personal views or human interests, and thus to fail to regard them with due respect as persons (Downey 1977). To be treated with consideration and respect by others is an important element in moral education. To feel respected as a person helps pupils to treat others similarly. Procedures adopted in the discussion and enquiry method can make just as important a contribution to the moral education of pupils as do the exercise of judgement and interpretation of material relevant to the controversial issues. But what pupils learn here is to form judgements based on their own reasons rather than on received opinions. The emphasis placed on enquiry and discussion procedures allows for the development of the kind of rational approach to moral issues that we discussed in an earlier chapter.

The value of the Humanities Curriculum Project lies partly in its impact upon other curriculum areas. Enquiry and discussion methods may well be adopted by teachers not concerned with the project itself. Eggleston (1976) refers to the contagion effect of curriculum innovation and mentions the influence of the Humanities Curriculum Project upon teaching methods elsewhere in the school. MacDonald (1973) points out that the introduction of non-authoritarian teaching styles within a school may prove attractive to teachers in subject areas that tend to overlap with the topics in the Humanities Project. Elliott (1975) explores the relevance of the aims and principles of the Humanities Project for vocational guidance within the school. He claims that to develop pupils' understanding of controversial social issues through the medium of reflective discussion where divergence of views is protected is consonant with one of the central aims of vocational guidance, namely to help school-leavers make rational decisions about publicly controversial issues in the world of work, such as strikes, the role of unions, equal pay, work and leisure and so on.

Early attempts at evaluating the effects of the project (Schools Council 1970) showed not only some improvement in language skills but also a shift towards the development of qualities we have highlighted as important in characterizing the morally educated person. It was found that pupils tended to replace expediency by a conscientious attitude towards moral issues, reflecting an advance in moral development in Kohlberg's terms. From being blindly obedient, they showed greater self-assertion and a considerably stronger awareness of social issues than they had previously done. Although many pupils found their new role initially difficult to accept and tried to force the teacher back into his traditional role, once they had accepted the change, many welcomed the new approach in spite of its shock effect.

The Humanities Curriculum Project was designed not as a moral education programme for all secondary school pupils, to take account of developmental stages, but to develop an understanding of certain topics in terms of their relevance to young people who were soon to leave school. The prime aim was to help fourteen to sixteen year olds through discussion to come to understand certain controversial areas in such a way that they felt committed to and responsible for their own decisions and would learn how to handle relevant evidence and to develop the kind of critical awareness we have stressed as important throughout this book. However, what has not been made clear by the project team is what precisely achievements like understanding or judgement imply in the context in which they are used. What would it mean, for example, to understand issues related to the family? It could be argued that understanding is more or less profound according to the number of perspectives a person can bring to bear on the issue. In this case it would involve perhaps a grasp of the facts about subcultural differences in family patterns or an appreciation of the conflicts tha go on in family life from an emotional point of view. In practice it is differences in family patterns or an appreciation of the conflicts that promote or indeed whether understanding is being promoted if they have no clear idea of what form this understanding might take. Yet again, no clear analysis is offered of what is involved in making a moral judgement. The question of whether pupils are able to make appropriate moral judgements without direct teacher guidance raises considerable doubt in the minds of some practitioners. Teachers themselves need to be clear about the nature and status of moral judgements and about the procedures for carrying on the kind of debate required by the project.

Wringe (1974) finds that, by contrast, the work of the Farmington Trust provides a good example of an attempt to analyse clearly what morality is and what is entailed in becoming a moral agent. Both the Humanities Curriculum Project and the Lifeline Project lack, in her view, the necessary epistemological groundwork required by teachers.

One of the main contributions made by the Humanities Project to our thinking about moral education has been to draw the attention of teachers and educators to the notion of teacher neutrality, itself a controversial issue.

The neutral teacher

In setting up the Humanities Curriculum Project, the team considered three possible positions that teachers might adopt in dealing with controversial issues. They could either follow a line laid down by the school in an attempt to ensure that all teachers followed the same procedure; or they might offer their own points of view to pupils; or they might adopt the role of neutral chairman in discussion groups. The third seemed to the team to be the only tenable position for teachers to adopt in this kind of area and thus criteria were set up to help teachers understand and enact this particular kind of role. An important distinction was made between the value position of the teacher on the issues themselves and his position as an educator. In respect of the former he is expected to remain neutral, not in the sense that he has no personal commitment to values raised by the issues discussed, but that he agrees not to reveal them to the members of the group. In respect of the second, he clearly does not remain neutral, in that he is committed to the procedures he adopts (discussion rather than instruction), to the selection of topics and material which he judges appropriate and also to the importance he attaches to developing an understanding of controversial issues and to maintaining and even raising the standards of discussion.

We find then that the role of the teacher as neutral chairman is fairly strictly laid down. He must not offer his own opinions, comment on the pupils' point of view or on the values conveyed by the materials being used. He is not permitted to offer factual information but is allowed to answer questions about the meanings of words and to ask questions to which he thinks he does not know the answers. He may direct pupils' attention to pieces of evidence from the resource collection which they have not considered at what he deems a suitable point in the discussion. The sort of neutrality being suggested then is procedural neutrality (Stenhouse 1975, Elliott 1971). Neutrality is seen by Stenhouse as a criterion by which to judge a teacher's performance; what he means by a neutral chairman is one working to certain criteria which he must make clear to his pupils at the outset so that they are able to comment upon his performance. Subsequent evaluation of the project showed that the neutral chairman's role was not without problems. Many teachers find it difficult to adopt but those who had access to training and were successful found the role rewarding and were learning to adopt a critical attitude towards their own work. Pupil reaction too presented problems in that many pupils found it initially unnerving to have to put forward their own views without teacher guidance or approval; in fact many of them showed that they preferred the teacher to play the familiar role of instructor.

Not only do many teachers find the concept of neutrality a difficult one to understand and implement, but those working at a more theoretical level, as we see from the literature, have questioned its whole validity. In fact, teacher neutrality itself has become something of a controversial issue, as we can see from the fierce debate which has raged over the concept during recent years. There appear to be three major questions to which we might address ourselves in an attempt to examine the problems raised. We must ask firstly whether teachers ought to adopt a neutral role; secondly whether this is possible; and thirdly what its practical implications are for children of different age ranges.

Those who advocate neutrality in relation to moral education usually do so for two related reasons. They do so firstly to avoid imposing their own views on their pupils and thus running the risk of indoctrinating them, even unwittingly or unintentionally. Secondly, their aim is to help pupils to learn through enquiry, discovery and argument and thus to form their own conclusions on issues where there is no clear-cut solution. Fundamentally then, they wish to avoid the kind of miseducation we discussed earlier which comes about as a result of failure to promote autonomy, understanding or critical awareness in pupils. Thus the view of neutrality that emerges is not one which leaves the teacher uncommitted to values; on the contrary, he is strongly committed to certain educational values which he considers important.

However, those critical of this approach will argue that neutrality is not desirable. McPhail (1972) claims that the teacher is failing in his responsibility towards his pupils if he does not make clear his value position over moral issues. To refuse to communicate his own values to those who are expected to share theirs is, he argues, to adopt a superior position and to an extent to discriminate between teacher and pupils, showing less than due respect for pupils as persons. Mary Warnock (1975) echoes this view when she voices a psychological objection to the thought of a teacher remaining neutral in a highly charged dispute about a topic which is supposed to affect everyone. If a teacher in this situation does not join in, he will seem either alarmingly remote or superior and perhaps patronizing. Moreover, she argues, teachers must be sincere. If they have moral beliefs, they ought to express them, otherwise they are failing as teachers. She disagrees too with the notion of procedural neutrality, suggesting that the only way for pupils to learn what counts as evidence in an argument and to develop the ability to form rational conclusions for themselves, is to witness a rational adult doing so. A teacher must take a leading part in the argument if he is to teach children to argue.

However, to claim that a teacher ought to participate in discussion and to act as a model in showing children how to draw conclusions on the grounds that they will otherwise not learn, is to raise an empirical problem. Have we any evidence to show that children fail to learn to discuss, to use evidence and to learn to form their own conclusions, if they do not see their teachers doing these things? The evidence collected from pupils using the Humanities Project over the years certainly suggests that it is possible for adolescent pupils to learn discussion techniques, to become critically aware and to form conclusions, though this ability very much depends upon the success of the teacher in adopting a neutral role (Stenhouse 1975). Wilson also adopts the view that children will not learn how to think morally merely by discussing issues of a social and ethical nature, unless they have first been taught an appropriate methodology and are versed in the techniques of discussion. Unless the whole matter is going to be left to chance, such skills must be imparted by direct teaching, so there is no place for a neutral chairman in his scheme.

The question of whether teachers can be neutral is fraught with problems unless we make a clear distinction between neutrality in relation to values in general and procedural neutrality. It could be argued that to be generally neutral is humanly impossible, since to take up any value position, even one of total lack of commitment, is to show one's values. To declare oneself politically uncommitted, for example, is in itself an indication of one's commitment. And in fact almost all the professional duties of a teacher force him to express his values. He does this in the way he treats pupils in his lessons and around the school; he reveals his values through his educational aims, his attitudes towards his colleagues and his selection or exclusion of teaching material. And even though he may claim that he is simply teaching facts, it is easy to teach facts in a biased manner, perhaps without even being aware of it. We return then to a definition of neutrality in procedural terms which Stenhouse has argued is desirable and which he has demonstrated is possible.

However, his work has involved only a limited age range of pupils, those who in general developmental terms have reached a stage where they are beginning to reason and to think hypothetically. It is likely that many of them, especially the more able, may have reached Piaget's stage of formal operations by the time they begin work of the type suggested by the Humanities Curriculum Project. But teacher neutrality must surely be interpreted rather differently with younger pupils who have not yet learned to reason and who very much depend upon adult guidance. Children's moral development can be arrested at an early stage if they are not given reasons for taking moral decisions. Kohlberg's research has shown that to present children with moral arguments slightly in advance of those they already use is the only sure way of promoting moral reasoning. For a teacher to stand back and adopt the kind of procedural neutrality we have been discussing would therefore seem inappropriate with children at the primary and lower secondary school stage. Many would argue that it is a teacher's duty to show children that lying and stealing are wrong, thus making quite clear what his moral values are. If we are concerned with moral development and reasoning, however, the teacher's main concern surely must be not simply to teach that certain actions are right or wrong but to help children to understand the full implications of such acts for themselves and for others and to appreciate the significance of different social contexts. Their concern should be not so much with the products but with the processes of moral thinking. And to promote moral thinking by understanding these processes involves playing an active part by prompting or questioning and encouraging the child to look critically at his own thinking. We argued in Chapter 5, however, that these processes cannot be developed in a vacuum; form must be based on content, manner on matter, so that some positive moral guidance is needed. It is not necessary, of course, that this should be offered in Humanities Curriculum Project lessons, provided that it is being attended to elsewhere in the provision the school makes for moral education. And it may be that in such lessons the teacher must be allowed to remain neutral for his own protection.

Summary and conclusions

In this chapter we have given a brief outline of three curriculum projects in moral education, designed for use in secondary schools. A further project, Startline, planned for the eight to thirteen age range is expected shortly.

The Farmington Trust Project, directed by John Wilson, is based on the premise that children should be offered direct teaching in the nature of morality. However, although Wilson claims that he himself has adopted this approach with a very broad age range, little guidance is offered to teachers to help them link the teaching of the moral components discussed with children's stages of development.

McPhail's Lifeline Project sets out to provide a five-year programme for secondary schools and includes materials for teachers to use with their classes, beginning with areas of personal import for younger pupils and gradually broadening in implication and scope to meet the growing social and moral awareness of older pupils. This material seems to parallel children's developmental stages, although no links are made by the authors with empirical research findings. Lifeline is designed for use within existing curriculum areas and needs ideally an appropriate school organization which allows its main aim, leading a considerate life, to be put into practice.

The Humanities Curriculum Project, originally intended for use with fourteen- to sixteen-year-old school-leavers, differs from the other two projects discussed in that the teacher plays a less direct role and responsibility for discussion of controversial issues of a social and moral nature is placed firmly with the pupils themselves. The role of the neutral teacher is discussed, together with its implications for moral education in general.

CHAPTER 8

IN CONCLUSION
MORAL EDUCATION AND THE TEACHER

A lot of ground has been covered in the earlier chapters of this book and the reader has been presented with a plethora of material. Throughout we have made every attempt to integrate this material, in some places at the risk of appearing repetitious, perhaps even boringly so. We must now try, even at that same risk, like good teachers, to round off our discussion by drawing all the threads together, by attempting some kind of synthesis and, in doing so, to focus attention on the importance and the relevance of all that we have hitherto discussed for the individual teacher, to pick out in summary the main things he needs to understand and to be aware of as he faces up to his inevitable responsibility for the moral upbringing of his charges.

We began by endeavouring to get a clearer view of what morality is and thus of what moral education should concern itself with. Our first step was to show what it is not. For the greatest weakness in what has passed for moral education in the past has been a misconception of its purposes. The concern of the moral educator should not be to instil moral precepts in an authoritarian manner. This, we argued, is one of the major reasons why it is necessary to explode the myth that it can be dealt with as an aspect of religious education. Rather, his aim should be to help pupils towards developing the ability to do their own moral thinking and to reach their own conclusions on moral issues. This, we suggested, is required both by the notion of "morality" and by that of "education". For our everyday judgements on behaviour imply that the intention of the agent is a crucial feature for any truly moral action along with a willing commitment to the principles and values upon which that action is based. Nor can either the intention or the commitment be there if the principles and values are not fully understood and freely adopted on the basis of autonomous thinking.

We then went on to consider some of the major elements in that process of moral thinking, stressing that the notion of moral autonomy does not entail that we cannot make valid assessments of the quality and the levels of moral judgements. A good deal of factual knowledge of many kinds is necessary if our moral judgements are to be sound. For we cannot make carefully thought out decisions if we lack that knowledge that will enable us to make a proper appraisal of the situation or that upon which predictions of the likely consequences of our actions can be made. We saw too that it is as important here, as in any sphere of human activity, to show a respect for truth and standards of rationality. In particular, we noted the dangers and the ever-present temptations to be selective in our choice of which evidence we will allow to count in reaching our decisions, of falling into the trap of what Freud called rationalization rather than adhering to strict standards of rationality. This led us, therefore, to a recognition of the need here, as in all aspects of education, for the development not only of knowledge but also of understanding and critical awareness. We acknowledged too that many kinds of skill, both social and practical, would be needed if our moral choices were to be translated effectively into moral action.

This consideration raised the question of the extent to which intellectual ability might affect the level of moral functioning an individual might be capable of reaching. Although accepting that this would inevitably have some effect, we warned against falling into the trap that so many education theorists from Plato to the present day have fallen into and assuming some pupils to be incapable of any kind of moral education. For not only did we point out that to assume this was to accept that such pupils were less than fully human, so that they could with justification be offered a moral upbringing that could only be described as indoctrination; we also drew attention to the fact that intellectual ability is not the only quality required for moral judgement or moral behaviour; other qualities are equally important.

Preeminent among these are qualities of an emotional or affective kind. We stressed that the morally educated person is one who has come to value moral behaviour, to recognize its importance and to be committed to it, not as a matter of mere prudence or expediency, a calculation of means to ends, but as something that has an intrinsic value, that is worth doing for its own sake. We also examined in some detail the emotional aspects of moral behaviour, emphasizing not only the need for that proper control of the emotions that can come from a full understanding of them and their effects on one, but also the necessity in any truly moral action for there to be a positive commitment to the object or objects of that action, a love of one's fellow man, what the Greeks called ἀγάπη (*agape*) rather than ἔρος (*eros*), without which moral behaviour is a mere loveless "going through the motions", behaviour of a kind that few would wish to describe as moral in any real sense. We suggested too that this is an area of human experience that merits much greater attention than it has hitherto received in discussions of morality.

If this is the kind of development that teachers must bring about in the process of promoting moral education, then they need as great an understanding as is possible of the psychological factors involved. We spent some time, therefore, outlining some of the major psychological theories in this field and especially those that have been based on the notion of stages of intellectual development through which each individual must pass if he is to reach the end state of moral autonomy. We considered in detail the evidence of the researches of men such as Lawrence Kohlberg which suggest that, although there will be variations between individuals and between societies in the rate of progress through these stages, the sequence of stages is invariant and no-one reaches the autonomous stage without successfully passing through the stages that precede it. We noted too that it is common for individuals to become stuck at early stages of moral development and to fail ever to reach the final goal of autonomy, a feature of moral development that we suggested is of particular relevance for the teacher.

It is also possible to see these stages not only in sequential and chronological terms but also as different forms or levels of response to moral problems and dilemmas that can be observed at any age. This suggests that we should not be too ready to assume that all young children are incapable of any kind of critical, autonomous response to moral issues. Conversely, it also suggests that we must recognize not only that some adults will not have reached the stage or moral autonomy in respect of any of their behaviour but that all of us, no matter how highly educated morally, are likely to reveal a level of behaviour, of thinking, of response to certain moral problems that is below that of freely thought out, autonomous choice. In many cases, this will be the effect of those fixations that result from certain kinds of childhood experiences, particularly those associated with unpleasant experiences. Often, however, it will be the result merely of the lack of the right kind of guidance towards moral development.

All of this highlights the need for the teacher not only to be familiar with what at the conceptual level might be claimed to constitute a moral education, but also with those psychological factors that affect the development of pupils towards this state. He needs to be aware of the characteristics of these successive stages of development; he needs to understand that children cannot operate at a stage they have not reached, that they cannot respond to demands they are not equipped to deal with; he needs to consider how he can most readily lead pupils on from one stage to the next and, in particular, to appreciate the significance of the "one stage above" theory, that pupils cannot understand the concepts of the stage two above theirs, that they cannot take seriously those of the stages below and that, in order to move beyond the stage they are at, they need to be presented with the kind of thinking that is only one stage above them; he needs finally to be aware of the dangers of those fixations that may result if he handles their moral upbringing ineptly, to be as conscious of the harm he can do as of the more constructive contributions he can make to moral education.

All of this has to be viewed against a backcloth of haphazard moral learning of all kinds. We examined many of the sources of this moral learning, in particular, the home, the peer group and the media. We noted too that moral learning of a similar kind goes on in the school, prompted by every aspect of its contact with its pupils, This learning, if not unconscious, is certainly unreflective and uncritical and one of its major difficulties is that it often results in double standards of behaviour, since parents often take the line that their children must not do as they do but as they say, the media also will often present conflicting standards of morality and it cannot be denied that schools and individual teachers can be equally ambivalent in what they communicate to their pupils in this area. All of this learning has to be converted somehow into moral education, primarily, of course, by being held up to conscious, critical and reflective appraisal.

However, we also suggested that this uncritical absorption of moral attitudes is not something to be deplored, that it should rather be regarded as providing the raw material of moral education. Children must behave morally from the earliest age so that they need a set of moral principles to guide them. It may also be the case, as Aristotle proposed, that we can become moral only by acting morally, a point that is reinforced by the claims of Lawrence Kohlberg that it is the content of the moral guidance that children receive that provides the only basis on which a moral education of the form we are advocating can be developed.

The provision of a content for moral education does create a number of difficulties for teachers. It is not possible to provide any kind of objectively established or universally agreed basis for such a content, so that any attempt to teach it must look like the kind of external imposition that could be described as indoctrination. However, we argued that a good deal of the moral content of our teaching might be justified by an appeal to the basic demands of community living, that the requirement that moral behaviour should evince "love" of one's fellow man might take us somewhat further and that we would not be going too far if we acted on the assumption that a moral education which has the form we have been advocating is likely to lead to an acceptance of those values that might be described as "human" values. Finally, we suggested that in any case the precise content we offer our pupils, unless it is totally bizarre and off-beat, is unlikely to be of enormous significance provided that it is always presented with the procedural requirements of moral education in mind, that, again, it is not the matter of what we offer that is crucial but rather the manner in which we offer it and that the most important things for teachers to remember are the dangers of being dogmatic in what they advise and the need to avoid doing harm rather than to work too hard at doing good.

It is not enough, however, to advise schools and teachers that they must assist their pupils to make moral decisions, that they must guide them towards a state of moral education by helping them to appraise critically the moral attitudes they have acquired through their varied experiences and to develop the skills, the knowledge, the understanding and the feeling for other people that is required, nor merely to suggest that, in order to do this, they must pay due attention to the psychology of moral development and the stages through which every child must pass. We must also offer some practical guidance as to how they might set about this complex and difficult task. For this reason, we turned in the latter part of the book to a consideration of moral education and the curriculum.

We began by reasserting that moral education is the concern of every teacher, regardless of the age of his pupils or his particular subject specialism; like language development, it goes across and through the curriculum. We then considered some of the particular ways in which this manifests itself, some of those aspects of the life and work of the school that we need to examine from the point of view of their contribution to the moral development of pupils. We suggested that few, if any, of the subjects we teach in schools could be regarded as having no moral dimension, so that we need as teachers to be aware of that dimension and of the import that our teaching of particular subjects has for the moral education of our pupils. We looked in particular at the moral issues that must arise in the teaching of literature and history, as examples of the humanities in general, and we had earlier considered the contribution that the expressive arts have to make to the development of those affective qualities that we have been at pains to stress throughout as important, if too often neglected, aspects of moral education.

We also noted the influence of the teacher's overall approach to his job, the impact of all the contacts, both formal and informal, that he has with his pupils and the kinds of relationship he develops with them. Emphasis was placed too on the role played here by the climate of the school and we examined some of the proposals that have been made to structure this in order to provide support for particular projects in moral education or, at least, to ensure that it would not undermine and be counter-productive to what such projects were endeavouring to achieve. In particular, we considered the contribution that can be made by certain kinds of organizational devices such as the institution of some kind of school council with resonsibility for the running of the school or for some aspects of school life, and we suggested that those counselling services, whose advent has been a feature of secondary schools in the United Kingdom in recent years, might be used not merely to assist pupils with specific problems but to make yet another kind of contribution to the overall responsibility of the school for moral education.

Finally, detailed attention was given to some of the major projects in moral education that have been developed in recent years, some attempts to establish this as an area of the curriculum in its own right, and we explored some of the general issues that this kind of approach raises as well as the specific problems and difficulties of particular schemes.

Several points must now be made in conclusion.

In the first place, it is important that we do not assume that decisions as to the practical content of any programme of moral education are to take the form of a choice from within these possibilities. Do we adopt an approach that is based on specific moral education projects or do we leave it to the English teachers or the history teachers or do we institute a school council or establish counselling services? Too often in education issues are polarized in this way — it is usually the fault of the theorists — and seldom is this a productive way of looking at things. The question is not which of these devices we should choose or plump for; it is a matter of reaching the most judicious combination of them all. We need to use all of these approaches if we are to attend successfully to the needs of our pupils in this sphere and the appropriate combination of them will depend as much on the needs of individual pupils as on the conditions prevailing in any particular school. It is crucial, therefore, that the school should make the right kind of varied provision for moral education.

Even more crucial, however, as always, is the role of the individual teacher. The moral development of children will be affected by the experiences they have of all the adults they meet but their moral education, no matter how carefully it is planned and organized by the school, will depend in the last analysis on the quality of their teachers, on the skill, sensitivity and awareness with which each teacher faces up to and fulfils his responsibility in this area.

There are several things that this requires teachers to consider very seriously. In the first place, as we have stressed throughout, the potential for doing harm here is immense. Not only can we create "hang-ups" that the individual may never be able to rid himself of; we can also very easily block the route to autonomous thinking generally. No matter how convinced we are of the rectitude of our own moral beliefs and principles, therefore, we can only do harm by imposing them on our pupils in a dogmatic, over-rigorous and authoritarian manner.

Secondly, the content of the teacher's own moral beliefs will be of great importance, whether he sets out to impose these on his pupils or not. For he will not be able to avoid communicating to them what he believes, what he stands for, and the more they respect him the more influential he will be in this respect, so that the teacher who relies on charismatic qualities to maintain his authority faces particular dangers here. It is essential, therefore, that every teacher give careful consideration to this matter and assure himself that he can regard this kind of influence with equanimity.

Of even greater importance, however, is the manner in which the teacher holds his moral beliefs, since, as we have stressed throughout, it is the manner in which pupils come to hold their moral beliefs that is crucial to moral education. To some extent, as we have already asserted, it does not matter what particular moral values pupils catch from their teachers if they also absorb a recognition of the need for reflective, critical and autonomous examination of them. The worst damage a teacher can do to his pupils is not to encourage them to some particular moral position but to cause them to hold to that position in an unreflective, authoritarian or heteronomous manner, to fail to appreciate the need for understanding, critical awareness and personal commitment. Teachers must do more, therefore, than examine their own moral principles; they must also examine the basis for them; they must endeavour to assess the quality, the level and the status of their own moral education.

In the end, the quality of the teacher is the most crucial ingredient in any recipe for moral education, as indeed it is for all forms of education. If the teacher himself is not a morally educated person, then he has nothing to offer his pupils but potential harm and danger in what may well be the most important area of their development as persons. It is as much to help teachers towards an appropriate level of moral education themselves as to promote a greater understanding of why and how they might contribute to that of their pupils that this book has been written.

Bibliography

Archambault, R.D., editor (1965) *Philosophical Analysis and Education*. London: Routledge & Kegan Paul.

Argyle, M. (1969) *Social Interaction*. London: Methuen.

Atkinson, R.F. (1965) Instruction and indoctrination. In Archambault (1965).

Ayer, A.J. (1946) *Language, Truth and Logic*. London: Gollancz.

Baier, K. (1975) Moral autonomy as an aim of moral education. In Langford and O'Connor (1975) and in Snook (1972).

Bandura, A. (1962) Social learning through imitation. In Jones (1962).

Bandura, A. and McDonald, F.J. (1963) The influence of social reinforcement and the behaviour of models in shaping children's moral judgments. *Journal of Abnormal and Social Psychology*.

Bandura, A., Ross, D. and Ross, S.A. (1961) Transmission of aggression through aggressive models. *Journal of Abnormal and Social Psychology*.

Bandura, A. and Walters, R.H. (1963) *Social Learning and Personality Development*. New York: Holt, Rinehart & Winston.

Bantock, G.H. (1968) *Culture, Industrialisation and Education*. London: Routledge & Kegan Paul.

Bantock, G.H. (1971) Towards a theory of popular education. In Hooper (1971).

Barker-Lunn, J.C. (1970) *Streaming in the Primary School*. Slough: National Foundation for Educational Research.

Barnes, D. (1976) *From Communication to Curriculum*. Harmondsworth: Penguin Books.

Belson, W. (1977) *Television Violence and the Adolescent Boy*, Farnborough: Teakfield.

Bernstein, B. (1967) Open schools, open society? *New Society*, 14 September.

Bernstein, B. (1971) On the classification and framing of educational knowledge. In Young (1971).

Blackham, H. (1975) The curriculum in moral education. In Taylor (1975).

Bloom, B.S. *et al*. (1956) *Taxonomy of Educational Objectives 1: Cognitive Domain*. London: Longmans.

Bowlby, J. (1975) *Attachment and loss*. London, Penguin Books.

Brennan, W.K. (1965) The foundations for moral development. In *Special Education*.

Bronfenbrenner, U. (1970) *Two Worlds of Childhood*. New York: Russell Sage Foundation.

Bruner, J. (1960) *The Process of Education*. New York: Vintage Books.

Bull, N. (1969) *Moral Judgement from Childhood to Adolescence*. London: Routledge & Kegan Paul.

Crittenden, B.S., Indoctrination as miseducation. In Snook (1972).

Dearden, R.F. (1968) *The Philosophy of Primary Education*. London: Routledge & Kegan Paul.

Dearden, R.F., Hirst, P.H. and Peters, R.S. (1975) *Education and Reason*. London: Routledge & Kegan Paul.

Dickinson, G.L. (1901) *The Meaning of Good*.

Downey, M.E. (1977) *Interpersonal Judgements in Education*. London: Harper & Row.

Durkheim, E. (1960) *Moral Education*. New York: Free Press.

Edwards, J.B. (1959) A study of certain moral attitudes amongst boys in a secondary modern school. Unpublished M.A. dissertation, University of Birmingham.

Eggleston, J. (1976) *The Sociology of the School Curriculum*. London: Routledge & Kegan Paul.

Elliott, J. (1971) The concept of the neutral teacher. *Cambridge Journal of Education*.

Elliott, J. (1975) Neutrality, rationality and the role of the teacher. In Taylor (1975).

Elliott, J. and Adelman, C. (1975) Teacher's accounts of the objectivity of classroom research. *London Education Review*.

Eysenck, H.J. (1960) The development of moral values in children — the contribution of learning theory. *British Journal of Educational Psychology*.

Eysenck, H.J. (1964) *Crime and Personality*. London: Routledge & Kegan Paul.

Ferri, E. (1972) *Streaming: Two Years Later*. Slough: National Foundation for Educational Research.

Flew, A.G.N. (1972) Indoctrination and doctrines. In Snook (1972).

Freud, S. (1905) Three essays on the theory of sexuality. *Standard Edition Volume VII*. London: Hogarth Press.

Freud, S. (1909) Two case histories. *Standard Edition Volume X*. London: Hogarth Press.

Freud, S. (1914) On Narcissism. *Standard Edition Volume XIV*. London: Hogarth Press.

Freud, S. (1933) New introductory lectures on psychoanalysis. *Standard Edition Volume XXII*. London: Hogarth Press.

Gatchel, R.H. (1972) The evolution of the concept. In Snook (1972).

Gesell, A., editor (1940) *The First Five Years of Life*. New York: Harper & Row.

Gesell, A. and Ilg, F.L. (1946) *The Child from 5 to 10*. New York: Harper & Row.

Gill, C.J. (1967) Counselling in schools. *Trends in Education*.

Green, T.F. (1972) Indoctrination and beliefs. In Snook (1972).

Haan, N., Smith, M.R. and Block, J. (1968) The moral reasoning of young adults. *Journal of Personality and Social Psychology*.

Hare, R.M. (1964) Adolescents into adults. In Hollins (1964).

Hargreaves, D.H. (1967) *Social Relations in a Secondary School*. London: Routledge & Kegan Paul.

Harris, A. (1976) *Teaching Morality and Religion*. London: Allen & Unwin.

Hartshorne, H., May, M.A. and Maller, J.R. (1929) *Studies in the Nature of Character*. London: Macmillan.

Havighurst, J.R. and Taba, H. (1949) *Adolescent Character and Personality*. New York: Wiley.

Henderson, D. and Bernstein, B. (1969) Social class differences in the relevance of language to socialisation. *Sociology*.

Himmelweit, H. *et al*. (1958) *Television and the Child*. Oxford: Oxford University Press.

Hirst, P.H. (1965a) Religious education and the maintained school. *British Journal of Educational Studies*.

Hirst, P.H. (1965b) Liberal education and the nature of knowledge. In Archambault (1965).

Hirst, P.H. (1974) *Moral Education in a Secular Society*. London: Hodder & Stoughton.

Hirst, P.H. and Peters, R.S. (1971) *The Logic of Education*. London: Routledge & Kegan Paul.

Hoffman, M.L. and Hoffman, L.W., editors (1964) *Review of Child Development Research*. New York: Russell Sage Foundation.

Hollingshead, A.B. (1949) *Elmtown's Youth*. New York: Wiley.

Hollins, T.H.B., editor (1964) *Aims in Education*. Manchester: Manchester University Press.

Hooper, R., editor (1971) *The Curriculum: Content, Design and Development*. Edinburgh: Oliver & Boyd in association with the Open University Press.

Howden, R. and Dowson, H. (1973) *Practical Guidance in School*. London: Careers Consultants.

Jackson, B. and Marsden, D. (1962) *Education and the Working Class*. London: Routledge & Kegan Paul.

Johnson, R.C. (1962) A study of children's moral judgements. *Child Development*.

Jones, M.R., editor (1962) *Nebraska Symposium on Motivation*. Lincoln, Nebraska: University of Nebraska Press.

Jones, R.M. (1972) *Fantasy and Feeling in Education*. Harmondsworth: Penguin Books.

Kay, W. (1968) *Moral Development*. London: Allen & Unwin.

Kay, W. (1975) *Moral Education*. London: Allen & Unwin.

Kellmer-Pringle, M.L. and Edwards, J.B. (1964) Some moral concepts and judgements of junior school children. *Journal of Social and Clinical Psychology*.

Kerr, J.F., editor (1968) *Changing the Curriculum*. London: University of London Press.

Kilpatrick, W.H. (1951) *Philosophy of Education*. London: Macmillan.

Kilpatrick, W.H. (1972) Indoctrination and respect for persons. In Snook (1972).

Kohlberg, L. (1963) Moral development and identification. *National Society for the Study of Education 62nd Yearbook*. Chicago: University of Chicago Press.

Kohlberg, L. (1964) Development of moral character and ideology. In Hoffman and Hoffman (1964).

Kohlberg, L. (1966) Moral education in the schools: a developmental view. *School Review*.

Kohlberg, L. (1968) The child as moral philosopher. *Psychology Today*.

Kohlberg, L. and Gilligan, C. (1971) The adolescent as a philosopher: the discovery of the self in a post-conventional world. *Daedalus*.

Kohlberg, L. and Mayer, R. (1972) Development as the aim of education. *Harvard Education Review*.

Kohn, M.L. (1958) Social class and parental values. *American Journal of Sociology*.

Kohn, M.L. and Schooler, C. (1969) Class, occupation and orientation. *American Sociological Review*.

Kuhmerker, L. (1974) We don't call it moral education. *Journal of Moral Education*.

Lacey, C. (1970) *Hightown Grammar: The School as a Social System*. Manchester: Manchester University Press.

Langford, G. and O'Connor, D.J., editors (1975) *New Essays in the Philosophy of Education*. London: Routledge & Kegan Paul.

Loughran, R. (1967) A pattern of development in moral judgements made by adolescents. *Education Review*.

Luria, Z., Godlwasser, M. and Goldwasser, A. (1963) Response to transgression in stories by Israeli children. *Child Development*.

MacDonald, B. (1973) Humanities Curriculum Project. In Schools Council (1973).

MacRae, C. (1954) A test of Piaget's theories of moral development. *Journal of Abnormal and Social Psychology*.

May, P. (1971) *Moral Education in the School*. London: Methuen.

McPhail, P., Ungoed-Thomas, J.R. and Chapman, H. (1972) *Moral Education in the Secondary School*. London: Longmans.

McPhail, P. (1973) *Our School*. London: Longmans

Moore, G.E. (1903) *Principia Ethica*. Cambridge: Cambridge University Press.

Moore, W. (1966) Indoctrination as a normative concept. *Studies in Philosophy and Education*.

Moore, W. (1972) Indoctrination and democratic method. In Snook (1972).

Morris, J.F. (1958) The development of adolescent value judgements. *British Journal of Educational Psychology*.

Mussen, P.H., Kagan, J. and Conger, J.J. (1969) *Child Development and Personality*. New York: Harper & Row.

Mussen, P.H., Langer, J. and Covington, M., editors (1969) *Trends and Issues in Developmental Psychology*. New York: Holt, Rinehart & Winston.

Nash, M. (1958) Machine-age Maya: The industrialisation of a Guatemala community. *American Anthropologist*.

Nettleship, R.L. (1935) *The Theory of Education in Plato's Republic*. Oxford: Oxford University Press.

Newbold, D. (1977) *Ability Grouping — The Banbury Inquiry*. Slough: National Foundation for Educational Research.

Newsom, J. and Newsom, E. (1963) *Infant Care in an Urban Community*. London: Allen & Unwin.

Niblett, W.R., editor (1963) *Moral Education in a Changing Society*. London: Faber.

Oakeshott, M. (1962) *Rationalism in Politics*. London: Methuen.

O'Connor, D.J. (1957) *An Introduction to the Philosophy of Education*. London: Routledge & Kegan Paul.

Peck, R.F. and Havighurst, R.J. (1960) *The Psychology of Character Development*. New York: Wiley.

Peters, R.S. (1960) Freud's theory of moral development in relation to that of Piaget. *British Journal of Educational Psychology*.

Peters, R.S. (1963) The paradox of moral education. In Niblett (1963).

Peters, R.S. (1965) Education as initiation. In Archambault (1965).

Peters, R.S. (1966) *Ethics and Education*. London: Allen & Unwin.

Peters, R.S., editor (1967) *The Concept of Education*. London: Routledge & Kegan Paul.

Peters, R.S. (1970) Concrete principles and the rational passions. In Sizer and Sizer (1970).

Peters, R.S. (1973a) Moral education in the secondary school. A review in *Journal of Moral Education*.

Peters, R.S. (1973b) *Reason and Compassion*. London: Routledge & Kegan Paul.

Peters, R.S. (1975) Education of the emotions. In Dearden, Hirst and Peters (1975).

Phenix, P.H. (1964) *Realms of Meaning*. New York: McGraw-Hill.

Piaget, J. (1932) *The Moral Judgement of the Child*. London: Routledge & Kegan Paul.

Rest, J., Turiel, E. and Kohlberg, L. (1969) The level of moral development as a determinant of preference and comprehension of moral judgements made by others. *Journal of Personality*.

Rusk, R.R. (1957) *The Doctrines of the Great Educators*. London: Macmillan.

Russell, B. (1908) *A History of Western Philosophy*, 2nd edition. London: Allen & Unwin.

Sartre, J.P. (1962) *Sketch for a Theory of the Emotions*. London: Methuen.

Schofield, A.J. (1977) Pastoral care and the curriculum of a comprehensive school. Unpublished M.A. thesis, University of London.

Schools Council (1968) *Young School Leavers*. London: H.M.S.O.

Schools Council (1970) *The Humanities Project: An Introduction*. London: Heinemann Educational for the Schools Council.

Schools Council (1973) *Evaluation in Curriculum Development: Twelve Case Studies*. London: Macmillan.

Schools Council (1977) *Discovering an Approach*. London: Macmillan Education for the Schools Council.

Sears, R. Maccoby, E. and Levine, M. (1957) *Patterns of Child-Rearing*. New York: Harper & Row.

Sizer, N.F. and Sizer, T.R., editors (1970) *Moral Education*. Cambridge, Mass.: Harvard University Press.

Smart, N. (1968) *Secular Education and the Logic of Religion*. London: Faber.

Snook, I.A., editor (1972) *Concepts of Indoctrination*. London: Routledge & Kegan Paul.

Solomon, R.L. and Wynne, L.C. (1953) Traumatic and avoidance learning. *Psychological Monographs*.

Spiro, M.E. (1958) Children of the Kibbutz. Cambridge, Mass.: Harvard University Press.

Stenhouse, L. (1975) Neutrality as a criterion in teaching: the working of the Humanities Curriculum Project. In Taylor (1975).

Sugarman, B. (1973) *The School and Moral Development*. London: Croom Helm.

Taylor, M., editor (1975) *Progress and Problems in Moral Education*. Slough: National Foundation for Educational Research.

Toulmin, S. (1950) *An Examination of the Place of Reason in Ethics*. Cambridge: Cambridge University Press.

Turiel, E (1969) Developmental processes in the child's moral thinking. In Mussen, Langer and Covington (1969).

Vigotsky, L.S. (1962) *Thought and Language*. Cambridge, Mass.: Massachusetts Institute of Technology Press.

Walsh, W.H. (1969) *Hegelian Ethics*. London: Macmillan.

Ward, J. (1971) Modification of deviant classroom behaviour. *British Journal of Educational Psychology*.

Warnock, M. (1975) The neutral teacher. In Taylor (1975).

White, J.P. (1967) Indoctrination. In Peters (1967) and in Snook (1972).

White, J.P. (1968) Education in obedience. *New Society*.

White, J.P. (1973) *Towards a Compulsory Curriculum*. London: Routledge & Kegan Paul.

White, J.P. (1975) The moral objectives of a uniform curriculum. In Taylor (1975).

Williams, N. and Williams, S. (1969) *The Moral Development of Children*. London: Macmillan.

Wilson, J. (1964) Education and indoctrination. In Hollins (1964).

Wilson, J. (1971) *Education in Religion and the Emotions*. London: Heinemann.

Wilson, J. (1972) Indoctrination and freedom. In Snook (1972).

Wilson, J. (1973) *Practical Problems in Moral Education*. London: Heinemann.

Wilson, J. (1975) Moral education and the curriculum. In Taylor (1975).

Wilson, J. Williams, N. and Sugarman, B. (1967) *Introduction to Moral Education*. Harmondsworth, Penguin Books.

Woods, R.G. (1969) Introduction to moral education. Review in *Journal of Curriculum Studies*.

Woods, R.G. and Barrow, R. St C. (1975) *Introduction to the Philosophy of Education*. London: Methuen.

Wringe, S. (1974) Some problems raised by the Humanities Curriculum Project. *Journal of Curriculum Studies*.

Young, M.F.D., editor (1971) *Knowledge and Control.* New York: Collier-Macmillan.

Official Reports quoted or referred to

Central Advisory Council for Education. *15 to 18* (The Crowther Report) H.M.S.O. (1959).

Central Advisory Council for Education. *Half Our Future* (The Newsom Report) H.M.S.O. (1963).

Central Advisory Council for Education. *Children and their Primary Schools* (The Plowden Report) H.M.S.O. (1967).

Index of names

Index of subjects